Satan in America

Satan in America

The Devil We Know

W. Scott Poole

ROWMAN & LITTLEFIELD PUBLISHERS, INC.
Lanham • Boulder • New York • Toronto • Plymouth, UK

ROWMAN & LITTLEFIELD PUBLISHERS, INC.

Published in the United States of America
by Rowman & Littlefield Publishers, Inc.
A wholly owned subsidiary of The Rowman & Littlefield Publishing Group, Inc.
4501 Forbes Boulevard, Suite 200, Lanham, Maryland 20706
www.rowmanlittlefield.com

Estover Road
Plymouth PL6 7PY
United Kingdom

British Library Cataloguing in Publication Information Available

Library of Congress Cataloging-in-Publication Data

Satan in America : the Devil we know / W. Scott Poole.
    p. cm.
Includes bibliographical references and index.
ISBN 978-0-7425-6171-7 (cloth : alk. paper) — ISBN 978-1-4422-0062-3
(electronic)
1. Devil—Social aspects—United States—History. 2. Devil—Political aspects—
United States—History. 3. Devil—Christianity. 4. Good and evil—Social
aspects—United States—History. 5. Good and evil—Political aspects—United
States—History. 6. United States—Religious life and customs. 7. United
States—Civilization. 8. National characteristics, American. 9. Political culture—
United States—History. 10. Violence—United States—History. I. Title.

BT982.P66 2009
306.6'35470973—dc22   2009020062

Printed in the United States of America

∞™ The paper used in this publication meets the minimum requirements of
American National Standard for Information Sciences—Permanence of Paper for
Printed Library Materials, ANSI/NISO Z39.48-1992.

for Beth

Contents

Preface

"Night Stalker": American Exceptionalism and the Reality of Evil

In the summer of 1985, Richard Ramirez, dubbed by the media "the Night Stalker," entered homes in Southern California, spray-painted occult symbols on the wall and killed and mutilated the inhabitants. Ramirez claimed to be a practicing Satanist, inspired and empowered by evil spirits to commit his ghastly crimes. Australian heavy metal band AC/DC, infamous for their anthem "Highway to Hell," provided his mental soundtrack. He had shot, stabbed, beaten, and raped in the middle of the night, attacking the elderly, women, and children in the most savage ways imaginable. In one case, he had gouged out his victim's eyes after her death. Ramirez would be convicted in 1989 of forty-three counts, thirteen counts of murder.[1]

Richard Ramirez was a living nightmare. He knew none of his victims, choosing them at random and sometimes attacking several homes on the same night in a berserk frenzy. When caught and brought to trial, he terrified even his judge and jury with his cold, impassive demeanor. The pentagram tattooed on his hand embodied his commitment to the occult. "You don't understand me," he told reporters. "You are not expected to. You are not capable of it. I am beyond your experience. I am beyond good and evil."[2]

Many in the media and in the American public saw Ramirez as part of a larger threat to society. He appeared on the scene at a moment in American cultural life when many Americans were willing to believe that tens of thousands of Ramirezes waited in the night, part of a large conspiracy of devil worshippers seeking to kill their children. Ramirez emerged at a time when America was profoundly fascinated with the alleged threat of

Satanism and psychopathic serial killers. What a number of authors have called "a satanic panic" seized the country in the early 1980s, a panic induced by a rash of false claims, media sensationalism, and religious entrepreneurs who either claimed to be reformed and redeemed ex-Satanists or to have knowledge of vast networks of conspiracy. Meanwhile, adult children discovered in "repressed memories" narratives of their parents torturing, raping, and initiating them into satanic rites. Religious leaders led crusades against rock music and role-playing games. Day care centers came under suspicion as fronts for satanic covens. Even some law enforcement bought into these claims, hiring "occult experts" to help them ferret out local Satanist cells. The scholarly interpreter of this phenomenon, Bill Ellis, notes that the Satanism scare, while in no way comparable to the witch hunts that killed tens of thousands in early modern Europe, still resulted in "a waste of expense and needless ruin of reputations and livelihoods."[3]

The "satanic panic" drew on a vast collection of historical images, and many Americans used the imagery of Satanism to express their anxieties about the nature of evil. This is a basic thematic element in our culture and in most human cultures. Nothing so assaults our highest ideals, our clarity about what it means to be human, and even our deepest moral commitments as acts of evil performed for their own brutal sake. And yet, "true crime" remains a popular and best-selling genre. Basic cable is packed with numerous exposé series that focus on bloody crimes. We let the serial killers of the world shock us, in part, because we and those we love are so unlikely to be victims of them that we believe, they cannot really touch us. Or perhaps we make ourselves spectators of evil because, at least in our minds, that way we will not become victims of it or collaborators with it. In other words, our hunger for cheap paperbacks that tell tales of vicious criminalities and television that focuses on similar ghastly acts may be a kind of talisman, a way to glance at ultimate evil in hopes that this means we will never have to confront it. Or become its dinner.

We embrace the sensationalism of individual violence rather than face the more imposing horror of established, systematic, institutional violence that perhaps resides at the very heart of our social order. We agree in principle with Josef Stalin, who is supposed to have quipped that the death of a single individual is a tragedy, but the death of millions is a statistic. Tales of grisly murder hide the frightening realities of our national existence. But whether we like it or not, whether we will face it or not, violence and terror intersect in our histories—our personal histories and our larger national history. The inhumane acts of Ramirez actually replicate in microcosm the behavior of historical forces that have shaped the modern world and the place of the United States in it. In fact, the acts of "the Night Stalker," combined with all the acts of known psychopathic murderers over the last century, pale in comparison to the acts of "nation building" often accepted as the price of American national identity, or simply American interests. Compare your knowledge of the worst acts of individual murderers to the following:

> William Bradford describes a Puritan attack on a Pequot village in which the village was set on fire and those who escaped the flames "were slain with the sword, some hewed to pieces, some run through with rapiers." Puritan minister Cotton Mather boasted that 600 Pequot souls had been sent to hell.
>
> An American news correspondent in Manila describes the American occupation of the Philippines in 1901 as the extermination "of men, women and children, prisoners and captives, active insurgents and suspected people, lads from ten up . . . our soldiers have pumped salt water into men to make them talk . . . have taken prisoners . . . and an hour later without an atom of evidence to show they were even *insurrectos*, stood them on a bridge and shot them down one by one."
>
> On March 16, 1968, a company of U.S. soldiers entered the village of My Lai, rounded up the inhabitants (mostly women, children, and the elderly), placed them in a ditch and turned murderous gunfire on them. Army investigators later found between 450 and 500 bodies, some of them infants in their mother's arms, buried in the ditch.[4]

Many more examples, some even more contemporary, could be added to this catalog of death and destruction, real historical evil that takes tens of thousands of lives. These actions have been variously interpreted through the lens of nationalism, pragmatism, and patriotism. But for most of American history, true evil has been believed to reside not in us but in the enemy that must be destroyed. America is the Unfallen Angel, secure in its innocence, but beset by thousands of dark foes.

The American nation is not alone in perpetrating evil. Moral evil is writ large in the story of the human experience. The suffering and meaningless death inflicted by the human tendency to destroy, maim, rape, and plunder is a central theme running through the history of every civilization on Earth. While every major religious tradition since the Axial Age (600 BCE to 600 CE) has celebrated the values of compassion, benevolence, and mercy, the societies that gave birth to these ideas have been built on mounds of corpses. The twentieth century, with all its vaunted technological process, saw modern states transforming that technology into a machinery of death, slaughtering ethnic minorities on a scale undreamed of in previous eras.

History does not allow us to stand apart from these realities, and yet our culture asks that we attempt to do just that. The goal of contemporary, white, suburban, American society is the isolation of the self from pain and the awareness of pain. At the very same time, American culture maintains a belief in lurking evil. The American self is actually divided within itself, as we refuse to acknowledge that the roots of horror and pain in the world lie in our own motivations, our own capacity for evil that finds expression in a thousand small choices. As Freud noted in *Civilization and Its Discontents* we "are not gentle creatures who want to be loved and who at the most can defend themselves if they are attacked." Instead, Freud asserts, human beings are creatures "with a powerful share of aggressiveness. As a result, their neighbor is often for them not only a potential helper or sexual object, but also someone who tempts them to satisfy their aggressiveness, to exploit his capacity for work without compensation, to use him sexually without his consent, to seize his possessions, to humiliate him, to cause him pain, to torture and kill him." Freud's savage assessment is startling, but true to any study of human society at any moment of its historical experience. "Who in the face of all his experience of life and history," Freud demands to know, "will have the courage to dispute this assertion."[5]

This distressing view of human nature and the societies shaped by human nature is not the answer to the problem of evil modern America would prefer. When not transforming the cultural enemy into the epitome of satanic evil, avoidance of the problem of evil and narcissistic posturing about its meaning are the most common responses. Some of the contemporary writing on religion in America illustrates this attitude. A recent book by Bart Ehrman, entitled *God's Problem*, takes on the question of evil in a religious context. The author purports to challenge traditional orthodoxies by insisting that monotheism provides no answer to the deepest question of human existence; if God is good, why do human beings suffer? This is indeed a powerful question, redolent of Dostoyevsky's devastating formulation that the suffering of a single innocent calls into question the justice of God. In raising these questions, Ehrman exposes how often our notions of the sacred are simplistic and ideological, easy platitudes that ignore the fundamental human problems of suffering and evil.[6]

And yet, Ehrman's "solution" to this problem, one only available to a small portion of the global community's inhabitants, is to retreat within the walls of a bourgeois fortress and "love and be loved . . . cultivate friendships . . . make money and spend money." Chris Hedges, in his review of this book in *Harvard Divinity Bulletin*, calls this a "celebration of middle-class comfort and wasteful consumption in the industrialized zones of safety." Ehrman has asked the wrong question, according to Hedges. Rather than shaking our fist at God and demanding to know why we suffer "the question is why we permit others to suffer." In other words, why do we do evil?[7]

Hedges has turned Ehrman's formulation of the question on its head, reminding us that much of the evil in the world is not really a mystery. There is something commonplace about actual evil, something that does not catch our eye at first and, for most of us, only becomes clearer with the passage of time. As philosopher Nel Noddings argues, real evil seldom comes "with all of the excitement conveyed by stories of devils, witches, demons, spells and possession. Evil does not have a stomach-churning stench, nor does it signal its presence with palpable cold and darkness." Hannah Arendt's famous, and controversial phrase "the banality of evil" in *Eichmann in Jerusalem* conveys this sense of moral horror, often wrapped in the most innocuous-seeming guises. American life is rife with examples. The televangelist whose words of hate incite violence against gays and lesbians. The politician whose desire to be thought patriotic leads to support for raining destruction on the heads of helpless civilians. The modern suburb's affluence and comfort that rests on a foundation of class violence and economic exploitation. These are the boring, pedestrian, everyday horrors, the savagery of the quotidian.[8]

Theologians and ethicists often picture evil as rooted and expressed in actions of violence, violence turned outward in empire building and inward in an effort to shape a harmonious social order (or a disciplined self). Rather than thinking through the complexities of the "problem of evil," why we practice aggression and violence or why suffering seems imposed on others even when human agency is absent, the human tendency is simply to declare the Other as evil. The image of the devil in human history has provided the simplest answer to the problem of evil in all its forms. How is it that human beings, capable of acts of self-sacrifice and moral magnificence, are also able to perpetrate the greatest of horrors? One answer has been the power of an evil, dark force that has helped to corrupt us from the beginning of time—a devil that embodies all of our aggression and rage without any of our capacity for moral imagination.

Ahriman, Shaytan, Iblis, Satan, the devil. In cultural regions of the world where the influence of monotheism has been most deeply felt, Satan has encoded humanity's most profound anxieties about violence, horror, and the inexplicable nature of suffering in a universe allegedly ruled by a loving God. A Tempter, but also a creative sadist, the monotheistic West's image of the devil has given us an embodiment of violence. Our dark impulses are us, but they are also not us, according to traditional beliefs about Satan. We act on our most vicious impulses, the logic of the diabolical tells us, because a Tempter pulls us into them, makes us live in our darkness, causes us to forget ourselves or even become a new, wretched self. For millennia, human beings have seen the serpent waiting in the darkness, waiting to encircle us and destroy us.

The United States emerged at a point in human history when dark fears of demonic spirits were seemingly on the wane. Mark Larrimore views the period of the Enlightenment as one of the "tectonic shifts" in the human understanding of evil that challenged older notions of demon spirits infesting a sinful world. And yet the birth pangs of the American nation also occurred at a moment when a powerful religious response emerged to challenge modernity. The growth of American evangelicalism brought the idea of spiritual rebirth and spiritual warfare to the forefront of the American consciousness. The nation conceived in the very heart of the Western Enlightenment became obsessed with the devil and his power.[9]

Satan in America: The Devil We Know insists that the devil played a significant, and at moments determinative, role in the shaping of the American religious and popular imagination. It looks at the devil in American history, his image and uses, at crucial turning points in the nation's social, cultural, and political history. America has been in love with the dark at almost every stage of its history, eager to view its enemies as satanic. Powerful social groups have used this image of evil to explain their enemies to them and to legitimize acts of violence against those they have constructed as demonic. A country such as the United States, deeply infused with a religious sense of its identity and mission, easily slipped into the tendency of rendering its enemies, foreign and domestic, as diabolical. The mentality of manifest destiny, interwoven into the American character, prevented this society from seeing the dark irony and deepest reality of its quest for empire. While launching crusades against demons abroad, and within the lives of its own citizens, American society has located itself at the intersection of violence and hubris. Its own landscape has become the terrain of hell, the kingdom of Pandemonium, and the abyss.

Satan will not go away. The devil plays a more significant role in our public vocabulary today than at any time since the seventeenth century. A multitude of forces—powerful religious movements, political and social realignments, the trends and obsessions of America's popular culture—have created a powerful image of Satan that influences the majority of the American people. A significant number of Americans hold the most infantile conceptions of Satan imaginable, views that have as their consequence a profoundly simplistic conception of the moral universe. Such ideas influence our domestic and international policy and corrode our spiritual and moral resources. We, and the leaders we elect, talk incessantly about the problem of evil, but almost always in the terms of an ancient mythology of a Lord of Darkness.

Not all cultural commentators agree with this view. William Hart, in his short, but thoughtful, series of reflections on the nature of evil, calls his chapter on the figure of Satan "the devil in decline." It is Hart's contention that, beginning in the nineteenth century, new ideas ranging from

Freudianism to Darwinism caused a general decline in religious belief and a more specific decline in beliefs about Satan (even though in the same chapter he notes polls showing an overwhelming majority of Americans believe in the devil). Hart believes that most moderns have come to agree with Freud that the devil is little more than "a child's repressed fantasies about being seduced by his or her father." But even Hart is forced to admit that "millions continue to believe in Satan . . . as a real supernatural entity and the chief agent of world evil."[10]

Andrew Delbanco argues the point even more strongly in his *The Death of Satan: How Americans Have Lost the Sense of Evil*. Delbanco, writing in the early 1990s, insisted that America suffered from a "crisis of incompetence" in its ability to articulate the meaning of evil. Satan, he writes, had once "been understood to be everywhere." Over the centuries of American existence, he (and the larger concept of evil) had retreated before the onslaught of growing secularization, finding expression in "the culture of irony." Belief in the devil, he suggests, has become one of modernity's orphans, unable to find a home in today's largely secular culture.[11]

The Death of Satan is a profound meditation on the nature of evil and, as with all of Delbanco's work, a guided tour of all the significant literary, philosophical, and even theological reflections on the topic. He does, however, focus on only a thin layer of American society, primarily American intellectuals, to prove that the devil has been losing ground. A perceptive review of the work by Richard Wrightman Fox notes that Delbanco "never looks at that part of the population that still believes in [the devil]." That part of the population grew enormously in the final decades of the twentieth century calling into question just how "secular" American society has truly become. As this book will show, the study of American history is not the story of what Delbanco calls "the devil's decline into invisibility." Rather, it is a study of his ascent.[12]

This book does not claim to be a comprehensive account of the role played by the devil in all aspects of American culture. Literary production related to the devil could alone fill a book several times this one's length. In the interest of keeping the focus on the role of Satan in shaping American identity, the material analyzed has been self-consciously limited. Notable for its absence is a discussion of the devil in American folklore, a topic deserving a separate treatment. Only in a few cases, specifically the Jersey Devil and the "satanic panics" of the 1980s and 1990s, did I make use of the mountain of work on the devil in American folklore. Important work has already been done in this field and will hopefully continue. The reader is also encouraged to explore the numerous books in the bibliography that will allow them to gain a more complete sense of how integral the image of Satan has been to all aspects of American culture.[13]

In terms of method, this work tries to forge a much-needed link between the study of American history, religious studies, and the study of popular culture. Historians have, in the last twenty years, come to see the importance of using religious belief as an interpretive variable. Scholars such as R. Laurence Moore and George Marsden have interwoven the study of theology seamlessly with the study of American history. Their work refuses to consider religious and theological questions in isolation from the historiography of the American experience.[14]

Satan in America examines religious ideas not only in relation to popular culture, but also as an aspect of popular culture. It presumes that popular culture often functions as an aspect of religious faith. Scholars such as Harry Stout and Frank Lambert are the pathfinders of this approach, studying not only popular religious belief but also how those beliefs sometimes break down the barrier between religious culture and popular culture. Michael Cuneo, in his study of the idea of possession in American history, argues that by the 1970s, popular culture actually informed and even helped to shape religious belief. My work builds on their insights. Like Cuneo, I see religion and popular culture interwoven in the minds of most Americans in the twentieth century, theological and religious beliefs informing expressions of popular culture and vice versa.[15]

The American devil created by a partnership of film and theology, comic books and popular religious movements, has become a ready metaphor for escapism and the denial of moral responsibility in the American experience. In a sense, this study of the diabolical metaphor is a study of the failure of a society to deal seriously with the problem of evil. In this, the book follows Jeffrey Burton Russell, who, in his monumental multivolume study of the image of Satan, found this to be an exceedingly common tendency in Western culture. A fascination with the supernatural, rather than a serious analysis of the problem of evil, has been the most common way that Western societies have tried to illuminate the shadows of life.

This examination of religion and popular culture assumes the American devil's close relationship to social and cultural violence, suggesting that he is the very engine of a mechanism that drives historical acts of cruelty and inhumanity. No modern thinker has examined the nature of evil and the violent roots of the social order more closely than the French literary critic and philosopher René Girard. In his groundbreaking *Violence and the Sacred, I See Satan Fall Like Lightning,* and *The Scapegoat,* Girard has argued that all mythological systems, and the societies that look to them for foundational narratives, are grounded in some act of violence, the destruction of some kind of "contagion." Only by destroying this contagion is the growth of harmony in the social order possible. Human beings' natural state, given their love of aggression and desire for supremacy, is "the war of all against all." Founding myths locate this violent urge in some mythic cause of disorder, some "scapegoat," which triggers a cycle of violence ending in the destruction and death of the source of disharmony. Society has purified and renewed itself so that the cycle of violence can begin again.[16]

Satan, according to Girard, has played a special role in the violent, society-forming mechanism. Satan is, in part, the force that brings unity to society by making sure that "the unfortunate victim is completely isolated." The victim becomes a devil. Girard also sees Satan as the actual destruction and violence performed on the victim, the idea of the devil is progenitor of the cycle of violence. In this mechanism, social unity is born from the fact that, once a victim has been chosen as the scapegoat, "no one in the community has an enemy other than the victim," and the destruction of that enemy brings a feeling of purity and release to the community. The enemy of society, the contagion that must be destroyed, the objects(s) of violence, are specific targets whose vilification, demonization, and death are the foundation of state and empire. Girard writes that "Satan has always been someone," the cycle of violence has always embodied its rage in specific victims.[17]

Some alternative voices have suggested that Satan has never been anyone or, indeed, anything other than a powerful metaphor. American theologians in the twentieth century often significantly revised traditional Christian teaching regarding the supernatural in general and Satan in particular. At times, this has risen out of a bland millennial optimism that characterized much of transatlantic Protestant liberalism in the early part of the century. In the aftermath of World Wars I and II and genocidal fascism, this rethinking of the idea of the devil grew out of a desire to confront the nature of radical evil. Paul Tillich, the enormously influential German theologian who came to the United States in the 1930s, refused to use the term "Satan" and preferred "the demonic." The idea of the demonic did not mean to him the existence of supernatural beings bent on the ruin of humanity. Instead Tillich used the traditional diabolical language to describe a destructive set of attitudes and forces in our experience that seeks to define the finite as the infinite. Ironically, Tillich defined an obsession with a literal belief in Satan as itself "demonic." Such beliefs, he asserted, over-literalize the nature of evil, making evil all the more insidious. "The devil made me do it" means, in essence, I didn't do it and I am not responsible for it.

However sophisticated this understanding of the category of the demonic may have been, we will see in chapter 4 that Tillich's ideas, and the ideas of other theologians who reworked traditional Christian symbols in conversation with modernity, arguably had little influence outside the seminary classroom and a few sophisticated pulpits. In contrast to the limited influence of these thinkers, twentieth century popular culture, in

some ways a peculiarly American synthesis of technological sophistication and collective democracy at work, churned out literalized representa-
tions of the demonic in films, comics, and cheap paperbacks. American religion made Satan a central figure in its worldview. The devil hid behind
myriad manifestations of pop culture. Satan as tempter, fallen angel, and
source of chaos and death surfaced in iconic figures from Tod Browning's
Count Dracula to George Lucas's Darth Vader.

The devil has become an essential part of the American cultural and
religious imagination. Chapter 7 will look at Hal Lindsey, an evangelist and self-proclaimed doomsday prophet whose odd and inhumane
speculations made for numerous best-selling books. Lindsey said more
than he knew in the title of a 1972 book: *Satan Is Alive and Well on Planet
Earth*. The devil is supremely popular and has had an especially good run
in the United States of America. Lindsey, with numerous others, helped
to keep him alive in what became the world's largest secular democracy,
that child of the Enlightenment, the United States.

The responsibility for Satan's latter-day triumph cannot be placed simply with popular evangelists, best-selling doomsayers, or even on their
significant number of followers. Belief in and obsession with the devil
are more than marks of American credulity, more than evidence that the
Enlightenment failed to create a healthy skepticism. The devil is more
than a creation of America's popular culture. Beneath the urban legends,
the comic strip Lucifers, and theological explanations of evil both sophisticated and crude lay the profound American experience with historical
evil, evil that seems greater than the sum of its parts.

Radical evil has been part of America's collective history, indeed has
helped to shape the nation we have become. The enslavement of human
beings, frequently in the most heartless and brutal forms imaginable,
coils at the very root of America's first flourishing. Moreover, the contemporary borders of the United States would look very different had
it not been for nineteenth-century America's territorial ambitions that
led to a preemptive, imperialist strike against Mexico in the 1840s and
the genocidal extermination of native peoples. Inside the boundaries of
the American empire, social power inflicted enormous suffering on the
marginal people. Only after a long century of struggle, often against racist and sexist violence allied with a profound and cruel apathy, did marginal people in America begin to seize the basic rights of citizenship and
basic protections under the law. The great gains won by the civil rights
struggle, the women's movement, the labor movement, and the emerging
alliance for gay and lesbian rights are still tenuous and frequently under
threat from conservative forces within American society.

America has failed to grapple with these basic facts about its historical
experience. Instead, the concept of America's profound innocence, the

idea that somehow the United States represents a great exception in human history, influences religious ideas and popular culture at every turn. Robert Jewett and John Shelton Lawrence have defined this attitude as the "Captain America complex," named for the Marvel Comics character first created in the 1940s who, through most of his history, has combined "explosive strength with perfect moral intuitions." This has been, unfortunately, the primary conception that Americans have had of their own nation, a view that obscures the many dark shadows over their country's national history and transforms every foreign policy decision into a moral crusade.[18]

Satan has had a special role to play in this historical melodrama. Much like biblical scholar Elaine Pagels has described the role played by the devil in early Christianity, America's social history of Satan has been one in which the devil has been used to "characterize human enemies." Satan, the ultimate evil, has been linked with perceived threats to our national order and national identity. This makes those threats diabolical in their reach, and thus any action, no matter how cruel or inhumane, becomes justified. We can do evil as long as our goal is the defense of our ultimate innocence. We can do the devil's work as long as we are fighting the devil. The United States, of course, is far from the only contemporary society with blood on its hands. The history of the twentieth century, a history of brutal conflict and technology placed in the service of genocide, offers a thousand examples of profound evil. The crimes of Nazi Germany or the Soviet Empire alone dwarf America's frequent collaboration with evil. Shouldn't these societies have a similar fascination with evil, perhaps even a tendency to create the same mythopoeic explanations of evil so common in the American experience? In some sense, shouldn't these societies be more obsessed with Satan, or some other symbol of radical, supernatural evil, than Americans have proven to be?[19]

A comparison with the historical experience of Germany in the twentieth century is useful in understanding the differences. More than any other nation, Germany has been forced to face the problem of evil. The crimes of the Nazi regime, and the collaboration of many everyday Germans with those crimes, has become for many the very symbol of historical evil. German culture has been forced to face the evil within, the evil that its people and its culture perpetrated through the demonization and murder of Jews, Slavs, homosexuals, and anyone outside the parameters of Nazi racial ideology. Tony Judt, in a 2008 essay, wrote that Germany, "was transformed in the course of a generation into a people uniquely conscious of the enormity of its crimes and the scale of its accountability." The secular nature of German society meant that the only demonic forces to be blamed were the "devils" of racist nationalism united with a fanatical militarism.[20]

America's confrontation with evil has been less explicit and filtered through a mythological framework structured by American religious experience. In the latter half of the twentieth century, American fascination with the Prince of Darkness grew to epic proportions in a society that was, arguably, becoming less secular with each passing decade. While fascination with Satan and his work grew among large swaths of American society, the public culture of the United States continued to insist on American innocence and basic goodness. American nationalism is closely connected to this deeply held belief, a central tenet of America's civil religion. The sense of newness in the settlement of colonial America combined with the promise of America encapsulated in the founding documents to make America's righteousness the official representation of American history for generations of schoolchildren, hopeful immigrants, historians, politicians, and foreign policy wonks.

This ideology of innocence long informed the writing of American history. Andrew Bacevich has referred to this idea of American innocence as "the myth of the reluctant superpower." In this reading of American history, America has only exercised violence when some great historical evil threatened peace and democracy. The whole notion of "American exceptionalism" among historians was born out of this sense of American uprightness and, though it sometimes took sophisticated forms, generally began with the premise that few historical analogies could be applied to the American experience since its democratic experience represented something truly new in the world, a social and political Eden where humanity had the opportunity to begin again. Other nations may seek to fashion empire; America has always and only represented, and fought on behalf of, democracy and freedom. This view has long been under attack, and indeed has no contemporary defenders among professional, academic historians. Nevertheless, the idea of American exceptionalism remains a popular folk belief and a handy rhetorical tool for politicians.[21]

The belief in American innocence is a failure of our collective moral imagination. There is some truth to the notion of American exceptionalism, but it is not a happy truth. To rephrase Judt's comment on postwar Germany, America is a nation uniquely *un*conscious of its crimes and *un*aware of the scale of its accountability. Cornel West puts it well when he writes that "the American democratic experiment is unique in human history not because we are God's chosen people to lead the world, nor because we are always a force for good in the world, but because of our refusal to acknowledge the deeply racist and imperial roots of our democratic process."[22]

A culture gets the devil it deserves. American ideas about the nature of evil, and its own response to or collusion with evil, emerged in the thematic elements of the American Satan. The rhetoric of newness and innocence has surrounded the United States from the beginning. So has the shadow side of this tradition, in which the American nation is itself a kind of fallen angel. American historical experience began with the rhetoric of democracy and equality but developed in the enslavement of 4 million black people in the first century of its existence, the brutal subjugation of its native peoples, and a twentieth century marked by a growing love of militarism; imperial expansion; and, by the standards of the developed world, an extraordinarily violent civic culture. The story of Satan, the angel who became a monster, expresses the contrast between the American promise and the American historical reality.

Does most of America perceive that its fascination with the fallen angels is a reflection of its own fall from innocence? A bright promise of innocence becoming corrupted by pride and lust for power is the story of both the devil and the United States. Indeed, America could learn moral wisdom from this mythic narrative if it received top billing in the American consciousness. Unfortunately, this aspect of the national story remains subterranean, only visible when we give American religious and popular culture a close and critical reading. In fact, in a very insidious way, America's conscious image of Satan legitimizes some of the nation's worst tendencies, even as Satan's narrative reflects anxieties about those same tendencies. An America drunk on notions of its own innocence and goodness has been able to identify the devil with its enemies, and its enemies with the devil, time and again. At one time or another in American history, the most influential religious movements, the most powerful politicians, and the dominant trends in popular culture have identified marginalized women, native peoples, slaves, Roman Catholics, Muslims, social progressives, alienated young adults, immigrants, and numerous other social and political groupings and identities as satanic, inspired by Satan, or even Satan himself.

Theologians and philosophers may ponder questions of theodicy, why evil exists in a universe created by a good God. But most popular thinking about Satan in modern America does not reach this level of sophistication. Unfortunately, Satan has provided an easy shorthand answer to the daunting problem of evil. There is evil because there are evildoers in league with the Evil One. In American society and history, this has been *the* most common response to the problem of evil. American political and religious leaders, and the masses that follow them, have not simplistically claimed "the devil made me do it." They have tended to claim, with an even more raw simplicity, the devil made *them, the outsider, and the enemy* do it.

Clyde Z. Nunn's study from the early 1970s highlights this emphasis in American demonology. Nunn looked at the correlation of beliefs about Satan with other variables and found that those who confessed a strong belief in the devil also believed that communism and the radical social movements of the 1960s threatened the American way of life. A strong belief in the devil further correlated with a belief that the restriction of civil liberties provided a way to keep America safe. A similar study conducted today might find that strong believers in Satan are those most concerned with "radical Islam" as a world threat. Or that extreme measures, including the suspension of civil liberties, might be required to prevent terrorist acts.[23]

The powerful metaphor of Satan has usually been at the service of the dominant forces shaping American society. The devil, however, has also been a shape-shifter in American culture. In an odd twist explored in this book, Satan has proved to be a protean enough image to be deployed by some of the very groups that the public culture identified with him. The powerless as well as the powerful found in him a useful tool. Enslaved Africans, whom southern planters accused of satanic inspiration when they attempted slave rebellions large and small, took the devil they met in their masters' churches and identified him with the master class and slavery itself. Pentecostals in the early twentieth century, drawn from the ranks of the socially and politically powerless, found in the devil a power they could "cast out," a force they could control through simple faith. In the late twentieth century, American teenagers alienated by boomer parents and boomer institutions, found in Satan the perfect symbol of rebellion and alienation.

Satan has always been someone in the story of American history. Native peoples, blacks, immigrants, "reds," transgressive women, and "terrorist evil-doers" have all been Satan for Americans at one time or another. Again and again, the community, rallied often by the emerging or triumphant nation-state, has cycled through the scapegoat mechanism, done violence to its victims, and found social unity again. And the cycle has begun anew.

This book examines this cycle through a close reading of American religion and popular culture from the first settlements to the present. The first half, "Diabolical Beginnings," emphasizes how the American Satan grew out of old-world conceptions of evil, especially informed by the Reformation, the rise of religious revivalism, and the tendency to identify the cultural other as a scapegoat and victim. The American devil took shape in the context of the rise of powerful religious movements, "great awakenings" that created a specifically American version of Christianity. The devil, as Lord of Evil, became the chief Enemy, the force behind every spiritual and moral anxiety. This cultural tendency in American history appears in the phenomenon of witch hunts and witch trials (more widespread than Salem), but also in the nineteenth century with white middle-class America's war against alcohol and immigrants.

Part Two, "The Satanic Century," looks at the experience of twentieth-century America through its fascination with the devil. The "American century" saw not only the birth of the United States as a global empire but also the emergence of Satan as a primary player in popular religious movements and popular culture. Both outlets for the demonic imagination provide us a window into the American love of violence and failure to come to grips with the power of evil in its national soul. Both allow us to see America as itself a kind of fallen angel who never knew it fell.

NOTES

1. Arthur Lyons, *Satan Wants You: The Cult of Devil Worship in America* (New York: The Mysterious Press, 1988), 4.
2. Richard Ramirez quoted in William Hart, *Evil: A Primer: A History of a Bad Idea from Beelzebub to Bin Laden* (New York: St. Martin's Press, 2004), 76.
3. Bill Ellis, *Raising the Devil: Satanism, New Religions, and the Media* (Lexington: University Press of Kentucky, 2000), 287.
4. These accounts are taken from Howard Zinn, *A People's History of the United States* (New York: Harper Perennial, 1995), 15, 469.
5. Sigmund Freud, *Civilization and Its Discontents* (New York: W.W. Norton and Company, 1989), 68–69.
6. Bart D. Ehrman, *God's Problem: How the Bible Fails to Answer Our Most Important Question* (New York: HarperOne, 2007).
7. Chris Hedges, "A Hollow Agnosticism," review of *God's Problem*, by Bart D. Ehrman, *Harvard Divinity Bulletin* 36, no. 2 (Spring 2008).
8. Nel Noddings quoted in Hart, *Evil: A Primer*, 15.
9. Mark Larrimore quoted in Hart, *Evil: A Primer*, 9.
10. Hart, *Evil: A Primer*, 56, 57.
11. Andrew Delbanco, *The Death of Satan: How Americans Have Lost the Sense of Evil* (New York: Farrar, Straus and Giroux, 1995), 3.
12. Delbanco, *Death of Satan*, 23.
13. On Satan in American folklore, see Bill Ellis, *Lucifer Ascending: The Occult in Folklore and Popular Culture* (Lexington: University Press of Kentucky, 2004).
14. This is especially true of two of their works, George Marsden's *Religion in American Culture* (San Diego: Harcourt, Brace and Jovanovich, 2001), and R. Laurence Moore's *Touchdown Jesus: The Mixing of the Sacred and Secular in American Culture* (Louisville, KY: Westminster John Knox Press, 2003).
15. Interestingly, much of this effort has been focused on the colonial era. See Harry Stout, *The New England Soul: Preaching and Religious Culture in Colonial New England* (New York: Oxford University Press, 1986) and Frank Lambert, *Inventing the Great Awakening* (Princeton, NJ: Princeton University Press, 1999).

16. See especially René Girard, *I See Satan Fall Like Lightning* (Maryknoll, NY: Orbis Books, 2001), 22–31, 69–70.

17. Girard, *I See Satan*, 36, 46, 152.

18. Robert Jewett and John Shelton Lawrence, *Captain America and the Crusade against Evil: The Dilemma of Zealous Nationalism* (Grand Rapids, MI: William B. Eerdmans Company, 2003), xiii.

19. Elaine Pagels, *The Origin of Satan* (New York: Vintage Books), xviii.

20. Tony Judt, "The Problem of Evil in Postwar Europe," *New York Review of Books* 55, no. 2 (February 14, 2008): 3.

21. Andrew Bacevich, *American Empire: The Realities and Consequences of American Diplomacy* (Cambridge, MA: Harvard University Press, 2002).

22. Cornel West, *Democracy Matters: Winning the Fight against Imperialism* (New York: Penguin Books 2004), 41.

23. Lyons, *Satan Wants You*, xiv.

Acknowledgments

Denis de Rougemont wrote *The Devil's Share*, one of my favorite books dealing with the symbol of the devil and the problem of evil. In the first few pages of that short work, de Rougemont wrote, tongue in cheek, about the possible dangers of writing about his chosen subject.

> It was not without some uneasiness that I felt the promptings of this book: between author and subject, does one ever know which chooses the other? To speak of the devil, to write about him—was this not an impudent way of provoking him publicly?

I'm happy to report that the pages that follow did not provoke any diabolical interest in me though they did give rise to numerous interesting queries and speculations from my students at the College of Charleston. Graduate students, as well as undergraduates in my Religion in American History course, provided me with a listening post for my ideas. Graduate assistant Katherine Jenkins helped compile research from twentieth century periodicals. Graduate assistant Amanda Mazur helped with the early stages of searching for images. Hilary Lentz's interest in early modern witch hunts (and in contemporary horror films) proved a source of inspiration for me. I look forward to the publication of her own research and scholarship.

Supportive friends encouraged me and, in some cases, provided valuable practical assistance. Alan Richard and Nina Kushner's interest in my research and writing is a constant encouragement to my work just as their friendship provides one of the bright lights of my life. Myra Seaman's critique of the first three chapters helped me work through those problematic sections. My friendship with her and Robert Grant gave me time out for good food, beach time, movies, and Rock Band. Cara Delay, Noelle Carmichael, and Tim Carmichael encouraged me more than they know by constantly asking me about my progress on the book. Niamh, my very special goddaughter, provided, along with her brother Finn, a needed respite from my dark reflections. Tami Boyce helped me with photographs and listened patiently to my strange ideas for graphic design and t-shirts she should produce.

I was very lucky in the editors and staff I have been able to work with at Rowman & Littlefield. Executive Editor Niels Aaboe guided the work on this project. Michelle Cassidy, editorial assistant to Niels, provided quick answers to my many questions. Melissa McNitt shepherded the work professionally through production. I was also lucky in the help I received from the American Antiquarian Society, the New York Public Library, the Peabody-Essex Museum, and the University of Michigan archives. I am grateful for their willingness to allow images from their collections to appear in this volume.

Most important to the writing of this book, far more than she realizes, is my partner Beth Phillips. Beth's complete support, constant encouragement, willingness to sacrifice in order to give me time to write and reflect has made all the difference in the writing of this book. I'm glad she is both my biggest fan and best friend. This book is dedicated to her.

I

DIABOLICAL BEGINNINGS

1

"The Devil Is Come Down in Great Wrath": The American Satan in the Colonial and Revolutionary Worlds

The Prince of Darkness reigns supreme.

Satan emerged in the ancient Near East as a minor character in Yahweh's heavenly court. Satan today enjoys celebrity status after a 4,000-year historical and literary transformation from God's envoy of disaster to God's archenemy. Horror films make us cringe at his power to corrupt the human personality, while best-selling books offer to tell his side of the story. Novelizations of Armageddon declare him a character of cosmic importance with an intricate and devious design on humanity. Tens of millions of America's evangelical Christians believe they are in constant daily combat with the same dark angel who has warred with God since the endless eons before creation.

Most Americans do indeed believe in him. A 2005 poll, conducted by Gallup under the aegis of the Baylor Institute for the Study of Religion, asked a cross-section of Americans whether they believed the devil to be a personal entity, an actual rather than simply a metaphorical source of evil. Fifty-five percent claimed they believe he is a literal being, a supernatural entity dedicated to evil and corruption. Another 19 percent said they thought such a being "probably" existed. Most of these Americans also believe Satan to be active through a host of demonic minions.[1]

More recently, a November 2007 Harris poll found evidence of growing belief in the devil. In fact, more Americans believe in the literal existence of Satan than in the theory of evolution. The poll, based on a much larger sampling than the Baylor Study, revealed that 62 percent believed Satan to be alive and well while only 42 percent accepted the Darwinian theory of evolution. Belief in the devil among evangelical Christians is especially high, including a sturdy belief in witches and warlocks. Even more notable, a large percentage of Roman Catholic and mainline Protestants shared similar beliefs even though the same poll revealed that these groups' rates of acceptance of modern ideas, such as Darwinian evolution, are much higher than that of evangelicals. In America, Satan has survived despite technological innovation and modern biology. In fact, he has more believers here than in any country in the developed world.[2]

The numbers who believe in Satan as a literal being have noticeably grown over the last four decades. In 1982, only 34 percent of Americans would admit they believed the devil to be a "personal being who directs evil forces and influences people to do wrong." Another 36 percent said they believed him to be an "impersonal force," perhaps a metaphor, for the work of evil in the world. Belief in demonic spirits, Satan's minions, has also grown. In 1982, only about half of those who confessed a belief in the devil acknowledged a belief in demons.[3]

These numbers become even more striking when compared with rates of belief in the devil in other developed nations. In 1973, polls conducted in Western Europe found that only 17 percent of the French, 21 percent of the British, and 25 percent of the citizens of the former West Germany acknowledged a belief in Satan. At even the lowest point of satanic belief on record in the twentieth-century United States, many millions more people have believed in the devil than in any European nation.[4]

This book attempts to analyze and explain why Satan has always been important in the American consciousness and frequently in the American unconscious, why Satan's story has been a success story in the United States. The land of new promise, rich with possibilities and always certain of its own goodness, has been a haunt of demons. At almost every crucial turning point in American history, at every moment of transformation in American social and cultural life, Satan has embodied, structured, and legitimized, America's self-identity. He has been the ghost at the American banquet, hiding in the "howling wilderness" that threatened the Puritans and giving rhetorical lessons at the elbow of American politicians. In recent years, he has gone into the entertainment industry, making music that voices rebellion and alienation and films that have had us screaming (and, in the case of one notorious film, vomiting and fainting) in the aisles. He is always with us, America's silent partner and the key to its secret history.

What exactly does the average American believe in when they profess a belief in Satan? It is, in fact, frequently unclear. Any contemporary person who asserts this belief actually accepts an amorphous set of beliefs born of various and often conflicting traditions constantly in flux. The American Satan draws as much on the entertainment industry as on ancient texts for his identity. Beliefs about the devil for the average American might come from sources as diverse as serious theological works, stories related by a Pentecostal grandmother, a viewing of *The Exorcist*, a stray passage heard from the Bible, or some well- and oft-told urban legend. All of these sources might, in fact, inform the beliefs of a single individual at the same time.

A composite description of the American devil of the twenty-first century must note the collusion between American religious movements and popular culture. Since colonial times, American religion has fought the devil and diverse strands in American popular culture have provided a running commentary on that fight. In turn, imagery in everything from comic books to film has added color and texture to the image of Satan proclaimed from pulpits and feared in the pews.

This cooperative partnership between religion and pop culture, evolving since the earliest settlement of North America, has created a Satan terrifying in his seductive power, a threat not only to humanity but to God Himself. The devil in America has emerged as the epitome of fallen innocence, a once-beautiful angel who chose pride over love of God. Unlike Milton's Satan, however, the American Satan was not forever twisted and made monstrous by his great fall. He appears as Billy Budd, handsome to his victims and with a powerful sexual aura, appealing especially to women. Also unlike Milton's Satan, it is hard to feel empathy for this American devil. His fall made him less an admirable rebel and more a beautiful monster, a cosmic serial killer.

America's Satan is far more powerful than his medieval European forebear. He is never, as he was sometimes viewed in the middle ages, a jester or a fool. Nor is he, as Dante imagined him, locked forever at the lowest depths of the inferno, burbling like an angry infant and impotently flapping his leathery wings. America's Satan is, instead, seemingly omnipresent, corrupting Christianity itself, seducing leaders in government and business, building an organizational structure of his followers to rival the church, hindering religious revivals, leading a huge army of demonic minions who can possess human beings, causing natural disasters, inspiring the enemies of the United States to acts of violence. Moreover, in a peculiarly American contribution to satanic lore, the devil is working overtime to bring about the end of the world and even to incarnate himself as a human being on Earth, the Antichrist. Satan, like modern America, has an interest in the geopolitics of empire. The American Satan does not see the end of the world as his final judgment and downfall. Instead, Armageddon is his last roll of the dice against the Almighty, a final conflict he seems confident of winning.

This American devil, for all his power, is a dark wine of recent vintage. But the biography of the image of the devil in religious thought, by the time of the American founding, had already had several millennia of development and historical evolution. Much of the previous work on Satan has focused on his origin and historical development. These works have generally stressed the enormous differences between the earliest biblical understanding of Satan and how Christianity came to imagine its greatest foe. Scholars such as Henry Ansgar Kelly and Jeffrey Burton Russell have examined the development of the literary, theological, and folkloric Satan, exploring his antecedents in the ancient near east and examining the development of his image into modern times. This is an image that has undergone significant historical revision.[5]

The devil, it turns out, has not always been the devil. In the Hebrew scriptures, the Christian Old Testament, Satan appears as a member of Yahweh's heavenly court, one of the "sons of God." No prince of evil, his name simply means "one who obstructs." Rather than being obviously malevolent, the Satan of early Hebrew thought performs the harsh work of God in the world, testing his servants, as in the book of Job. The Hebrew scriptures even use "Satan" as a verb to describe the direct action of God. As Elaine Pagels notes, the Hebrew scriptures do not imagine Satan as "the leader of an evil empire." He functions instead as God's son of a bitch, an enforcer who does God's dirty work.[6]

Only in Hellenistic Judaism did Satan begin to appear as a "fallen angel" in direct conflict with God and God's people. Beginning in the third century BCE, an apocalyptic literature emerged within the Jewish tradition that suggested that some angels had fallen from Yahweh's favor. These evil angels engaged in a struggle against God and God's people until the end of the world. The historical context facilitated this concept of metaphysical conflict. The political situation in Hellenistic Palestine fostered the growth of numerous sectarian movements within Judaism, each sect producing religious texts that promised the quick arrival of the end of time, a moment of judgment for their enemies and justification for their own views. Satan as a "prince of evil" opposed to God proved very appealing in this context. Sectarian Judaism tended to define its enemies as allied with the head of the rebel angels. This begins the long history of identifying one's religious and political enemies as not only misguided, but as servants of a supreme evil power.[7]

Hellenistic Judaism's ideas about the devil proved formative for the Christian concept of Satan. Even in these mythic tales, however, we don't meet the fully conceptualized Christian devil. The rebel angels of Jewish apocalyptic literature are frequently given a leader, though his identity varies. Sometimes he is named Belial or Azazel, with "Satan" listed only as the name of one of his minor colleagues. Moreover, in these works the rebel angels are sometime less enemies of God than enemies of humanity, whose evil acts serve God's larger purposes. They are not independent operators, challenging God. They are forces primarily opposed to human beings and used by God to instruct or chastise.[8]

The specific conditions of the Christian era, in Jeffrey Burton Russell's view, provides the blueprint for the modern Satan, Prince of Darkness and evil incarnate, foe of God and enemy of all that is good. Christians inherited late Judaism's idea about enemy angels but also had these notions sharpened by the experience of being a persecuted minority and by their struggle against "heresy," false beliefs the emerging Church saw as threatening true Christian doctrine. The Christian Church imagined an evil angel, rather than the Roman Empire or heresiarchs, as their true enemy. This did not remove culpability from the Church's human opponents. If anything, it darkened their guilt, since they were acting as the very instruments of Satan rather than simply as misguided human beings.[9]

Elaine Pagels's work *The Origin of Satan* strengthens Russell's argument in her close dissection of early Christian thought about the Evil One. The Princeton scholar introduces her study as a "social history of Satan" that explores not only the historical origins of the symbol of Satan, but also the uses to which the ancient world put the powerful metaphor for evil. Again and again, identifying one's enemies with demonic power provided a psychological strategy for dealing with anger, chaos, and various social and political anxieties. A Prince of Darkness proved a ready answer to the problem of evil that did not require personal or societal moral transformation. Evil inhered in the supernatural and in those corrupted human beings who had made league with it.[10]

The most original contribution of *The Origin of Satan* is Pagels's examination of the role played by the devil in the construction of the Christian Gospels themselves. Rather than a bit player in the account of Jesus' life and ministry, Pagels notes that Satan's influence determined the dramatic direction of the gospel accounts. During the course of his earthly life, Jesus appears to meet hundreds of people who have been possessed by demonic spirits and even by Satan himself. This is significant not only for New Testament scholars seeking to interpret early Christianity, but also for understanding what Satan came to symbolize. Earliest Christianity evolved out of a sense of profound confrontation with evil. This idea continues to influence global Christianity but, as we will see, has special resonance in the American context.[11]

In the decades following the writing of the gospels, Justin Martyr (100–165 CE) laid the groundwork for much of the Christian church's notions about Satan. He, for example, made the all-important connection between the serpent that tempted Eve in the third chapter of Genesis and "the dragon," the devil of the New Testament. He also attributed to Satan enormous power, insisting in his exegesis of the early chapters of Genesis that the punishment of Adam and Eve included God granting Lucifer significant power over humanity and the cosmos.[12]

Justin Martyr and other early Christian figures provided some of the basic assumptions for what would become the Western world's "devil." However, as Jeffrey Burton Russell notes, early Christian theological thinking on the question of evil remained diverse and more sophisticated in its beliefs about Satan than is often supposed. Some early Christian thinkers actually disdained the concept of the devil. St. Augustine, a fifth-century Christian bishop whose body of work proved determinative for the course of Latin Christendom's doctrinal development, emphasized the sovereignty of God in the universe, leaving only narrow space for the devil to operate. Satan remained insignificant in Augustine's vast theological corpus, even though the problem of evil deeply concerned him. As Russell notes, Augustine thought that introducing Satan into the discussion of evil raises more questions than it answers. It is bad enough that God made cancer cells, sharks, and hurricanes. Why would a beneficent deity also "give the universe a lord of evil?"[13]

Most medieval Christians did not ponder Augustine's philosophical concerns, but they did ponder the devil. Most of what Americans see today when they envision the devil emerged out of the popular folk culture of the Christian Middle Ages. Medieval folklore fastened on Satan some of his primary accouterments, including cloven feet, horns, and a tail. Beliefs about Satan never became systematic, in part because, not unlike today, Satan gathered to himself many of the attributes of popular tales about evil. Medieval beliefs about the nature of the devil tended to shade into beliefs about other destructive mythological beings such as trolls and dragons, in the same way that today's ideas about the devil are freely influenced by screen images of vampires, werewolves, and even serial killers.[14]

If the medieval devil provided comedy relief in popular culture, medieval theology had little concern for the devil at all, giving him little attention or respect. Dante's *Inferno*, inspired in part by scholastic theology, gives us a Satan that, Russell writes, "appears more pathetic than terrifying." Popular culture reflected this scholastic view. Late medieval drama tended to transform the devil and his demons into comedic figures that frolicked, fell, and farted in the background of medieval mystery plays. How, these images asked, could these demonic jesters be anything but an annoyance to God's triumphant Catholic and Apostolic Church?[15]

Nevertheless, the frequent appearance of Satan in medieval culture signaled his growing importance in European popular culture. In fact, by the dawn of the Renaissance, Christianity showed a greater fascination with Satan than at any time since the early centuries of the faith. In the thirteenth and fourteenth centuries, a forest of theological and pastoral documents sought to define Satan's activities on Earth, with a special emphasis on the possibility of possession and human cooperation (often including conjugal relations) with demons. In 1326, Pope John XXII released the bull *Super illius Specula*, which condemned magical practices as consultations with the devil.[16] Folk practices related to divination and fortune-telling came to be regarded as "pacts with hell" instead of as religiously neutral "white magic." The very notion of the "infernal pact" and consequent "satanic conspiracies" became fodder for ecclesiastical pronouncement and popular legend in the late Middle Ages. This cultural legacy, filtered through the Reformation, Puritan concerns, and the rise of evangelical revivalism, remains with us in many of modern America's conceptions of Satan and his work on Earth.

This early modern fascination with Satan overlapped with, ironically, the birth of the Age of Skepticism. The age of Montaigne was also the age of the witch hunts. While we rightly connect early modern Europe with the scientific revolution and the rise of the nation-state, it was also a historical moment in which age-old fears and folk beliefs suddenly and horrifically made their way into emerging jurisprudence. In fact, as historian Robert Muchembled notes, it is frequently "forgotten that the actual burnings were the work of the civil power." New nation-states made possible the prosecution of witches on a scale unimagined in the medieval period. Church and state collaborated in the "liturgy of fear" that burned across Europe in the new, enlightened age.[17]

Witchcraft panics erupted in the late fifteenth century in France and Germany and had not been tamped down long when a new panic in the mid-sixteenth century spread to Switzerland and England. A final vicious phase began in the 1620s and lasted until the last quarter of the century. Scholars are divided on the numbers executed by the witch hunts, though most would place the victims somewhere between 50,000 and 100,000 people. Brian Levack has estimated the number at 60,000, a figure reached by taking the number of known trials and multiplying it by the average rate of trial and conviction.[18]

Marginalized women faced the brunt of the violence that emerged from Europe's love for demonology and satanic conspiracies. Women had long been viewed by celibate churchmen as spiritually suspect, at least when not properly ensnared in either marriage or religious life. These attitudes continued with the Protestant Reformation. Indeed women's options became even more limited in the Protestant sixteenth century, as marriage became the only possible sphere of action. Women who, in various ways, challenged Catholic and Protestant conceptions of true womanhood risked becoming a scapegoat for community ills. In such a context, widows who lived off of community charity, financially independent women, women who ignored sexual conventions all risked facing an accusation of witchcraft after a drought, a sudden death, an outbreak of contagion, or some other community misfortune. Christina Larner concludes that in areas of Europe where the witch hunts were most severe (such as Germany, France, and Scotland) women accounted for about 80 percent of the accused. In peripheral areas such as England and Russia, the percentage was between 95 and 100.[19]

The witchcraft trials gave horrific proof of early modern Europe's fascination with the devil and its willingness to define the marginalized as his servants. This fascination altered in the eighteenth century. Challenges to religious belief from the pen of Hume, Diderot, and Voltaire included a challenge to the belief in Satan. Voltaire, for example, called the English poet John Milton's *Paradise Lost* a "disgusting fantasy" and saw belief in both hell and demonic beings as one of the many tricks the Church had played over the centuries on the peasant classes.[20]

This attack on belief in the devil did not result in a rapid decline in popular belief in the demonic. The scientific revolution that informed Enlightenment values had its own share of fascination with the occult. Robert Boyle, the English scientist largely responsible for the creation of the modern discipline of chemistry, interviewed miners in the 1670s in an attempt to discover whether the men had met with any "subterraneous demons . . . in what shape and manner they appear; what they portend and what they do." During the same era, advice on so-called practical magicks made up a significant part of English publishing. In 1720, well into the "Age of the Enlightenment," one of the most popular English books in print was *The New Fortune Book*, which offered magical cures and love potions.[21]

Once the very concept of belief in the devil had been challenged, cultural critics could borrow his imagery more freely, wielding him as a weapon against the very orthodoxy that had first created him. The critical reexamination of satanic belief had the ironic effect of bringing the devil a fresh class of recruits eager to use satanic imagery for social and cultural purposes. Satan became not a figure of evil but rather a subversive force that challenged oppression by secular and sacred authorities. The devil of the romantics did not replace the devil of Christian tradition, but he did influence Western popular culture in a variety of ways.

English visionary poet William Blake saw Satan as a symbol that could be used by the forces of political radicalism, indeed could embody political radicalism, rather than simply serving to support through fear-mongering systems of power and oppression. In his 1790 *Marriage of Heaven and Hell*, Blake portrays Satan as a subversive spirit who embodies human emotion and the possibility of liberation from reason and orthodoxy, twin engines of oppression in Blake's view. Blake celebrates Satan as the ultimate rebel. It was Blake who famously commented that Milton was "of the devil's party without knowing it" because in his literary Satan he had created a powerful image of the struggle against unjust authority.[22]

Romantic conceptions of the devil helped promote the birth of a kind of satanic chic in the nineteenth century West. Particularly potent in France, satanic chic joined a strident anticlericalism with an emerging gothic romanticism to make the devil both a figure of fascination and a symbol of rebellion. Jeffrey Burton Russell points out that the so-called "satanism of the nineteenth century" did not become a true religious satanism but rather a theatrical expression of gothic evil used for aesthetic effect and shock value. Charles Baudelaire took this tendency to its literary heights, finding in Satan a symbol of everything from human brutality to a representative of a dark, frightening, and seductive beauty. His 1857 collection of poems *Les Fleurs du Mal*, containing his infamous "Litanies to Satan," must be read as a work of ironic reflection, an irony drawing on the rich imagery surrounding Satan in Western culture. Baudelaire, whose spiritual interests eventually led to his return to the Roman Catholic Church, helped to spawn the Decadent movement.[23]

Satanic chic also created a powerful effect outside the literary world, presaging emergence of the American Satan as a pop culture phenom. Belgian "magic lantern" operator Etienne Robertson built his tomblike *Phantasmagoria* theatre in 1830s Paris to meet popular demand for satanic thrills. The magic lantern projected light through colored glass slides, enabling Robertson to create a hellish diorama of shadows in his theatre. Satan, portrayed as a giant, leathery-winged beast, flew above the heads of terrified spectators.[24]

Satan came to humanity in many manifestations, from the ancient Middle East to eighteenth-century Europe. None of the images and symbols of the devil have been purely dominant at one moment in the history of the West. For example, while some Parisians thrilled to the entertaining devils of the Phantasmagoria, others devoutly prayed to the Virgin and saints for deliverance from evil. Others probably did both. Throughout the long history of the devil, different and often competing images from religion and popular culture have helped to shape his symbolism and thus the human understanding of evil.

A biography of the American devil must take into account the longer history described above while also analyzing the diverse forces peculiar to the American experience that have shaped Satan's current incarnation among us. Theologians have played a role in giving the United States its devil, but so have popular religious movements with little time for theology. Complicating the image of the American Satan even further, our complex and variegated popular culture has used theology according to its needs for color and effect. This process appears even in contemporary America but can be traced to the earliest days of American settlement.

Satan's arrival on North American shores, like Dracula relocating from his ancestral Transylvania to London, had to be prepared ahead of time.

Before the early European settlement of America, the Reformation had splintered Christendom and opened up centuries of conflict. Catholics and Protestants waged war on one another, imprisoned dissenters, and tortured heretics in what each side believed was a titanic struggle against the devil. This period, viewed by some as a rebirth of Christianity from dead medieval forms, also gave birth to a new and powerful devil.

These conflicts, and the Prince of Darkness they produced, can be seen in some of the earliest European explorers and conquerors of the New World. Spanish explorers in the American southeast and southwest brought with them a profound belief in the operation of Satan on Earth, nurtured by centuries of devout Catholicism and put into practice through the inquisition and expulsion of heretics and Sephardic Jews. After one generation of exploration and conquest in the New World, Spanish ecclesiastics began organized efforts to root out the works of the devil among the Amerindians. An Office of Inquisition was instituted in the 1530s by Juan de Zumarraga, Archbishop of Mexico. Indian religious rituals, especially those that in some ways resembled Christian sacraments, came to be seen as "satanic inversions" of Catholic rites.[25]

The Spanish conquerors brought their own idea of heresy, satanic pact, and the witches' sabbat with them to the New World to interpret the native religious ceremonies they witnessed. Hernando Ruiz de Alarcón, writing against the perceived "idolatry" of the Indian in 1629, believed that the native peoples had made an "infernal pact" with Satan. Indeed, the emphasis given to animal spirits in many native religions led him to conclude that most of the Indian shamans were shape-shifters along the lines of the European werewolf. Even Friar Bartolomé de Las Casas, though a strong proponent of the rights of Native Americans under Spanish occupation, described the New World as full of the activity of demonic spirits. La Casas literally saw the air above the Americas teeming with devils and Satan coming to Earth to tempt witches to kill the unbaptized infants.[26]

Notably, not all New World missionaries took it for granted that the Amerindian cultural traditions were lost to Satan. The Thomistic tradition within Catholic theology viewed nature (all aspects of human life and culture) as containing some elements of the good and perfectible by grace (God's supernatural intervention in human life). Some Spanish Franciscans viewed Indian religious rituals as preparatory rites, "training wheels" for the practice of true Catholic doctrine. Las Casas himself, though seeing the devil everywhere in the New World, believed that even many European cultural traditions belonged to the world of nature and could be corrupted by the devil if God's grace did not intervene. In New France, the Thomistic tradition held sway. Jesuit missionaries, while appalled by some of the Indian's social practices, generally viewed them as pagan innocents whose traditions had helped prepare them for the gospel. While the devil could turn these natural traditions to his own dark ends, God's grace could also intervene. This somewhat tolerant view certainly contributed to the relatively positive relations that the French in the New World maintained with their native neighbors.[27]

This is not to say that Jesuit missionaries did not use the language of diabolism to describe certain aspects of Amerindian cultural life to themselves and to their superiors. Jesuit missionaries tended to attribute Iroquois beliefs related to dreams and divination to the devil. Indeed, some seventeenth-century Jesuit missionaries believed that "big dreams" represented real supernatural evil, devices used by Satan to keep the Iroquois from turning to the Church.[28]

The decline of Spain's international empire in the late 1500s opened the door for the emergence of new Atlantic powers. English settlers, comparatively latecomers to the new continent in the seventeenth century, came to the New World directly from a context of a home country riven by religious conflict and poisoned with folk beliefs about Satan. The devil, in English folklore, could intervene in any human life or human community, creating chaos through human agents. In 1566, one of the earliest English texts on witchcraft appeared, entitled "The Examination of John Walsh." Containing all of the canards common to witch trials, the author claimed that Walsh had confessed to intercourse with "Feries" and had used a "familiar" that came to him in the form of a black dove, a dog, and a man with cloven feet. Walsh was alleged to have used the powers granted him by Satan for thievery and to curse and bewitch.[29]

Queen Elizabeth herself, perhaps understandably worried about assassination, imprisoned a number of suspected "sorcerers and olde witches." In her reign, she replicated a larger European tendency of linking the work of the devil with threats to the state. King James I also brought an obsession with the works of the devil to the English throne. Convinced that witches, in league with Satan, had tried to kill him in a "tempest" upon the North Sea, James remained certain that he was the center of the evil one's concern in the early seventeenth century.[30]

The Puritan movement in sixteenth- and seventeenth-century England had sought to rid Anglicanism of the last vestiges of the Roman Church. The war against Rome was, in part, a war with the devil. The Puritans grounded their conception of true religious faith in the need to struggle against the wiles of Satan. English Puritan leaders in New England brought with them an anxiety about the devil's influence, as well as a belief that he worked through a host of malignant servants. Strong believers in the power of the supernatural, they proved able to find the work of Satan as readily, perhaps more readily, than the providences of God. The Puritan clergy viewed both the Indians who dwelt in the New

England woods and transgressive women within their own settlements as conduits for satanic power, parts of a larger conspiracy against the work of God on Earth. The "city on the hill" was beset on all sides by the forces of hell.

The Puritan conviction of Satan's activity on Earth provided the ideological context for the infamous Salem Witchcraft trials. In 1692, nine-year-old Elizabeth Parris and eleven-year-old Abigail Williams, respectively the daughter and the niece of Puritan minister Samuel Parris, began hearing stories of Caribbean and African folk magic from Parris's slave Tituba. It is probably hard for us today to grasp the entertainment value these stories had for the young women of Salem village, most of them teenagers, who flocked to the Parris kitchen to listen to Tituba recount these tales. In fact, the young women became so overwrought by the stories that some entered ecstatic, trancelike states, falling to the ground and frothing at the mouth.[31]

Local physician William Griggs, at Parris's request, examined the young women and rather quickly concluded that they had been bewitched. The girls readily agreed with his prognosis and began to issue accusations, unleashing long-held village prejudices and anxieties of their own and of their parents. Their deadly accusations began with Tituba herself and then focused on two marginal women in the village, Sarah Osborne and Sarah Goode. Goode was a poor woman who lived on the village's charity, but who often responded to that charity with rancor. Osborne was a mentally challenged woman with a hint of sexual scandal in her past.[32]

The young women's accusations quickly spun out of control. In May 1692, the royal governor of Massachusetts established a special court to ferret out what appeared to be a large and threatening satanic conspiracy. One hundred forty-one people would be arrested as suspects. No one, ultimately, was safe. The accused included Rebecca Nurse, a church member and perhaps the most respectable elderly matron in Salem village. It also would include Dorcas Goode, Sarah Goode's daughter, a four-year-old child, who would be chained for seven to eight months in the darkness of Salem Town jail.[33]

The Salem witch trials proved that the Old World obsession with satanic pacts and supernatural evil had come to colonial America. Historians who have examined the events in 1692 have detailed a diverse collection of causes and effects, including the significance of social tensions over the control of property and the role played by gender and social expectation in the choice of targets for witchcraft accusations.[34]

The most recent work on Salem emphasizes the role that folk traditions of "cunning folk" played in the background of the events of 1692. David D. Hall and Richard Godbeer have opened to us the world of Puritan popular culture and complicated any simple definition of how the Puritans viewed the supernatural, witchcraft, and the nature of the devil. While the Puritan ministry condemned all manner of traffic with the occult, popular religious traditions gave some place to the role of charms, amulets, and even astrological speculation. Puritan popular culture, as well as Puritan theology, influenced their view of the devil and his works.

The Puritan blending of the popular and the theological meant that, much as in contemporary America, contradictory beliefs about Satan and his influence jostled with one another in the New England mind. Many Puritans thought in terms of "good magic" versus "evil magic," as opposed to the Puritan ministry's idea that magic, or "cunning" belonged by definition to the realm of Satan. Gradually, folk belief and Puritan theological belief coalesced into a single system of thought that regarded Satan as active in all aspects of life. In this way, the witch trials presaged a deadly American pattern in which theology and popular folk belief would unite in a conspiracy of paranoia that could only end in persecution and violence.[35]

Salem reveals what would become another typical American tendency in the deployment of satanic imagery. The effort to root out evil from the Puritan "city on a hill" took place within a context of terror inspired by a recent destructive Indian war and the possibility of renewed violence between the Puritans and the native peoples. In 1675, the Puritan settlements had recently fought a bloody war with the Wampanoag under a sachem known as Metacomet (called "King Phillip" by the Puritans). Historians have estimated that perhaps as many as 20,000 whites and Indians died in this conflict, a huge number by seventeenth-century standards. Salem Village had lost 30 percent of its male population. Direct connections existed between the witchcraft trials and this terrible conflict. Mercy Lewis, one of the young accusers whose screams, fainting fits, and tales of demonic attack began the hysteria, had been orphaned in a recent Indian raid.[36]

The war only fed the Puritan concept of evil that fueled the witchcraft hysteria. The heightened anxieties created by ongoing conflict with natives help explain why accusation of radical satanic evil in the heart of the Puritan settlements met so readily with belief. Puritans had always assumed that evil crouched on the shadowy outskirts of their settlements even before Metacomet's War. One of the earliest references to satanic influence in the documents of American Puritanism is not a witchcraft accusation, but rather a description of a meeting of Indian leaders that, Puritan clergy claimed, included an appearance by Satan himself.[37]

The Puritan understanding of the Indians made the threat they posed more than human, transforming it into a threat from the satanic and monstrous. An entire discourse among early American theologians concerned itself with why the natives had never heard the Christian message. Most concluded that it was because the devil had thoroughly enslaved them and held them in his power. This view was strong among the Puritans but could be found throughout the American colonies. Captain John Smith of Virginia, for example, said of native religion that "the Chief God they worship is the Devil." Virginian William Crashaw agreed, saying of the New World that Satan "visibly and palpably reigns here."[38]

Puritan divine Cotton Mather created an elaborate demonological mythology to explain why the native peoples were the special servants of Satan. According to Mather, the natives had been a people seduced by Satan to come to the New World, a world where the gospel had not been revealed and Satan could rule. This made them "the children of the devil" in a world where Satan ruled as "prince and power of the air." A few years before the beginning of the trials, Mather had called the Indians Satan's "most devoted and resembling children." Later, Jonathan Edwards would explain the Amerindian presence in the New World in a similar way, writing that "the devil did here quietly enjoy his dominion over the poor Indians for many generations."[39]

In 1691, these "children of the devil" had launched yet another assault on New England in a series of raids on northern Puritan settlements. This had followed an abortive Puritan military expedition to Maine in 1688–1689 in which the unpopular Royal governor, Edmund Andros, had failed to bring Native American forces to heel. Accusers in the Salem trials soon claimed that many of those suspected of witchcraft had worked as secret allies of local Indians and, in several cases, that the devil himself had the appearance of a Native American.[40]

Puritan narratives of their war with local Indians returned again and again to satanic imagery to explain, and legitimize, their violent incursion into New England. Cotton Mather described how it was time "for the devil to take alarum" when the Puritan settlements spread through New England since, in Mather's mind, the conquest of Indian territory was a victory over Satan. In the Pequot War, Satan's supposed alliance with the Indians provided legitimacy for the worst atrocities. In 1637, Puritan forces set ablaze a native palisade on the Mystic River, burning to death many of the defenders. They then killed, drowned, or enslaved the survivors. Mather actually referred to "the bodies of so many natives barbequed" as a "sweet sacrifice to God." Those who survived to be taken captive "were the pictures of so many devils in desperation."[41]

This background ensured that Mather, obsessed with the activity of the devil in the Puritan settlements (and within the human heart), quickly attributed the perceived outbreak of witchcraft to the devil's larger plan to destroy New England:

The story of the prodigious war, made by the Spirits of the Invisible world, upon the People of New England . . . made me often think that this inexplicable War might have some of its Original among the Indians, whose chief Sagamores are well known unto some of our Captives, to have been horrid sorcerers, and hellish conjurers such as conversed with demons.

Mather described the devils as swarming around the Puritan settlements "like the frogs of Egypt." Only moral and spiritual vigilance could save the saints, vigilance and the willing use of violence to prevent corruption. Deodat Lawson, preaching in Salem village, proclaimed that "the devil is come down in great wrath . . . awake, awake, I beseech you!" For Lawson, "to awake" meant to perpetuate violence on those infected with satanic evil.[42] The devil also took on a feminine shape in the Puritan imagination. Women represented a majority of those executed for witchcraft in colonial New England in the seventeenth century. In Salem, women accounted for all but one of the executed. Just as early modern European witch hunters had done, Puritan's gendered the demonic as female. In the New England context, women who failed to live up to Puritan standards of behavior came to represent a powerful symbolic threat. Just as native peoples outside the settlements represented the possibility of satanic attack, women who rejected their role in the New England towns represented a diabolical fifth column. The accusations brought against one Salem woman, Bridget Hobbes, included many of the misogynistic ideas of Western culture about women's weakness to satanic influence combined with the diabolical nature of sexual allure. "Witnesses" accused Hobbes of becoming a powerful succubus-like creature who appeared to them in the night wearing a "red paragon bodice."[43]

Salem represents an especially toxic outbreak of America's fascination with the devil. American historians, especially in the writing of textbooks, have rightly emphasized the Salem witchcraft trials as a key moment in the history of the colonial United States. Here, misogyny and fear of the Other came together to produce needless cruelty and suffering. This emphasis on Salem has, however, also had some unfortunate consequences. Scholars Owen Davies and Jonathan Barry have noted Salem has received tremendous attention in the teaching curriculum of American history, which, they say, has the positive effect of creating a "commendable public awareness of the basic historical issues" involved while also tending to dilute its impact by focusing on a single event. In the minds of many, Salem has come to represent an anomaly in the American experience, a brief flirtation with the irrational past of European folk traditions.[44]

In truth, Salem embodies a broader colonial fascination with Satan and his work. The focus on this single incident has the unintended effect of suggesting that Americans gave up their fascination with the devil and his agents on Earth after the debacle of 1693. Not only did America not give up its belief in Satan, it continued to look for witches to burn as well. Americans embarked on witch hunts throughout the colonial period, each one containing all the horrors of Salem in microcosm. Accusers willingly used the machinery of colonial justice to prosecute their targets, much as their European forbears had asked civil authorities to investigate, convict, and execute on theological premises. The panic in Salem was not even the only outbreak of witch hunting in New England. In fact, more than 344 New Englanders were charged with witchcraft in the first century of the colonies' existence. Puritan courts hauled in many of these victims on charges of religious heresy and then indicted them as witches. About three-quarters of them were women. They all, in various ways, represented some threat to the tenuous Puritan settlement in the New World.[45]

Puritans proved quick to identify religious outsiders as allies of Satan and examples of his work in the world. Increase Mather, the father of Cotton Mather, insisted in his *Essay for the Recording of Illustrious Providences* that Quakers had been deluded by Satan and even suggested that "Evil and Infernal Spirits of Hell" possessed their missionaries. Numerous other anti-Quaker tracts accused Quakers of being led astray, or even possessed by demonic spirits. Even Roger Williams, generally regarded as a beacon of tolerance in early American history and himself accused of being demonically deluded, insisted that the "quaking and shaking" of the Quakers under religious inspiration was not the work of the Holy Spirit, but of the devil.[46]

Colonial Americans did not limit the devil's activity to New England or to the seventeenth century. In many of these instances, the same tendency to link the marginalized and the powerless to Satan created the conditions that made a witch hunt, and sometimes a prosecution and execution, possible. While never as intensive or involving the same number of people as the Salem trials, worries about Satan's influence over colonial life generally grew from the same racist and misogynist roots as New England's horror.

One example is Grace Sherwood of tidewater Virginia, who, in 1706, found herself called before the Court of Princess Anne County to answer charges brought by her neighbors. Sherwood had a reputation as an odd, unmarried woman who spoke little to her neighbors and kept to herself. Her marginal social status seems to have constituted the only basis for the accusations brought against her. Absurd rumors, including that she had "voyaged across the Atlantic, as far as the Mediterranean, in an eggshell," circulated freely. Some claimed that she had brought back "exotic herbs" from her mystical voyages and that this was why rosemary grew so freely around her house.[47]

Sherwood was both dunked into the water and strip-searched by several "ancient women," who asserted, surely intriguing the court, that "she was not like them nor any other women they knew of." This evidence in hand, Colonel Edward Mosley and John Richardson, the chief justices of the Princess Anne court, sentenced her to an indefinite stay in prison. She languished for eight years until, in what almost seems an afterthought, she was finally released.[48]

The deadly combination of belief in witchcraft and misogyny created one of the most enduring of American folkloric traditions in the eighteenth century. The so-called Jersey Devil, rumored even today to haunt the pine barrens of southern New Jersey, grew out of a set of folk stories circulating in New England in the decades following the Salem executions. Usually reported as a large, leathery creature with glowing eyes and the power of flight, more than 2,000 sightings of the creature have been reported, some as recent as the last decade of the twentieth century.

A marginalized woman, accused of cavorting with Satan, is at the heart of these fantastic stories. In 1735, according to one tradition, a woman named Mrs. Shroud, known locally in Leeds Point to be a witch, claimed that she was about to give birth to her thirteenth child, a child who would be a demon or perhaps even the devil incarnate. In one version of the story, Mrs. Shroud is described as rejecting her husband's patriarchal authority and refusing to have child number thirteen. She curses him, and herself, by this domestic rebellion and gives birth to a demon. Shroud supposedly attempted to hide the creature but it escaped into the night by flying up through the chimney. New Jersey had its devil.

Other traditions place the birth of the Jersey Devil somewhat later. One claims that a young girl having an affair with a British officer was cursed with a monstrous birth. Yet another, perhaps the most fantastic, says that the child's grandmother, a witch, and even Satan himself, attended the creature's birth, a being with "a forked tail, hooves, horse-like head and the wings of a bat."[49]

Folklorists frequently seek to find common threads in variegated versions of legendary material. Ideas or images that appear in multiple versions of the same tale can help them piece together the origins of stories such as that of the Jersey Devil. Notably, the word *Leeds* appears in all of the accounts of the Jersey Devil, either as a place name or as the last name of the female responsible for the creature's birth. Alfred Heston, the local historian for Atlantic County, New Jersey, has traced the Leeds family back to both Great Egg Harbor and the place that would take their name, Leeds Point, New Jersey. Heston also notes that in 1735, a Samuel Shrouds lived directly across the street from a Mrs. Leeds. If an affair occurred between the two, an illegitimate birth of a deformed child could have given rise to the legends.[50]

This explanation, while intriguing, is based largely on speculation. Whatever the actual origins of the various stories, all of them encode a profound misogyny that reflect a context in which women had been burnt as witches just a generation before these stories circulated. Women, and particularly their ability to give birth, are blamed for loosing a frightening, deformed evil upon the world. Indeed, the tradition of monstrous births in European folklore about demonic influence frequently included the idea that such anomalies represented punishment for sin. In 1580, for example, neighbors accused an Austrian woman named Barbara Striglin of "intercourse with the Devil" after it was alleged that "her pregnancy ended when a demon flew from her body in the form of a large raven, leaving a gaping wound in her side." Witches, the folk belief suggested, gave birth to demonic creatures, beings either reptilian or avian (or some combination). Such narratives encoded male fears and fascination with female fertility. All of these ideas emerge in early American folklore about the Jersey Devil.[51]

Religion, folklore, and popular culture became mutually reinforcing sources for the story of the Jersey Devil. In the early nineteenth century, illustrious figures, including Commodore Stephan Decatur and Joseph Bonaparte, brother to Napoleon, reported seeing a strange creature while hunting in the Jersey woods. The mysterious death of livestock in the 1840s apparently led to an impromptu exorcism that kept the creature away, according to local lore, for fifty years. By the early twentieth century, the Jersey Devil had returned. On January 19, 1909, the Evans family of Gloucester, New Jersey, reported to police that a creature "with a head like a collie and a face like a horse" appeared outside of their window, hovering by flapping its two-foot-long wings. Luckily for the Evanses, the creature did not act especially devilish and flew away when Mr. Evans opened the window and yelled "shoo!"[52]

Sightings of the creature continue, as do reports of its "screams" or "wailing" that can be heard in some of the more deserted sections of the Jersey woods. The story itself reveals that the American fascination with Satan survived the witch hunts and indeed kept some of its basic premises. The devil still lurked in "the howling wilderness" for many eighteenth-century New Englanders. Moreover, the folk traditions about this creature show an eagerness to define the Other, the marginalized, as satanic. Not only could unruly women practicing witchcraft or trying to control their own sexuality attract the attention of Satan. They could literally give birth to demonic monstrosities to haunt the American night.

Racial oppression, along with hatred of women, further forged a fascination of the demonic in early America. In the midst of the American Revolution, the institution of slavery provided the context for one witch hunt in 1779. What would become the "Land of Lincoln" included a number of southern Illinois slaveholders in the earliest settlement period. Authorities in the Cahokia settlement executed numerous slaves for the offense of witchcraft and poisoning. They hanged one slave, Moreau, for his alleged crimes; others were reportedly shot and then burned. Colonel John Todd, lieutenant commandant of the early Illinois settlements under the Commonwealth of Virginia, wrote that Moreau had been executed because "he poisoned his master but his mistress was too strong for his necromancy."[53]

The sketchy details of the Illinois incident are supplemented by a long history of slave owners whose fears connected poisoning to witchcraft. American slave owners throughout the eighteenth and nineteenth centuries depended on enslaved blacks to prepare and serve their food. Knowledge of powerful poisons in the African herbal tradition had acquired new strength in the Caribbean, becoming part of the vodun tradition that came to colonial America primarily through New Orleans and, in a more limited way, through the Carolina and Georgia low country. This fact continually struck terror into the hearts of white slaveholders, especially when some major slave conspiracies had supposed African "sorcerers" at their heart. In the late eighteenth century, accusations of poisoning took up a significant amount of time on the colonial docket. According to Yvonne P. Chirau, North Carolina issued thirteen indictments from 1715 to 1785 for such offenses, while in Virginia "more slaves stood trial for poisoning than any other crime except theft." While white authorities did not always link poisoning and witchcraft, a typical trial from Louisa County, Virginia, in 1783 found a slave "guilty of poisoning and conjuring." In Charleston, South Carolina, the 1822 Denmark Vesey plot, a failed conspiracy of hundreds of low-country South Carolina slaves, was headed in part by "Gullah Jack," a practitioner of "Hoodoo" referred to in court documents as a "sorcerer" and a "necromancer."[54]

The witch hunts, particularly through blending popular beliefs with theological ideas, provide the background for the contemporary American belief in, and indeed fascination with, the Prince of Darkness. In almost all of these examples, Satan is seen as conspiring with someone marginalized by the community. Accusations of witchcraft became a convenient shorthand for all of the young, and increasingly imperialistic, nation's anxieties about racial and gender hierarchies. Women who did not live according to traditional standards of marriage and family surely colluded with Satan. Slaves who challenged the system that kept them in bondage did so at the instigation of the original rebel against hierarchy, Lucifer himself.

Clearly the eighteenth century did not bring an end to American speculations about the work of Satan. The European Enlightenment had come to American shores, but so had the heritage of the Reformation and the

Wars of Religion. While the founding generation certainly framed American government on Enlightenment principles, many Americans viewed the Revolutionary War itself as a religious struggle. In urban America, rational deists made common cause with evangelical Christians, and while one side perceived the struggle as in part the destruction of "Old World superstitions," the other believed the "Old World" had not been far wrong in believing that Satan fought on behalf of one's political opponents.[55]

American colonists quickly linked their British imperial enemies with the devil. In 1765, anger over the Stamp Act in Charleston resulted in the burning of effigies of a British stamp collector, the pope, and Satan. Pennsylvania minister (and later founder of the University of Pittsburgh) Hugh Henry Brackenridge wrote in his 1778 *Six Political Discourses Founded on the Scripture* that King George III had been inspired directly by Satan. God clearly had also chosen sides and would fight on behalf of America.[56]

Satan had set up house in American cultural politics, a house that he would keep in the early national period. Many in the founding generation doubted that Satan, and similar "superstitions" would have much longevity. Thomas Jefferson fervently believed that a new rational religion would replace the outmoded superstitions of the Old World in the American experience, just as a rational political system had replaced the alliances of throne and altar that ruled Europe. Thomas Paine asserted, in his 1794 *Age of Reason*, "I do not believe in the creed professed . . . by any church I know of. My mind is my own church." Paine, like his sometime ally Jefferson, believed that America represented a new imperium of reason where "the stupid Bible of the churches" would be forgotten by a new deist creed. Paine and Jefferson could not believe Satan would live on in the brave new world of an enlightened American republic.[57]

They were wrong. In fact, Jefferson and Paine themselves would be accused by their political opponents of orating under the influence of the Dark Lord. Paine's deistic ideas became the target for numerous attacks by the American clergy, many of them suggesting that he wrote under satanic inspiration. The second volume of *The Age of Reason*, published in 1795, provided much fodder for those who viewed Paine as an agent of the devil. Mocking biblical stories from Jonah and the whale to the virgin birth, Paine's sarcastic tone zeroed in on the Christian faith as, in his words, "too absurd for belief, too impossible to convince and too inconsistent for practice."[58]

Paine received special attention from Timothy Dwight, a Congregational minister who served as president of Yale University and who used his position to critique all aspects of the Enlightenment as inspired by Satan. Paine came in for special treatment because of his influence in America. In 1788, even before the publication of the *Age of Reason*, Dwight had published a satirical poem entitled *The Triumph of Infidelity* in which Satan, after the completion of the American Revolution, makes his way across the Atlantic in a "gloomy car" (chariot) drawn by dragons. He brings with him, like a Roman emperor displaying his spoils in a triumph, all the major figures and works of the British and continental Enlightenment, including Hume, Voltaire, Diderot and, prominently, Thomas Paine himself.[59]

The sheer popularity of Paine's work accounts for some of this response, with *Age of Reason* appearing in no less than seventeen American editions between 1794 and 1796. Robert M. S. McDonald has written that "attacks on it emanated from pulpits from Maine to Georgia" and fear of Paine's religious ideas conjoined with many Americans' fears of the "godless" spirit of the French Revolution. France had become, for many Americans convinced that Protestant religious orthodoxy and political righteousness could not be separated, a kind of "evil empire" that fomented ideas threatening to America's moral fiber. Tom Paine, in the eyes of many, became a conduit for this river of godless pollution.[60]

Political conflict initiated the next round of accusations of satanic inspiration. America in the 1790s faced a crisis over the meaning of the American Revolution. Following the adoption of the Constitution in 1787, differing interpretations of the role of governmental power split the new nation's leadership, even as President Washington attempted to skirt conflict and remain above party and partisanship. Meanwhile, the aggressive tendencies of the young republic and the perception of new threats overseas served to further divide the American people over issues ranging from expansion into what is today the Midwest to how best to respond to the French Revolution and the government it had produced.

The presidential election of 1800, a watershed election that pitted Federalist John Adams against Republican-Democrat Thomas Jefferson, assured that political parties and rough-and-tumble elections would play a permanent role in American life. Indeed, the election year 1800 proved one of the most tumultuous in American history, with partisans of Jefferson and Adams engaged in fisticuffs in Congress and editors of rival party newspapers fighting in the streets. Political rhetoric would prove just as outrageous. Democratic-Republicans accused John Adams of desiring to establish a monarchy. On the other side, Timothy Dwight asserted that the Jeffersonian Republicans desired to replace the Christian faith with faith in rationality and warned his listeners, "we may behold a strumpet personating a Goddess on the altars of JEHOVAH." New Englanders literally worried that a Jeffersonian political triumph would force them to bury their Bibles in kitchen gardens or hang them down wells to prevent them from being confiscated by the "godless" new regime.[61]

The author of the Declaration of Independence represented the perfect target for Dwight and others who believed the devil plotted against the United States. Jefferson rejected Christian orthodoxy of all stripes, his own religious views shaped by the Enlightenment tradition of gentlemanly deism. Jesus of Nazareth remained a significant figure in Jefferson's personal religious thought, though the Virginia deist suggested that orthodox Christians had been mistaken in giving Jesus too much prominence, even as a figure of historical importance. Jefferson saw Jesus as part of a general movement toward reform and enlightenment in human history, teaching an ideal of "benevolence" that extended beyond tribal boundaries and embraced humanity. He was neither the Son of God nor even the perfect man, but rather a good but deeply flawed human being whose messianic delusions and "enthusiastic mind" lent itself to misinterpretation by 2,000 years of religious power-brokers.[62]

In the American context, Jefferson viewed the influence of clergymen with a baleful eye. Deeply fearing the alliance of church and state, he took it as a truism that religious leaders sought to extend their influence into the realm of politics. These ideas opened Jefferson up to criticism as both a religious truant and a dangerous political figure infected with "French atheism." The connection that his harshest critics made between Jefferson and the French Revolution became a theme in American political discourse and held its power and resonance into contemporary times. Time and again, partisans of particular religious and political systems have linked their opponents with a powerful symbolic triad of religious error, supernatural evil, and foreign collaboration. The attacks on Jefferson became the paradigm, if not the sole origin, of this type of political and cultural propaganda in America.

One of the most famous editorial images from the election of 1800 illustrates how this symbolism could be used with great effectiveness. In a famed lithograph entitled *A Providential Detection*, Jefferson is pictured kneeling before the altar of the French Revolution, an altar supported by none other than Satan himself. Jefferson seeks to burn the U.S. Constitution as an angry American eagle tries desperately to wrench it out of his hands. The fire that will destroy the founding document is fed by the writings of Enlightenment philosophers (the works of William Godwin, husband of early feminist author Mary Wollstonecraft, are especially prominent). The Satan who upholds Jefferson is medieval in his conception—talons and horns emerging from darkness to corrupt the American experiment. The eye of God looks down on the struggle, presumably sending the eagle to save America from the threat of Jefferson's satanic rationalism.

The inclusion of Satan in this image is much more than an allusion to political vice. The flood of anti-Jefferson propaganda used strong religious feeling throughout the 1800 election. Ministers across the country railed at Jefferson and his party with the same fervor they had used to attack Paine, convinced that Jefferson represented a supernatural threat. Timothy Dwight, emerging as the young nation's first important propagandist of satanic conspiracy, deployed the symbolism of satanic evil in an especially powerful way that hints at later American developments in religio-political polemic. In a sermon delivered on July 4, 1800, Dwight quoted at length from an obscure passage in the Book of Revelation that refers to an angel pouring out "a vial of God's wrath" that includes "spirits of devils, working miracles, which go forth unto the Kings of the earth." In Dwight's interpretation of this passage, the year 1800 was the year in which the contents of the vial were being poured. Dwight saw the "vial of God's wrath" as a prophesy of the wars of Revolutionary France, which he saw a destroying "the Anti-Christ," or the Roman Catholic Church. In a not altogether lucid pattern of thought, Dwight declared that God's wrath on earth also took the form of Enlightenment deism in Europe or, as he called it, "irreligion and atheism."[63]

Dwight believed that a triumph for Thomas Jefferson at the polls meant the triumph of France's political and religious errors in the new American Republic. A republican government could only be led by a Christian, he insisted, or else it would have "no point of rallying or confidence." In the wake of a Jeffersonian victory, the churches would become "temples of reason" and morals would collapse. "We may see the Bible cast into the bonfire," Dwight harangued, "we may see our wives and daughters the victims of legal prostitution."[64]

Timothy Dwight's belief that unclean spirits had been unleashed upon the earth, and that one of America's Founders might be one of those damned spirits, included an assertion that a large satanic conspiracy birthed much of the darkness supposedly coming on the world in 1800. Dwight specifically mentioned the Order of the Illuminati, allegedly a secret organization with satanic origins that had been responsible for the Revolution in France and for the general spread of Deism. Dwight, like many of his contemporaries and many conspiracy-minded religious leaders who came after him, was convinced that biblical prophecies regarding the Antichrist, Satan's messenger who would oppose Christ at the end of time, would be fulfilled in part by this secret and powerful organization.

In fact, an actual historical organization known as the Bavarian Illuminati dated back to 1772. Organized by Adam Weishaupt, a young law professor at the University of Ingolstadt, the group met to discuss enlightenment ideas, especially, but not exclusively, in relation to literature and politics. Weishaupt, who would later be demonized in hundreds of right-wing tracts, pamphlets, and booklets, hoped to create an organization that would, according to its own statutes, "encourage a humane and sociable outlook" and "spread useful knowledge among the broad mass of people who are at present deprived of all education." Modeled on the Masons, the organization would make its appeal as a "secret" fraternal order. Enlightenment historians suggest that, at its height, the organization may have had as many as 2,000 members. Luminaries such as Herder and Goethe were counted among its membership. In 1787, the Bavarian government suppressed the order along with other groups deemed dangerous to the Church and the Monarchy.[65]

The Bavarian Illuminati, also known as the Order of the Illuminati, would have been merely a footnote in the history of European revolution, reform, and reaction if not for the almost two centuries of conspiracy theory that has swirled around its role in human history, theories that emerged within a decade of the organization's extinction. This relatively small group of European cognoscenti had little to do with what the group came to be imagined as in the fevered imagination of America's evangelical ministers. Dwight's protégé, the Yale-educated minister and important American geographer Jedediah Morse, created even more colorful versions of his teacher's conspiracy theories. Morse told his Massachusetts congregation that "secret societies" had influenced the direction of the French Revolution and now threatened to bring "impiety and immorality" to the shores of America. Morse, in McCarthyite fashion, claimed to hold a list of Americans who were "officers and members of the Illuminati," including over one hundred members in Jefferson's home state of Virginia.[66]

Dwight cannot be ignored as a backwoods prophet spinning conspiracies. His presidency of Yale College made him one of the most influential eighteenth-century American churchmen, whose students filled prestigious pulpits across the young nation. Dwight's belief in secret satanic conspiracy, even his specific belief in a devilish "Order of Illuminati" functioning as an international, satanic conspiracy pulling the strings of government and finance, has remained a staple of doomsday prophets into recent times. It was an idea widely held at the beginning of the nineteenth century. In 1798, the major convention of Congregational clergy in New England condemned the "atheistical" policies fomented by France and brought to America by secret societies. Abigail Adams, wife of President John Adams, encouraged her friends to read some of the latest literature that explained the Illuminati's satanic plot against America. George Washington himself was pulled into the discussion and once assured a Lutheran pastor that the fraternal order of which he was a member, the American Freemasons, had no relationship to the "nefarious and dangerous plan and doctrines of the Illuminati."[67]

Despite his opponent's efforts to link him with a secret satanic order, Jefferson won the hotly contested election of 1800. Jefferson's election ensured both the birth of political parties in American society and the peaceful transition of the presidency between those parties. When he assumed office in 1801, he declared that the young nation had entered a new period of amity, "we are all Federalists, we are all Republicans." No Bibles went into the bonfire.

The devil did not leave the political scene, however. In what would become a typical American response to charges of diabolical influence, Jefferson's allies had learned to give their opponents as good as they got. Virginian D. A. Balcom turned the tables on the Federalists when he claimed that they, not Jefferson and the Democrats, acted as true agents of the devil. In his *The Devil on Politics; or, the History of Political Religion*, Balcom allows Satan to voice his plans for the American continent, describing how he had done his best to transport Old World tyranny to colonial America. When his efforts failed, he claims he attempted to subvert the American experience by "creating a picture of France that shows Infidelity sporting with liberty." This false picture allowed the Federalists to portray true democracy as allied with the devil. Balcom insisted that Satan further crafted his "political religion" by encouraging the growth of Federalist partisanship that arises "with a mist of darkness . . . from the bottomless pit." Balcom was not alone in using satanic imagery to turn the tables on the Federalists. Democratic propagandist Abraham Bishop mocked the claims of Dwight and his Federalist cohort, asking if they had managed to find any of the "sophistical workshops of Satan in America" or indeed a single, actual member of the Order of the Illuminati. Concern over Jefferson's membership in an apocalyptic and satanic cult disappeared into the history of bizarre political rhetoric. The idea of Satan at work in American society did not.[68]

The nineteenth century soon dashed Jefferson and Paine's hope that their brand of enlightenment religion would become the religious expression of the American Revolution. At the time of their deaths, a series of revivals, later styled as "the Second Great Awakening" swept the young republic and made evangelical Christianity the dominant religious expression in America. These revivals, and the religious worldview they inspired, contained at least as many threats of damnation as promises of salvation. Evocations of Satan became common. Christine Heyrman, writing about the religious awakening in the South, says that "as soon as evangelicals began in earnest to proselytize among southerners, Satan, in some form, suddenly seemed everywhere, a name that dropped easily and often from the lips of every convert."[69]

In the century following the deaths of Paine and Jefferson, millions of immigrants from Ireland, Italy, and Eastern Europe brought with them a deeply held and vibrant Catholic faith that taught, along with the beauty and power of the Church, the dangers and perils of supernatural evil. The crisis of the Union would find slaveholders evoking satanic evil as the inspiration for abolitionism. Religious revivalism would flare periodically and, just as periodically, Satan would play a central role in the vocabulary of newfound faith or faith under threat.

The American devil came ashore in the colonial fascination with witchcraft and threats to the early settlements. He gained in strength, indeed acquired powers of deception and destruction undreamed of in earlier times, in a series of eighteenth- and nineteenth-century religious revivals often referred to as "The Great Awakening" and "the Second Great Awakening." This emergence of an identifiably American Satan occurred in the midst of, and in a sense because of, the growth and influence of the particular brand of American revivalism. Even as the public culture of the United States became devoutly Christian and decidedly Protestant, Satan lurked around the edges of camp meetings and among the church pews. As chapter 2 will show, American religion was going to the devil.

NOTES

1. Association of Religious Data Archives, "2005 Baylor Survey," at www.thearda.com/quickStats/qs_70_p.asp (accessed June 1, 2008).

2. "Poll Finds More Americans Believe in the Devil Than in Darwin," *Reuters, UK*, November 29, 2007, at http://uk.reuters.com/article/lifestyleMolt/idUKN 2922875820071129?pageNumber=2&virtualBrandChannel=0 (accessed June 20, 2008).

3. Arthur Lyons, *Satan Wants You: The Cult of Devil Worship in America* (New York: Mysterious Press, 1988), xiii.

4. Lyons, *Satan Wants You*, xiii, xiv.

5. A number of scholars have examined the origins of Satan in recent years, including Elaine Pagels, Henry Ansgar Kelly, and Gerald Messadie. Messadie's work is the most problematic of these examples. Messadie spends only four of his seventeen chapters focusing on the devil in the Western experience, while the rest examines "Satan-like" beings in a variety of other cultural contexts. Other problems emerge in the author's accounts of biblical and historical narrative. For example, the unwary reader will go away believing the Hebrew Bible suggests that Adam and Eve were forced from the garden for sexual intercourse (a notion that appears in the interpretive tradition and not in the text) and that the Salem witch trials, a clearly Puritan affair, provided an example of how "The Church and the Inquisition" exploited popular hysteria for its own ends. See Gerald Messadie, *A History of the Devil* (New York: Kodashna International, 1993), 228–29 and 292–93. Certainly the most important work on the history of the devil is Jeffrey Burton Russell's four volume series, used extensively in this work. A less well-known, but incredibly thorough, insightful, critical, and creative work is Neil Forsythe,

The Old Enemy: Satan and the Combat Myth (Princeton, NJ: Princeton University Press, 1987).

6. Henry Ansgar Kelly, *The Devil, Demonology, and Witchcraft: The Development of Christian Belief in Evil Spirits* (Eugene, OR: Wipf and Stock Publishers, 1974), 14–15.

7. Elaine Pagels, *The Origin of Satan* (New York: Vintage Books, 1996), 47, 48.

8. Henry Ansgar Kelly notes that one of the most important of these books, *The Book of Enoch*, provides much of the backstory for Christian ideas about Satan's fall from heaven. In this telling of the tale, angels known as "Watchers" lust after human women and seduce them. The result is a race of giants. For this crime, they fall from God's favor. See Kelly, *The Devil, Demonology and Witchcraft*, 25–28.

9. Jeffrey Burton Russell, *Prince of Darkness: Radical Evil and the Power of Good in History* (Ithaca, NY: Cornell University Press, 1988), 52, 53. Russell also places heavy emphasis on the Hebrew idea of mal'ak Yahweh (messenger of Yahweh) being reinterpreted with the Greek idea of *daemonia*, or demons, as being central to this period's development of the satanic idea.

10. Pagels, *The Origin of Satan*, xxii.

11. Pagels, *The Origin of Satan*, 19–34.

12. Russell, *The Prince of Darkness*, 63–64.

13. Russell, *The Prince of Darkness*, 110–12.

14. Russell, *The Prince of Darkness*, 111.

15. Russell, *The Prince of Darkness*, 111.

16. Alain Boreau, *Satan the Heretic* (Chicago and London: University of Chicago Press, 2006). Boreau notes that this bull was meant to correct an earlier pronouncement by Pope Alexander VI that placed magical practices outside the purview of the Office of the Inquisition.

17. Robert Muchembled, "Satanic Myths and Cultural Realties," in *The Witchcraft Reader*, ed. Darren Oldridge (London and New York: Routledge, 2002), 136, 144.

18. Brian P. Levack, *The Witch-Hunt in Early Modern Europe*, 2nd ed. (London and New York: Longman, 1995).

19. The best studies of the role of misogyny in the witch hunts include Lyndal Roper, *Oedipus and the Devil: Witchcraft, Sexuality, and Religion in Early Modern Europe* (London and New York: Routledge Press, 1994); Carol Karlsen, *The Devil in the Shape of a Woman: Witchcraft in Colonial New England* (New York and London: W. W. Norton, 1987); Marianne Hester, *Lewd Women and Wicked Witches: A Study in the Dynamics of Male Domination* (London and New York: Routledge, 1992). Larner's statistics are found in Christina Larner, "Was Witch-Hunting Woman Hunting?" in Oldridge, *The Witchcraft Reader*, 274.

20. Jeffrey Burton Russell, *Mephistopheles: The Devil in the Modern World* (Ithaca, NY: Cornell University Press, 1986), 136.

21. Darren Oldridge, *Strange Histories: The Trial of the Pig, the Walking Dead, and Other Matters of Fact from the Medieval and Renaissance Worlds* (London: Routledge, 2007), 9, 14.

22. Russell, *Mephistopheles*, 179, 180.

23. Russell, *Mephistopheles*, 206–9.

24. Nikolas Schreck, *The Satanic Screen: An Illustrated Guide to the Devil in Cinema* (London: Creation Press, 2001), 11–13.

25. Fernando Cervantes, *The Devil in the New World: The Impact of Diabolism in New Spain* (New Haven, CT: Yale University Press, 1994), 13–15.

26. Cervantes, *The Devil in the New World*, 35.

27. John H. Kennedy, *Jesuit and Savage in New France* (Hamden, CT: Archon Books, 1971), 140, 141. A full discussion of how European theological traditions, especially Thomism, contributed to the reading of Indian religion, see Cervantes, *The Devil in the New World*, 16–39.

28. Allan Greer, *Mohawk Saint: Catherine Tekakwitha and the Jesuits* (New York: Oxford University Press, 2005), 53–55.

29. John Ashton, *The Devil in Britain and America* (Detroit: Gale Research Company, 1974), 202.

30. Ashton, *The Devil in Britain*, 201–2.

31. Marion L. Starkey, *The Devil in Massachusetts* (New York: Doubleday Anchor Books, 1949), chap. 4.

32. Frances Hill, *A Delusion of Satan: The Full Story of the Salem Witchcraft Trials* (New York: Da Capo Press, 1995), 36. It is worth noting that a debate exists about the cultural background of Tituba. This topic is explored in Chadwick Hansen, "The Metamorphosis of Tituba or Why American Intellectuals Can't Tell and Indian Witch from a Negro" in *The New England Quarterly* 47 (March 1974): 3–12. Elaine Breslaw examines this discussion in *Tituba, Reluctant Witch of Salem: Devilish Indians and Puritan Fantasies* (New York: New York University Press, 1996). Current discussion about the elasticity of Atlantic world identities makes this debate less compelling, but thoughtful work is still being done on it. Special thanks to graduate student Hilary Lentz for calling my attention to this debate with her own excellent study that suggests Tituba should be regarded as having an Arawak Indian background.

33. Hill, *A Delusion of Satan*, 96–99.

34. The historiography on Salem is voluminous. One of the best introductions to how property, social status, and community conflict affected the trials can be found in Paul Boyer and Stephen Nissenbaum's *Salem Possessed: The Social Origin of Witchcraft* (Cambridge, MA: Harvard University Press, 1971). Other works worth examining include Larry Gragg's *A Quest for Security: The Life of Samuel Parris, 1653–1720* (New York: Greenwood Press, 1990) and Peter Hoffer, *The Devil's Disciples: Makers of the Salem Witchcraft Trials* (Baltimore: Johns Hopkins University Press, 1996).

35. Richard Godbeer fully maps out the Puritan conception of "white magic" versus "black magic" and how theological ideas about demonology came into conflict with these views in *The Devil's Dominion: Magic and Religion in Early New England* (Cambridge: Cambridge University Press, 1992).

36. Hill, *A Delusion of Satan*, 39.

37. Ashton, *The Devil in Britain*, 319.

38. Both of these quotes come from an excellent article by David S. Lovejoy, "Satanizing the American Indian," *New England Quarterly* 67, no. 4 (December 1994): 603–21.

39. Godbeer, The *Devil's Dominion*, 192.

40. Godbeer, *The Devil's Dominion*, 192.

41. Mather quoted in James A. Morone, *Hellfire Nation: The Politics of Sin in American History* (New Haven, CT, and London: Yale University Press, 2003), 78.

42. Mather block quote taken from Robert C. Fuller, *Naming the Antichrist* (New York: Oxford University Press, 1995), 49–50. Following quotes both taken from Morone, *Hellfire Nation*, 86.

43. Hill, *A Delusion of Satan*, 118, 119.

44. Owen Davies and Jonathan Barry, introduction to *Witchcraft Historiography* (New York: Palgrave Macmillan, 2007), 4.

45. Godbeer, *The Devil's Dominion*, 151.

46. Godbeer, *The Devil's Dominion*, 194–95.

47. Ashton, *The Devil in Britain*, 310–12.

48. Ashton, *The Devil in Britain*, 313–15.

49. Jerry D. Coleman, *Strange Highways: A Guidebook to American Mysteries* (Alton, IL: Whitechapel Press, 2003), 120, 121.

50. Coleman, *Strange Highways*, 121.

51. Edmund Kern, "Confessional Identity and Magic in the Late Sixteenth Century," in Oldridge, *The Witchcraft Reader*, 184.

52. Coleman, *Strange Highways*, 122.

53. Ashton, *The Devil in Britain*, 312–13; Yvonne P. Chirau, *Black Magic: Religion and the African American Conjuring Tradition* (Berkeley: University of California Press, 2003), 71.

54. Chirau, *Black Magic*, 67, 70.

55. See Patricia Bonomi, *Under the Cope of Heaven: Religion, Society, and Politics in Colonial America* (Oxford: Oxford University Press, 2003). See especially chapter 7.

56. Perry Miller, "From Covenant to the Revival," in *Nature's Nation* (Cambridge, MA: Harvard University Press), 95.

57. Eric Foner, *Tom Paine and Revolutionary America* (New York: Oxford University Press, 1976), 246–47.

58. Foner, *Tom Paine and Revolutionary America*, 247.

59. Jane Donohue Eberwein, "The Devil and Dr. Dwight: Satire and Theology in the Early American Republic," *Christianity and Literature* 2 (Autumn 2002): 52.

60. Robert M. S. McDonald, "Was There a Religious Revolution of 1800?" in *The Revolution of 1800: Democracy, Race, and the New Republic* (Charlottesville and London: University of Virginia Press, 2002), 176.

61. McDonald, "Was there a Religious Revolution of 1800?" 173; See also John Ferling, *Adams vs. Jefferson: The Tumultuous Election of 1800* (Oxford: Oxford University Press, 2004), 153–55.

62. Peter S. Onuf, *The Mind of Thomas Jefferson* (Charlottesville: University of Virginia Press, 2007), 146–47.

63. Edward T. Larsen, *A Magnificent Catastrophe: The Tumultuous Election of 1800, America's First Presidential Campaign* (New York: Free Press, 2007), 168–69.

64. Larsen, *A Magnificent Catastrophe*, 169.

65. George Johnson, *Architects of Fear: Conspiracies Theories and Paranoia in American Politics* (Los Angeles, CA: Tarcher, 1983), 44–49.

66. "A Sermon of Jedediah Morse," April 25, 1799 (Printed and Sold by Cornelius Davis, 1799).

67. Johnson, *Architects*, 58–60.

68. D. A. Balcom, *The Devil on Politics; or, the History of Political Religion* (Printed for the author, 1817) Early American imprints, 23, 33.

69. Christine Heyrman, *Southern Cross: The Beginnings of the Bible Belt* (Chapel Hill and London: University of North Carolina Press, 1997), 53.

2

Darkness Invisible: The Devil and American Revivalism

Since the eighteenth century, evangelical Christianity has shaped American culture, particularly the national culture's conception of its identity and purpose. The growth of American evangelicalism represented the spread and triumph of some of the core values of Puritan New England, especially their view that their "city on a hill" had a special, providential destiny. This sense of providence, indeed of being chosen, helped create an ideology of American particularity. Since Revolutionary times, many historians, ministers, and politicians have seen in America a special religiosity that sets it apart from other human societies.

It is impossible to argue that the United States has been somehow "more religious" than other societies and cultures. This has not prevented scholars, preachers, and ideologues from claiming a special religious devotion for America, a piety recognized and rewarded by God. As early as the 1780s, Ezra Stiles could proclaim the success of the American Revolution as a reward for American religious devotion, a moment in which God had chosen a new Israel. Stiles's assertion has found its champions in every era of American history. At the beginning of the twentieth century, Senator Albert Beveridge, celebrating American expansionism in the Caribbean and the Pacific, proclaimed that "Almighty God has marked the American people as a chosen nation to finally lead in the generation of the world. . . . We are the trustees of the world's progress, guardians of the righteous peace."[1]

The belief in America as a "chosen people" has served to legitimate some of the nation's worst tendencies. But while any notion that America has an organic or congenital religiosity may be simplistic, it is indisputable that

33

the country's religious trajectory has been peculiar. Early American Christian communities developed in new directions, while religion suffused America's popular culture in a fashion unknown to the Old World. New religious movements, many with a heavy emphasis on the need of personal conversion, proliferated on the new continent. The tradition of American revivalism, the idea that God worked through godly ministers at specific times to bring about mass conversions, accounts in large part for this difference. Revivalism weakened, and in some cases severed, the religious ties of Americans to the older Christian traditions of Europe. Theological ideas that would influence generations of Americans emerged from the early colonial revivals. Evangelicalism, with its overwhelming focus on conversion as a powerful, explosive, transformative experience, became the most enduring of these ideas.

The image of the devil found renewed life in this new religious world of powerful conversions, even as the European Enlightenment called into question his very existence. American Christianity fully developed the concept of "spiritual warfare" in the revivalist context, a view of the Christian experience that emphasized the martial struggle with Satan and his demons. The transformative experience that millions of Americans experienced in churches and at camp meetings became a supernatural experience in which they stepped out of the mundane and into the cosmic battle between God and the fallen angels. By the nineteenth century, the devil was not restricted to contracting and cavorting with witches. He could attack and possess individual souls who had made no pact with him in the way witches allegedly had done. Most frightening to evangelicals, Satan could hinder the spread of the gospel and damn souls who had not heard the Good News. The devil of American evangelicals turned his wiles primarily toward the purpose of preventing conversion, of aborting the new birth.

The belief in personal conversion as a cataclysmic spiritual transformation, combined with the need to proclaim to others the possibility of such an experience, remains the central tenet of evangelicalism even today. The ethos of evangelicalism dates back to the Reformation. The Lutheran movement had stressed the idea of *sole fide*, faith alone, as the path to salvation, in contradistinction to the Catholic sacramental system. Interior faith in the gospel had the consequence, unintended by most Reformation thinkers, of placing enormous emphasis on the religious experience of the individual and the moment of the individual's conversion. Conversion could occur suddenly and powerfully. Medieval Christianity's gradual path to sanctification, aided by the sacraments within the Church, gave way to the individual's experience of transformative conversion.

The emphasis on individual religious experience helped create the Pietist movements of continental Europe. Ted Campbell has called these movements examples of a "religion of the heart," since they emphasized the role of emotion and of the affections in the religious experience of the individual. The idea of "heart religion" spread rapidly through the churches of the eighteenth-century West, in part as a response to the rational skepticism of the Enlightenment. Large numbers turned to Pietism in Germany, the Methodist tradition took England by storm, and Calvinists in Northern Ireland and Scotland began to experience emotional personal transformations. Revival meetings, public preaching that occurred outside the standard schedule of religious services and emphasized the need for immediate conversion, became the public theater in which Americans publicly performed their religious transformations.[2]

A series of revivals in the New England and mid-Atlantic colonies brought "heart religion" to the American colonies in the 1730s and 1740s. Jonathan Edwards, a Yale-educated Massachusetts minister, became the sophisticated voice that described, and advertised, the evangelical movement in America. Edwards's *A Faithful Narrative of the Surprising Work of God* detailed how, in 1734, a sudden stirring of religious affections brought salvation to numerous young people in his parish who, according to Edwards, had previously been interested in "company-keeping" rather than religious truth. This new religious enthusiasm spread to all parts of Edwards's parish and beyond, including perhaps as many as thirty-two New England towns by 1735.[3]

The revival described by Edwards contained thematic elements that have appeared again and again in American religious history. Edwards noted that many of those converted under his preaching evinced powerful emotional ecstasies that included joyful laughter. Others had mystical experiences, including visions of both heaven and hell. These emotional raptures and otherworldly experiences, common in all the colonial revivals, made it possible for evangelists to publicize their efforts. Outward expressions of inward faith also allowed the evangelist to keep tabs on the numbers being converted. Although Edwards's Calvinism made him shy of declaring a quantitative calculation of the "saved," he nevertheless suggested that supernatural conversion had come to "about 300" in Northampton alone. All participants viewed their conversion as a psychological earthquake, a moment in which the interior self had been transformed and irrevocably "saved" by God. It represented an experience so definitive that it forever divided them from their family, friends, and neighbors who had not experienced it. Those who did not accept the evangelical worldview remained in bondage to Satan.[4]

"The Great Awakening" and the growth of an American evangelical movement gave Satan a new lease on life at a time when Enlightenment thinkers mocked belief in him. A mere generation after the end of the Salem witch trials, it seemed that the devil suddenly was at work everywhere. Revival participants viewed the powers of the supernatural world swirling around the human soul, invading rural and urban communities with incredible transformative power. These supernatural powers, they believed, were not all from God. Satan lurked around the dark edges of every proclamation of the evangelical message, hungry for souls.

Edwards's account of the devil's work during the revivals seemed, at first, to call into question the extent of his influence. As the revivals began, Edwards claimed that Satan was "restrained" by the work of God in New England. Not only did Satan have difficulty interfering with the revivals, he also failed in his efforts to assault the faithful with sickness and depression. Nevertheless, there is a dark undertone in Edwards's account and even a suggestion that the power of the devil helped bring the revivals to an end.[5]

The mystical experiences of the newly converted in Massachusetts included encounters not only with the Holy Spirit, but also with the demonic. Troubled souls came to Edwards terrified of a dark angel who had tempted them to suicide. One person very graphically described a satanic voice urging, "Cut your own throat; now is a good opportunity, now now!" Joseph Hawley, a deeply religious merchant and an uncle of Edwards, actually did commit suicide, having become deeply depressed from believing that he was not truly converted and would go to hell.[6]

This perception of the torments delivered by the devil did not remain in the New England countryside. Religion and popular culture became partners even at this early stage of American life. The symbiotic relationship between American Christianity and American popular culture emerged in the 1730s with the arrival of George Whitefield. Whitefield, an Anglican minister who embraced the evangelical message of the need for powerful, inward conversion, visited the colonies in both 1738 and 1739. Whitefield had caused a stir in England by preaching to thousands in "open air" meetings about "the new birth." In September 1740, a crowd of 15,000 gathered to hear him near Boston. Historians have seen in Whitefield one of the first, true celebrities in America due to his widespread popularity and the numerous printed accounts of his activity. His popularity throughout the colonies, combined with the circulation of religious tracts and other publications, created a public image of the revivals that ensured their pronounced effect on American life. The writings of Edwards, Whitefield, and their imitators became best sellers, while public meetings received sensational coverage in colonial newspapers. Pop culture and religion had formed a strong and enduring alliance.[7]

Whitefield inspired the work of other preachers throughout the colonies. These preachers, styled "new lights" as a description of the new power and enthusiasm of their message, began small movements in New Jersey, Pennsylvania, and as far south as Virginia and North Carolina. African Americans heard the preaching of the new birth, and many, both enslaved and free, adopted a form of evangelical Christianity that they would soon make their own. On the colonial frontier, Presbyterian "new lights" infused a new life into the Scots-Irish congregations of the backcountry. Meanwhile, so-called Separate Baptists left their Calvinist roots and grew into a substantial movement in the northern and southern colonies.[8]

Edwards, Whitefield, and others became publicists of the idea of a single transforming religious experience for the American colonies. In their account of events, they linked diverse revivals and religious movements in different places as if they represented a single movement. Nineteenth-century historians, eager to inculcate a positive version of American peculiarity, further popularized the idea that the Revolutionary era had been preceded by a major religious awakening. Historian Joseph Tracey, writing in the 1840s, invented the term "Great Awakening" to describe this confluence of events. The notion of a congenital American religiousness became a powerful part of the ideology of American exceptionalism.[9]

Satan played an integral role in the "new light" movement. The evangelicals of the Great Awakening saw themselves engaged in a war with the devil while seeing those who opposed the "new birth" as allied with the Dark Lord. This view appears in one of the more famous evangelical sermons of the era, Gilbert Tennent's "The Dangers of an Unconverted Ministry" (1740). In this highly controversial sermon, Tennent clearly placed "new light" revivalists like himself on the side of God while insisting that those who challenged the recent waves of conversions fought for the Evil One. "Satan himself is transformed into an Angel of Light," Tennent declared, "Therefore, it is no great thing if his ministers also be transformed into ministers of righteousness." Tennent makes it abundantly clear that those who criticized the revivals found their inspiration in the infernal regions.[10]

The revivalist's opponents, meanwhile, accused the "new lights" of stirring up unhealthy emotions that severed religion from reason. Ironically, given that some of these opponents believed the "new lights" focused too much on the supernatural, some also raised the possibility that Satan could make use of the overwrought emotional responses to evangelical preaching. The Harvard faculty warned that Christians must measure spiritual experience by reason and the Bible or risk being deluded "by the suggestion of an evil spirit."[11]

The case of Martha Roberson in the Connecticut River valley illustrates the role played by the devil in the conflict over the revival's meaning. Roberson, age twenty-three in 1740, heard both Whitefield and Tennent proclaim the new birth. She apparently found the preaching of Tennent especially upsetting. When Tennent and several other ministers prayed over her, she experienced an emotional convulsion that she and others

present attributed to the devil. Her own description of her powerful reaction shows a combination of violence and barely disguised sexuality.
Roberson confessed to Joseph Pitkin, a traveling Connecticut merchant
whose diary provides the primary source of the incident, that when she
met Tennent "the devil filled me with such rage and spite against him that
I could have torn him to pieces and should have torn his cloathes off if my
friends had not held me."[12]

Roberson's allegedly possessed body became contested ground for the
advocates and opponents of the "new birth." Opponents of the revivals
found in incidents like her experience yet another reason to condemn the
revivals. Tennent had it wrong, they asserted, it was the new preachers of
the new birth who represented the work of the devil. The false religious
excitement of evangelical preaching had unhinged the mind of Martha
Roberson and others. Joseph Pitkin responded to these challenges by asserting that Roberson's possession showed that the Holy Spirit was very
much at work in Tennent ministry. After all, didn't Satan put most of his
energy into destroying the work of God on Earth?

Kenneth Minkema notes that the public reading of Roberson's possession marks a definitive change in the conception of the devil's relationship to the human soul. Her public ravings are not significantly different
in style and tone from those of the oppressed young women of Salem
whose accusations sent their neighbors to their deaths. Roberson, however, accused no one of having bewitched her. In part this reflected the
post-Salem attitude in New England in which accusations of witchcraft
became all but culturally impossible in that region. But the conception
of Satan and his work had also changed. Minkema points out that Satan,
for American evangelicals, had acquired significantly more "arbitrary
power" than he had been believed to have in Puritan New England. The
Dark Lord could directly possess a human soul. He could attack humanity without the aid of a witch or warlock. The devil was growing stronger
on the American continent.[13]

The final phases of America's first great burst of revivalism came during
the American Revolution. These revivals manifest two themes that became
part of the enduring legacy of the eighteenth-century revivals: Satan's influence and the near approach of the apocalypse. What Thomas Kidd calls
"the new light stir" of 1776–1783 began with fears of the Day of Judgment.
On May 18, the sky darkened in the middle of the day. Modern meteorolo-
gists suggest that a heavy concentration of soot in the atmosphere from
massive forest fires caused the phenomenon, but to the people of New
England it seemed a harbinger of the Day of Judgment. What became
known in New England folklore as "the dark day" convinced many that
biblical prophecy had been fulfilled and the final battle between God and
Satan had come. In fact, as late as 1842, an apocalyptic preacher would

describe how, in the lifetime of many of his hearers, "the sun had been darkened" just as had been predicted in biblical prophecy.[14]

Apocalyptic paranoia fostered the growth of revivalist preachers with a strong sense of Satan's influence. Henry Alline, a New England new light who moved to Nova Scotia in 1760, had been converted not by a vision of God's grace, but by a vision of the devil and of hell. As a teenager walking in the haunted New England woods, he found himself surrounded by "a blaze of fire. . . . I thought I saw thousands of devils and damned spirits." Alline's preaching during the Revolutionary era included both an emphasis on the soon-coming end of the world and the devil's role in dragging souls into an apocalyptic hell.[15]

The "new light stir" represented a moment of religious creativity in the evolution of American evangelicalism. Not all millennialist visionaries saw a dark fate awaiting many, if not most, human souls. Caleb Rich, who began his religious career as a Separate Baptist, would be dismissed from his congregation because he had come to believe in universal salvation, salvation for all humanity, rather than a strict division of the saved and the unsaved. Rich reported a series of visions in which the defeat of Satan represented not only a new birth for a few souls, but salvation for all. Rich's views were idiosyncratic and had almost no influence on the progress and direction of American evangelicalism. Most evangelical preachers agreed with him that the Antichrist would be defeated. But they also believed that millions upon millions of human souls would join the devil and his angels in torment.[16]

New birth revivalism developed further as the young nation changed dramatically in the late eighteenth and early nineteenth centuries. Following the Revolution, the population of the United States exploded, pressing on the boundaries of the young nation and spilling over into the old southwest and northwest. By the 1830s, traditional patterns of farming and artisan work gave way to an agricultural revolution and the beginnings of industrialization. A "market revolution" was underway that would transform America's economic life and have enormous implications for its social and cultural experience.[17]

The new national market reshaped America's class structure, its politics, and even its physical landscape. The independent artisan slowly disappeared as new techniques in manufacturing created a working class to labor in factories owned, insured, built, and supervised by a rising middle class. Politics focused on the emerging market's need for "internal improvements" such as railroads and canals. These improvements altered the countryside and transformed rural regions and sleepy villages into bustling commercial centers. Rochester, New York, essentially uninhabited at the time of the War of 1812, had become a market and manufacturing center of 10,000 people by 1830, primarily due to the opening of the Erie Canal.[18]

These changes in American life coincided with a new series of powerful revivals, more widespread and diverse than the Great Awakening of the eighteenth century. Beginning in some small ways in New England during the 1790s, revival fervor exploded on the American frontier in 1801 with the Cane Ridge revivals in Kentucky. Led by Presbyterian Barton Stone, the mass outdoor meetings at Cane Ridge attracted thousands from the lonely farmsteads of frontier Kentucky. These massive gatherings, combined with powerful preaching, resulted in a deluge of powerful, emotional conversions that led even Stone himself to comment on the "many eccentricities" that became part of the conversion experience in this and other backcountry revivals.[19]

Some historians have used the idea of the "Second Great Awakening" to describe the religious revivals that began in the early national period and lasted throughout the antebellum era. Nathan Hatch perhaps best captures the spirit of this era when he interprets it in terms of a bumptious new religious entrepreneurship that extruded numerous new American Christianities. Even less a single, unitary movement than the first Great Awakening, the revivals of nineteenth-century America had diverse beginnings and even more diverse consequences. Religious creativity, dynamism, and entrepreneurship became the major theme of America's Second Great Awakening, giving rise to everything from massive Methodist camp meetings to the birth of Mormonism and spiritualism.[20]

The concept of spiritual warfare with the devil grew in importance in the new religious world of the nineteenth century. Older ideas about the supernatural combined with revivalism, market ideology, and moral fervor to shape the image of Satan for a new generation of evangelical Christians. Most Americans inherited the folk beliefs of earlier generations concerning Satan's activities on Earth, including the idea that he sought to ensnare souls in infernal pacts to further his ends. The evangelical tradition had raised the possibility that Satan was even more active on Earth than the Puritans had supposed. He could possess and oppress souls without the help of evil human agents. He fought actively to prevent the proclamation and acceptance of the gospel of the new birth. Above all, America's evangelicals learned from their great awakenings that they, not just church authorities, fought in the arena of combat against the Dark Lord and his minions. The pious Christian served in God's army as a holy warrior.

The concept of spiritual warfare has had a long genealogy in the history of Christianity. The idea first appears in the Pauline epistle to the Ephesians, where the writer exhorted the early Christians to "put on the whole armor of God, so that you may be able to stand against the wiles of the devil. For our struggle is not against of flesh and blood." This minor theme in the writings of the New Testament acquired added force in the fourth century with the beginnings of the monastic movement. St.

Anthony of the desert was well-known for his belief that devils tempted him with the pleasures of the world. Demons, he claimed, appeared to him as dancing girls seeking to seduce him into renouncing his vows or as spectral shapes meant to strike fear into his heart and ruin his prayers. St. Anthony's struggle with evil spirits remained an important theme in monasticism (and much later in Renaissance art). Many of the saints throughout the medieval period saw themselves engaged in a spiritual struggle with Satan, though this tended to be a minor theme in hagiography before the modern era. In general, the saints' spiritual warfare was a struggle against sin, ultimately a struggle against themselves.[21]

The Reformation gave new life and meaning to the concept of spiritual warfare, in large part because many of its leaders believed themselves engaged in daily combat with the devil. In seventeenth-century England, the Puritans' conflict with their enemies helped make spiritual warfare a key theme. Puritan William Gurnall's three-volume *The Christian in Complete Armour*, published between 1662 and 1665, extended the Pauline metaphor of spiritual warfare to cover every aspect of the Christian experience. The same can be said for John Bunyan's 1678 *Pilgrim's Progress*, which portrayed the inner life as a struggle against powerful, mythic monsters seeking one's soul. In Bunyan's imagination of the spiritual life, Christians became knights slaying demonic dragons.[22]

American preachers and publicists of the early revivals traded heavily on the concept of spiritual warfare, making it a central theme in evangelical Christianity. They believed not only that they fought against the devil but also that the devil fought against them, taking a special interest in defeating the spread of their message. Evangelical minister Samuel Stebbins, in his 1806 pamphlet entitled *The Policy of the Devil*, wrote that the devil's primary work was to prevent the spread of the gospel, especially the gospel understood, from Stebbins's perspective, as the evangelical revival movement sweeping the young nation.

Stebbins's pamphlet introduces a theme that would become common in the demonology of nineteenth-century revivalism. The devil worked everywhere and with a much more insidious plan than most eighteenth-century evangelicals realized. Satan had tactical finesse. The Satan of the Hebrew Bible may have lashed out at Job with disease and disaster. The devil of Puritan and eighteenth-century New England enthralled souls with witchcraft and later direct possession of their bodies. But the American Satan of the early nineteenth century used more subtle tactics. He filled minds with, according to Samuel Stebbins, an "invincible prejudice" against revivalism while simultaneously spreading slander and suspicion that created disrespect for ministers of the gospel. The devil, to again quote Stebbins, was a "politic genius" and sought the most successful, rather than the most dramatic, means of attaining his ends.[23]

If Satan is imagined as an evil cosmic warlord, hindering the preaching of ministers might seem a minor hobby rather than his central concern. For the preachers of America's evangelical awakening in the eighteenth and nineteenth centuries, however, no other task would have been more important to the Prince of Darkness. Their preaching saved souls and thus prevented Satan from dragging the lost away to eternal damnation. Satan had a vested interest in destroying the Methodist camp meetings and Baptist frontier missions. This was in no sense a new idea, since the preachers of America's first Great Awakening saw Satan as their central opponent. But what Nathan Hatch calls "the democratization of Christianity" in the nineteenth century took this idea a step further. If a powerful existential conversion represented the core of Christianity, and if the primary duty of the converted was to spread the evangel message, then certainly Satan worked overtime to hinder conversions and to twist the message of the gospel. Moreover, if every evangelical Christian was to be a "preacher of the gospel," then Satan surely played a substantive role in the interior life of every Christian believer. The internal logic of this idea resulted in a strongly held belief that every Christian believer, whether a minister or a humble layperson, fought a daily war against powerful demonic forces.[24]

Accounts of early American folk beliefs about Satan, sorcery, and possession suggest that the devil was a terrifying force, a cosmic lord of evil whose presence meant destruction and death. And yet evangelicals of the nineteenth century, who believed he interacted with their souls daily, evince none of the panic and terror one might expect to flow from this belief. This did not mean that the nineteenth-century devil's power had become flaccid and impotent. Instead, antebellum believers combined a belief in Satan as an ever-present force working against the success of the evangelical message with the idea that they could gain victory over him with that very same message. Satan's morphology had changed significantly. Rather than a distant figure that involved himself only in the darkest and most unspeakable of endeavors, he became a close and personal devil, attempting to subvert the progress of the gospel. And yet the very message he sought to subvert worked his undoing.

The most notable aspect of this change for evangelicals emerged in their interpretation of alleged apparitions of Satan. Certainly Jonathan Edwards's parishioners perceived the deadly danger of the devil appearing to them physically or whispering temptation in their ear. They also knew that they could escape his clutches if they opened their hearts to God and experienced the regeneration preached by Edwards. Converts in the nineteenth-century revivals would see struggles with Satan, sometimes of a very physical variety, as a precursor to their own conversion, almost an initiatory rite into the evangelical experience. This understanding of

Satan's relationship to the individual Christian continued into twentieth-century American evangelicalism.

When we compare this new view to the Puritan understanding of the devil's interaction with the human soul, the differences are striking. The witch hunters of Salem convicted twenty-two-year-old Abigail Hobbes in large part because she confessed that she had seen the devil on her walks in the New England woods, telling Judge John Hathorne that she had held conversations with "the Old Boy." Puritan elites saw such a confession as part of the traditional proof that an "infernal pact" had been created between the human soul and the devil. But in contrast, revivalist, evangelical Christianity saw a close encounter with Satan as a basic rite of passage for any believer. For the Puritans, the appearance of the devil itself signaled that one's soul had been irretrievably lost. But by the early nineteenth century, a vision of the devil meant that you had begun a struggle that would ultimately save your soul.[25]

Many of the new converts in the second wave of American revivalism began their spiritual journeys convinced of Satan's enormous power over their soul, power so absolute that only a direct intervention by the Holy Spirit could possibly save them. In 1807, Methodist itinerant John Early told his hearers that at the time of his conversion he had screamed in fear, anxious that the devil was about to take him body and soul into hell. Christine Heyrman discusses the account of a young Virginian who, in 1797, became convinced that Satan haunted his bedroom. The terrified young man screamed out to his nephew, who shared the room with him to "Behold the approaching Fiend . . . sleep not . . . the Monster is coming!" Only a powerful conversion to the evangelical message saved him from the devil's power.[26]

Although a note of fear and panic at the approach of the devil is to be expected, a note of confidence fills the descriptions of those who have experienced conversion. In this conceptualization of Christian experience, "spiritual warfare" became the favored metaphor for religious experience. "The new birth" could free the soul from Satan's power, but the infernal prince would do all he could to prevent this from happening. Spiritual warfare became part of the trail of conversion and the fruit of a dedicated evangelical soul. No work better illustrates the new emphasis on the evangelical war with Satan than Caleb Jarvis Taylor's religious tract *News from the Infernal Regions*, first published in 1803. Set in the form of a gothic traveler's tale, the narrator tells of finding a crumbling house in "ruinous condition." Seeing it empty, and unable to find another place to stay as the sky darkened, he enters the frightening place and tries to sleep. He is awakened, quite literally, by pandemonium. A great "plurality of devils" appears before him. He has had the bad luck of falling asleep in the devil's headquarters on Earth.[27]

Taylor's unlucky traveler has stumbled upon a meeting between Satan and his top managers, and much of the work concerns demonic quarterly reports on the efforts to halt the evangelical revivals in America. Several of Satan's executive leaders are charged with corrupting and manipulating specific evangelical denominations and have nicknames like "Brother Baptist," "Brother Methodist," and "Brother Presbyterian." All of the progress reports of the "Black Brotherhood," and most of Satan's advice to his underlings, concern how to prevent local ministers and traveling evangelists from converting more souls. "They have taken away many of my subjects and still continue to depopulate my kingdom," Satan confesses to his capos, "but I am determined to dispute the ground inch by inch with them."[28]

Satan imagined as struggling for each individual soul created significant terror about the possibility of eternal damnation. One New Englander, H. A. Watts, described his own interior struggle in the 1757 poem "A Wonderful Dream." Watts's dream does not begin in an especially wonderful way, as he meets a "black infernal prince . . . Proudest of rebels who did once Heaven's mighty realms invade." Watts's image of Satan as a powerful warlord conflicts with the "infernal prince's" interest in Watts. The devil tells Watts that he is on his way to "the awful bar of God" to hear Watts's own doom pronounced for his failure to observe the Sabbath. Read from today's vantage point, Watts's pamphlet seems a parody of simplistic moralism, but for the writer and his first readers, this was deadly serious business.[29]

Perhaps the most striking feature of Watts's poem is how easily Satan is defeated. Watts has been saved by the message of God's grace. He triumphantly informs Satan that he no longer has a fear of hell. This assertion of the evangelical message causes "the frightful monster" to throw an impotent tantrum in which "with impetuous fury he tore up the trembling ground/and with his dismal cloven paws/did throw the clods around." The evangelical gospel functioned as a kind of exorcism, the message itself overthrowing the devil's power.[30]

Watts's *Dream* and Taylor's *News* present paradoxical images of the devil's power. On the one hand, he appears as a powerful Miltonic figure who once challenged God and still leads a host of evil angels. On the other, he seems interested in the most quotidian of matters (like Sabbath observance) and evangelical ministers defeat him by a simple mention of the grace of God or the name of Jesus. This contrast became a permanent characteristic of the evangelical devil in America, surviving into contemporary times. Modern evangelicals emphasize martial images of the Christian life and portray spirituality as a struggle against a powerful prince of evil and his works on Earth. At the same time, they assert that confident Christians can easily vanquish him. The 2006 film *Jesus*

Camp, a documentary exploring evangelical beliefs within the context of a camp for preteens that teaches spiritual warfare, embodies this dynamic. The camp's leaders "wrestle in prayer" with Satan as he engages in poltergeist-like pranks such as causing sound systems to break down and interfering with computers and fax machines. And yet the camp's adult leaders see every social ill as evidence of Satan's work on Earth, indeed as part of a global satanic conspiracy. This Dark Lord who can both corrupt an entire culture and take time out to interfere with a PowerPoint presentation can be defeated by Christians at prayer and the proclamation of the gospel. These attitudes carry forward the paradoxes of spiritual warfare born in the early nineteenth century.[31]

Why had the devil, or at least the nature of his work, changed in antebellum America? In the seventeenth century, Satan had been blighting crops and causing unnatural death through his pacts with witches. By the late eighteenth century, interfering with the work of the evangelical ministry had become his primary concern. Had the devil lost his power or changed his methods? Andrew Delbanco argues that Enlightenment currents in American thought created a devil shorn of much of his supernatural power in the eighteenth century. For some skeptical elites, witch hunting became something to be satirized (although, as we have seen, it endured long past Salem). Delbanco further notes that some of these same elites produced a literature of clinical writing on the idea of "lunacy" that had significant bearing on the conception of the supernatural. In this literature, any trance, vision, or fit previously ascribed to supernatural operations was read as a mental disorder.[32]

Much of Delbanco's evidence relies on what we know about elite opinion in the eighteenth century, and he, in fact, introduces significant evidence that supernatural beliefs remained sturdy for most Americans. Certainly witchcraft trials became less common, and as we have seen, the evangelical revivalists certainly saw Satan operating differently than had the Puritans or the people of early modern Europe more generally. The entrepreneurial demands being placed on Methodist circuit riders and Baptist preachers provide one explanation for this change. Christine Leigh Heyrman has argued that, in order for evangelicals to sell their message, they had to make certain adaptations to that message. She finds some evidence that the devil of rural American folklore, a being able to physically manifest himself to saints and sinners alike, took on a much more subtle role and that Methodist and Baptist evangelists came to emphasize his dangers to the individual soul rather than the possibility of a physical manifestation.[33]

Heyrman's argument has a great deal of merit when examining the direction taken by the leaders of individual institutions, some of whom sometimes seem embarrassed by their co-religionist's fascination with the sinister side of the supernatural. Still, the devil plainly had a powerful hold on the American imagination. Even as some ministers shied away from claiming that Satan could make physical appearances, other propagandists of the revivals emphasized that the subtlety of Satan's work made it all the more insidious. The devil became arguably more powerful as he shed his horns and cloven feet and began to work on the inner psyche of individual believers. The nineteenth-century preachers of the new birth may have questioned tales of satanic appearances, but they never questioned the role of Satan in their lives.

This belief in the devil's subtle but destructive influence is reflected in one popular 1805 account from South Carolina entitled *The Devil Let Loose, or a Wonderful Account of the Goodness of God*. The author of the pamphlet unwittingly shows how Americans ignored massive moral evil in their midst and asserted that the damnation of the soul remained the devil's central concern. This strange account further reveals the complicated attitudes that Americans held about the supernatural here on the cusp of the age of reason and the new age of revivalism. The supernatural power of the devil is, *pace* Voltaire, very much a threat.

The account begins by relating the story of the anonymous South Carolina planter "Mr. W___ K___" who, though known as "a good husband and master," also has a deep hatred of religious faith, especially in its evangelical variety. What especially animates this "good husband and master" is the idea that the women of his slave quarters attend the camp meetings and have powerful, emotional conversions. "O you d-mned bitches," he rages when he finds them at a revival meeting, "you are getting converted are you!" Though presented to us as one of the kindly slave owners, the pamphlet's author describes this "good master" as "cutting them with his whip in a most inhuman manner." Returning them to his plantation, he suspends them from tree limbs, with stones weighing down their ankles.[34]

So outraged does the irreligious planter become at the effect of the revivals on his slave property that he devises a bizarre plot to mock his evangelical neighbors and put the camp meetings out of business. Assembling a costume of black cloth, he adds "a frightful mask" crafted by "an eminent artist in Charleston." The costume comes complete with nineteenth-century special effects, including Medusa-inspired wooden snakes affixed to the mask and manipulated by a lever that causes them to writhe. W___ K___ takes to the roads with this elaborate costume, and according to the author, terrifies the "country people," who hold a firm belief in "ghosts, hobgoblins and the like." The narrator relates that word quickly spread that "the devil walked at twilight."

Delighted with his success, W___ K___ decides to take the fight directly to the hated camp meetings themselves. Enlisting the aid of some of his slaves, who are portrayed as willing to take part in the fun, the creative planter waits until the minister mentions how the people have been under attack by "the monster" that has been seen walking in the half-light. On cue, the slaves pound the walls with limbs and poles while K___ explodes phosphorous from which he appears garbed in his Satan costume "in the midst of the people who shrieked, screamed and fled in all directions."[35]

Until this point in the narrative, the author takes a typical eighteenth-century attitude toward the credulity of the "country people" who could believe that they were seeing a physical manifestation of Satan at twilight. He begins the narrative by noting that the early nineteenth century was "under the benign influence of the Sun of Reason." His telling of the satanic prank is also put to maximum comic effect as he describes the congregants running in all directions and huddling in the brush, fearful of moving.

It is here that the narrative takes a decisive turn and we see the author's true purpose. The slaves who aided their master flee home to escape detection but find no sign of W___ K___. When they search for him the next morning, he is found lying catatonic in the woods with no sign of visible injury. He refuses to break his silence over several days and nights, except in "screams of horror" and babblings about horrific nightmares. He remains abstracted until, near death, he lets out cries of "despair and horror" that terrify his gathered neighbors. "Save me! Save me!" he howls, testifying to those gathered around him that he has been in hell itself, dragged there by the fiend he had had the temerity to impersonate. In his final moments, he pronounces his belief in the evangelical gospel, dying with a "heavenly, placid serenity" on his formerly tortured visage.[36]

The Devil Let Loose brings together some of the central themes of America's revivalist traditions. The author fully recognized that belief in the devil in the nineteenth century, while fervent, also came with an awareness of a more skeptical tradition. The "Sun of Reason" had called into question earlier beliefs about Satan's influence. This forces the author to keep an ironic distance about the "appearances" of Satan to gullible rural folk. Nevertheless, the author also wants to assert the reality of Satan and that he represents a malevolent power concerned with the smallest of matters. Satan inspired W___K___ to impersonate him and used him to subvert the local revivals. He then dragged at least an abstracted version of W___ K___ into hell itself in an effort to damn him. His subtle methods make him appear more, not less, real.

Satan is a defeated enemy in this account, defeated by the power of evangelical conversion. Not only does he fail to dampen the fires of revival, he unwittingly contributes to its success. Yet even in defeat, he has incredible power. The text clearly assumes that Satan inspired W___K___ to don his diabolical costume, allowing the Prince of Darkness a human instrument to do his work. Moreover, Satan possesses the power to drag a soul into hell for at least a brief visit while the person's body remains alive. The devil was indeed let loose in this account. Even if the author really wanted to show his readers "a wonderful instance of the goodness of God," what he constructed, instead, was a powerful Satan who could toy with human souls.

The morally obtuse nature of much evangelical speculation about the devil also manifests in this account. The evils of slavery appear throughout although they are offered to the reader with no comment. The planter's unbelief and hatred for religion, not his inhuman cruelty to his slaves, becomes the symbol of his "lost" state. He doesn't repent of the sin of slavery, but only unbelief and blasphemy. Evangelicalism had learned to accommodate social injustice in the United States; Satan's influence was primarily felt in the soul struggling with conversion rather than with the realities of oppression. This would have significant implications for America's understanding of "the work of the devil" into the twentieth century. Political efforts toward moral reform would become another avenue to fight the devil, another aspect of spiritual warfare. But the politics of reform would tack away from questioning larger oppressive structures in American society, focusing instead on efforts to control and discipline the individual self.

Finally, *The Devil Let Loose* reminds us that slaves, in large numbers, had begun to accept the claims of evangelical faith. In this process, the institution of slavery itself became the context for the enslaved African's acceptance of the Christian faith. Evangelical awakening occurred in the African American as early as the 1760s. By the nineteenth century, Christianity, especially in its Baptist and Methodist forms, had come to the slave quarters. Satan emerged as a complex figure within the matrix of African American religion. This complex devil would hold an important place in African American Christianity and culture, his imagery redacted in the context of African folkways and the hardships of slavery itself. Traditional African religion had no real concept of Satan. Instead, trickster-deities whose work was sometimes malicious, if not irredeemably evil, had played an important part in African theology. The general African worldview has been to see the cosmos interrelated in an orderly pattern, with even opposing supernatural powers ultimately complementing one another. In traditional Yoruba religion, for example, Shopana, the god of smallpox, peacefully resides with the beautiful river goddess Oshun and the all-important Ifa, the god of divination. In this conception of the universe, even "evil" spirits have their place in the fabric of reality.[37]

Enslaved Africans, newly introduced to the Christian conception of the devil, assimilated the idea of a lord of evil into their traditional beliefs. This led to a creative demonology clearly separate from the more general evangelical understanding held by their masters. Satan could be fearful but functioned as a powerful, supernatural trickster instead of an evil, cosmic force. Slaves in North America brought with them an elaborate technology of magic that came to be called "conjure." The concept of the power of "conjure" defined Satan as a powerful sorcerer, as in the words of one spiritual:

> De debbil am a liah and a conjurer too.
> If you doan look out, he conjure you too.

At other times, Satan as trickster could be an even more morally neutral power who brought laughter and celebration. Many slaves viewed both the fiddle and the banjo as the devil's instruments. This did not put them off limits. To the contrary, this simply increased their value since their connection with the world of the supernatural gave them added power. Both instruments, rather than being forbidden, were believed to contain a special power due to their association with Satan.[38]

The complex nature of the demonic complicated the role of Satan in emerging African American theology. He was the enemy of God and of the human race, just as in white Christian thought. But his trickster nature also gave him something in common with the powerless slave who could not always challenge the master outright but could still find ways to subvert the racist social order. In slave folk tales, the devil appears more clever than powerful, reflecting the respect that traditional African society, and Southern slave society, gave to intelligence and cleverness.

The devil clearly worked in the rural South, both among slaves and free. In the North, where the market revolution reshaped the region's economic and social history, Satan emerged in the new world created by canals, railroads, and the new middle class. Western New York State, called the "burned-over district" in the nineteenth century because of the continuous waves of fervent revival sweeping over it, became a laboratory of religious experimentation. In one generation, this region saw the rise of the Finneyite revivals, the birth of Mormonism in Joseph Smith's visions, and the emergence of the American tradition of spiritualism in the night sounds heard by the Fox sisters.

The Finneyite revivals take their name from Charles G. Finney, an upstate New York lawyer who, after a powerful experience of conversion in 1821, began a remarkable career defined by his efforts, in his own words, "to pull men out of the fire." Finney went about this effort with gusto, the dramatic effect of his six-foot, two-inch frame and powerful voice converting thousands.

Finney introduced what he called "the new measures" to American revivalism, a set of techniques for successful religious entrepreneurialism intended to have powerful emotional and intellectual effect on the unconverted. Finney spoke directly to those outside the fold of believers, using all the forensic techniques of a trial attorney to convince them of their damned state. He even arranged the space of his meetings to provide the penitent with a clear course of action, setting up an "anxious bench" where those "convicted of sin" sat and prayed till they had achieved conversion. Finally, rather than resorting to the rural camp meeting, Finney brought the Second Great Awakening to the urban environments springing up all along the newly opened Erie Canal. Finney introduced the "protracted meeting," religious meetings organized on weeknights in connection with local, urban churches. The evangelist intentionally prolonged these meetings to allow time for the inquirers on the anxious bench to feel they had become fully converted.[39]

Satan represented the evil force Finney felt must be destroyed, as well as the chief obstacle to his revivals. The Finneyite tradition of revivalism did, however, mark a subtle change in the way many evangelicals viewed conversion. The ideas of spiritual warfare remained, but unlike the pre-1830 period, direct struggles with the devil became more complex, occurring on the societal as well as the individual level. In 1831, Finney opened the Chatham Street Chapel in the Five Points district of New York City. One of the most ethnically diverse intersections of America, it also featured some of the nation's worst urban poverty. Middle-class reformers since the 1820s had viewed Five Points as an open moral sewer. The effort to reform it became as much a struggle with the devil as an effort at saving the lost soul. Discussions between Finney and his allies about the opening of what would become the Chatham Street mission are couched in terms of a struggle with Satan over souls, spiritual warfare carried on in the streets of the Lower East Side. Lewis Tappan, an evangelical leader who leased the property to Finney, saw it as a kind of a beachhead in the devil's territory. You will, he assured Finney, be "rescuing from Satan one of his haunts." To men like Tappan, and to hundreds of thousands of evangelical Christians, such language was not a figure of speech. Finney had really challenged Satan on his own geography.[40]

Tappan's understanding of Finney's efforts in Five Points illustrates how the concept of spiritual warfare would broaden throughout the nineteenth century. The first evangelicals in America increasingly viewed the struggle with the devil as a struggle within the individual soul, and spiritual warfare became the responsibility of every Christian. Finney and others in the 1830s came to see spiritual warfare as both the struggle of the individual soul and the efforts of individual Christians to challenge evil within the larger society. This change would find expression first in the temperance movement and, throughout the century, marked a clear change in the Christian understanding of Satan's role in history.

This view did not become universal among American evangelicals. Many Christians, especially in the South, continued to view the devil's primary work as going on in the individual soul. After all, seeing Satan at work in the larger society might raise questions about social practices, such as slavery, that many preferred not to ask. Even in the North, the change came slowly and by degrees. In the 1830s, conversion of the individual remained the primary effort of evangelists like Finney and his imitators. The divisions between the saved and the lost sometimes led to interdenominational cooperation but just as often to evangelical infighting as minor doctrinal points became issues of ultimate, indeed eternal, importance. Sectarian divisions emerged in both individuals and families. This religious fragmentation midwifed one of the most creative religious systems in American history, a true "American Original" in the words of Paul Conkin. The Church of Jesus Christ of Latter Day Saints, the Mormons, would adopt a system with radically different ideas about God and the devil, though one in which many of the themes common to all American religious movements are prominent.[41]

In 1830, Joseph Smith published the *Book of Mormon* in Palmyra, New York, a work he and his followers understood as a final testament and a completion of earlier Jewish and Christian revelation. Smith claimed a supernatural source for these writings; indeed, he claimed they had been shown to him in the form of "golden tablets" by an angel. This new revelation became the basis for the Mormon movement and made it, by far, the most successful new religious movement of the 1830s outside the burgeoning evangelical traditions.[42]

The demonology of Mormonism clearly showed the imprint of its American origin. Although Mormon thought about Satan drew from themes in Christian theology, there are also significant departures from the traditional Christian mythos. As in traditional theology, Mormon theology views Satan as a fallen angel who challenged God out of hubris. Pride became his chief sin, a claim made in the Christian tradition from St. Augustine to John Milton. But Mormon teaching further conceptualized the "war in heaven" as a struggle within a dysfunctional family. Lucifer, like all created beings, is a child of God, a son of God. Jesus, as "the first-born of all creation," is the most favored of these sons, while Lucifer runs a close second, the "son of the morning," who, for all his beauty, has to look to Jesus as a divine elder brother. Out of jealously of Jesus and the human race, as well as pride in his own salvific competency, Lucifer and his fellow rebels fall when they challenge God by offering humanity an alternative plan of salvation. In the devil's plan, human beings can surrender their free will and become little more than robots programmed to carry out God's will. God punishes Lucifer and his followers by forcing them to remain as "ghosts of heaven" who will neither know physical incarnation nor, consequently, resurrection (this is an important idea in Mormon thought, as even God is imagined as having a kind of physical body).[43]

Protestant leaders attacked Mormonism's theological ideas about the nature of God and of the devil. Nevertheless, they shared with them certain commonalities with regard to the nature of evil. Mormon reflections on Satan's "alternative plan of salvation" can be viewed as a kind of mythic reflection on the claims of Calvinism. Evangelicals, many of whose forebears came out of the Calvinist tradition, struggled with the question of free will. Could human beings freely accept Christ, or were they bound by sin? Did conversion represent a free choice, or, as Reform theology had claimed, did the Holy Spirit ultimately make the decision to move, convict, and redeem the human soul? Almost all evangelicals, with the Methodist churches in the lead, sloughed off the Calvinist tradition and adopted the view that every human soul had the freedom to choose salvation or damnation.

Mormonism's view of Satan's temptation of humanity reflected these concerns about free will and salvation and offered a compelling critique of Calvinism. Satan offered to the human race a path to salvation that robbed them of their freedom and made easy the path of obedience to God. Robbed of free will, human beings would become extensions of the divine will. This idea included more traditional ideas about the causes of Satan's fall, emphasizing that it was pride and vanity on Satan's part that led him to suggest this alternative plan of salvation. But according to Mormon theology, Lucifer offered to humanity a satanic form of predestination and election in which human beings would be ushered into the kingdom of God without the struggle of making a free choice. Here Mormonism suggests that Satan was, in some sense, the first Calvinist. The first sin meant the loss of free will as Satan attempted to "predestine" souls for damnation. Satan represented the antithesis of the democratic individualism that became a primary cultural concern in Jacksonian America. The devil of the Mormon movement acted as kind of despot, seeking to steal the liberty of individual human souls and promising them salvation in return.

The effort to understand theological and moral freedom within American Christianity was not the only influence of the Jacksonian era on Mormon thought. American concerns over the nature of the native peoples of North America also found expression in Mormon conceptions of the devil. *The Book of Mormon* creates an elaborate mythology of pre-Columbian America in which two groups, the Nephites and the Lamanites, struggled for control of the continent. The Nephites are the righteous, prepared for the birth of Christ through portents and wonders. Their enemies, the Lamanites, are children of Satan. Mormons believe that Christ visited the American continent in the time period between his resurrection and ascension and in this time he appeared to both groups, though he faced rejection from the evil Lamanites.[44]

Here Smith had an idea strikingly similar to Cotton Mather's mythology of native peoples who had a special relationship with the devil. Smith believed that all contemporary Native Americans descended from the satanic Lamanites. In fact, demonic descent served as an explanation for their darker skin, which Smith viewed as a divine curse. Mormon thought also included people of African descent under a similar curse, an idea that led to the exclusion of African Americans from the Mormon priesthood until 1978. The Mormon devil, like the evangelical devil, came embodied as the cultural and racial Other.

The religious ferment of upstate New York produced movements that constructed even more creative cosmologies than Mormonism. In 1847, Katherine and Margaret Fox began to tell their parents and neighbors of the mysterious knockings or rappings they heard in the family's Hydesville, New York, farmhouse. Both claimed the ability to interpret these "rappings" and quickly became media sensations both in the United States and in Europe. By 1849, Margaret Fox would be making public appearances for paying customers and P. T. Barnum signed the Fox sisters in the same year. Their popularity marked the emergence of modern spiritualism as a movement, and soon a significant segment of the Victorian middle class in America became hooked on séances.

The occult noises heard by the Fox sisters would, in an earlier American context, have marked them as either bewitched or demon possessed. In fact, in their first public performances, they summoned the spirits with a clear allusion to the devil, "Hear, Mr. Split-foot, do as I do." Not surprisingly, many evangelical leaders condemned spiritualism as the work of Satan. Christian theologians rushed to proclaim the Fox sister's visions as either demonic manifestations or delusions. Historian Jon Butler notes that evangelicals condemned the spiritualists for being either frauds or servants of Satan and sometimes as both. Evangelical ministers threw spiritualists out of their congregations and initiated legislative efforts to ban séances and other occult activities.[45]

At least one evangelical writer saw spiritualism as an expression of the power of the Antichrist. In a booklet published in 1866 entitled *The European Sphynx: Or, Satan's Masterpiece*, Rev. Clinton Colgrove suggested that spiritualism played a part in a larger satanic conspiracy to introduce the Antichrist to the world. "What spirits then are these, whose entertainment and whose social instincts are accommodated? Spirits of the dead? Souls of once animated human dust? Certainly not! . . . Be sure they are demons and seducing spirits." Colgrove believed that spiritualism, along with the "diabolical enginery" of electricity, would be used in the apocalyptic "last days" to animate "the image of the Beast" prophesied in the Book of Revelation. Colgrove, beginning a tradition that has continued through Hal Lindsey and beyond, identified a contemporary political figure, Louis Napoleon of France, as the Antichrist, who would receive special help from the spiritualist movement.[46]

The earliest spiritualists, for their part, tended to see their beliefs as an extension rather than a repudiation of their Protestant faith. Most came from Episcopal, Methodist, or Presbyterian backgrounds. They viewed themselves as having commerce not with evil spirits but simply with spirits of the departed. The attitude of evangelicals to this movement shows both a division within American society and the continued strength of earlier ideas about the devil. While many Americans, influenced by the religious creativity of the nineteenth century, saw the séance as either a spiritual experience or as entertainment, most viewed the occult as nothing more than the raising of devils.

The interest in the occult and in alternative religious traditions may have remained the concern of only a small segment of Victorian America, but it did not disappear. In 1875, spiritualist Henry Olcott joined forces with Madame Petrovna Blavatsky to form the first Theosophical Society of America. Blavatsky, a Russian woman of noble standing who had left her husband and homeland in the 1830s to travel the world and explore her fascination with esoterica, came to America in 1872 with a system composed from bits of Daoism and Buddhism and joined with various aspects of the Western occult and Rosicrucian traditions. Her popular 1877 work *Isis Revealed* became the basic textbook of American occultism, extending the life of spiritualism even after the 1880s when the now adult Fox sisters declared their earlier commerce with the dead to have been fraudulent.[47]

Blavatsky criticized many aspects of traditional Christian orthodoxies. She reserved special venom for the notion of the devil. What she calls "the devil myth" had become for the churches, in her view, "the prop and mainstay of sacerdotism—an Atlas holding the Christian heaven and cosmos upon his shoulders." She viewed "the devil myth" as not only a false understanding of the spiritual world but as the linchpin for both Roman Catholicism and evangelical Protestantism. Her special animus against the idea of diabolical spirits may have been because of how commonly she and other religious experimentalists were accused of consorting with demons.[48]

The growth of interest in the occult in the late nineteenth century suggests that the spiritual dynamism of the 1830s and 1840s took Americans in creative directions far beyond the evangelical understanding of conversion. Even among evangelicals, the religious creativity of the period took forms far removed from the conversion paradigm. The idea of "spiritual warfare" against powerful metaphysical evil shifted to a struggle against societal evil. The earliest struggles for the rights of women and workers and the emergent abolitionist crusade all viewed evil as corrupting institutions and then harming human beings. This marked a change from the long-held evangelical view that evil emerged from individuals, aided and abetted by the devil. While this idea, explored more fully in the next chapter, did not influence all evangelicals, it did work a subtle influence on the role the devil assumed in their worldview.

In fact, even the powerful waves of evangelical revivalism that continued to wash across America in the latter half of the nineteenth century provide some evidence of a reconsideration of Satan's role. Mid-nineteenth-century evangelicals in no way denied the devil, but some older folk beliefs did wither in the urban environments of the post-1850 revivals. This resulted in a change of emphasis rather than a change of content. The preachers of the "Businessmen's revivals" in the urban north during the late 1850s never denied the influence of Satan, and they sometimes attributed small events to his diabolical efforts. And yet references to his power waned, and unlike earlier moments of revival, there were fewer claims of a cosmic struggle going on in individual souls. Indeed much of the mention of Satan comes from opponents of the revival who spoke his name with little more than irony. James Gordon Bennett, publisher of the *New York Herald*, mocked the influence of the revivals by printing the number attending revival meetings in the city compared to those attending the theatres. The lop-sided statistics allowed him to joke that "it would seem that Satan still has a majority."[49]

Satan may have played less of a role in the late nineteenth-century conversion narrative, but he stilled provided a handy way to portray one's religious enemies. Theodore Parker, the great Boston Unitarian preacher, challenged the revivals (and American revivalism in general) for being devoid of real moral content. Parker, deeply involved in the radical abolitionist movement by 1857, expressed exasperation that the revivals seemed to make a supernatural conversion experience the acme of the Christian experience at a time when radical social action was called for. Revival proponents, in the words of Kathryn Teresa Long, "believed Parker a direct representative of the devil." An aging Charles Finney called the respected minister an "evil influence," and some participants in the revivals took it upon themselves to pray daily that Parker would experience conversion or that God would "remove him out of the way, and let his influence die with him."[50]

Outside the world of the revivals, the growing realm of popular entertainment showed real change in America's concern over the Prince of Darkness. This began early in the century. By the 1830s, a number of traveling performers used ventriloquism, magic lantern shows, acoustic tricks, and natural magic not only to entertain and befuddle but also to cast doubt on the reality of the supernatural world. Scottish magician John Rannie originated this trend in his travels across America from 1805 to 1811. Rannie used both optical illusions and ventriloquism to entertain and, in his own estimation, to enlighten. Leigh Eric Schmidt quotes one of Rannie's handbills that promised to "expose the practices of artful imposters, pretended MAGICIANS and EXORCISTS and open the eyes of all those who still foster an absurd belief in GHOSTS, WITCHES, CONJURATIONS and DEMONIACS."[51]

Spiritualists sometimes became the special target of these efforts. Madame Blavatsky in *Isis Revealed* complained of ventriloquists disrupting the work of spiritualists. P. T. Barnum echoed the sentiments of Rannie and users of "natural magic." Barnum, as Leigh Eric Schmidt notes, viewed "magic" as "a playground of skeptical rationality and bold enterprise." His 1866 work, *The Humbugs of the World*, represents an odd mixture of entrepreneurial interest in the weird and pop-enlightenment skepticism.[52]

Leigh Eric Schmidt argues that mid-nineteenth-century anti-Catholicism also drew on this fund of enlightened suspicion. Evangelicals viewed Catholics as deceived by priests imagined as "corrupt magicians" who peddled sacramental occultism. In the earliest days of the Reformation, Protestant polemic had presented priests, bishops, and popes as something on the order of witches, and Catholics as deluded and ignorant. These views had a long cultural life in the Protestant world. In the nineteenth century, most of American middle-class Protestantism viewed Catholicism as equal parts theological impurity, prescientific ignorance, and satanic influence. A Methodist pamphlet published in 1848 made this link explicit. *Magic, Pretended Miracles, and Remarkable Natural Pherroma* described the alleged "miracles" connected to Catholicism as being performed through ventriloquism and sleight-of-hand. Interestingly, this Sunday school tract could see Catholicism as both a demonic fraud and a superstitious system that could be explained through purely natural means.[53]

The nineteenth century also saw Satan making an appearance in the growing world of popular entertainment. "Satanic" exhibits of one kind or another became increasingly popular at dime museums and "museums of wonders" then emerging in urban America. A popular exhibit at the New York Peale's Museum promised a tour of the "infernal regions" where fully costumed actors escorted visiting "souls" into the fires. Some visitors reported being deeply affected by the demonic imagery, one describing the eerie effect of the "mournful shrieks" in this "scene of horrors." On the other hand, there is no evidence that the exhibit inspired religious or theological reflection of any sort.[54]

Joseph Dorfeullie and Hiram Powers created one of the more elaborate of these exhibits for the "Western Museum of Cincinnati." Taking wax figures that had been damaged during shipment (as well as creating a number of original ones), Dorfeullie and Powers created a terrifying set of tableaux centered on Satan and the terrors of hell for their Midwestern patrons. Their depiction, called "Infernal Regions," included "mechanic wax effigies" that, according to historian of drama Andrea Stulman Dennet, "literally jumped out at the passerby while emitting horrific cries."[55]

Satan himself held the place of honor within the "Infernal Regions" exhibit. At first, Hiram Powers played "the King of Terrors" outfitted with a tail and pitchfork. He later created another mechanical figure. Dennet notes that Powers soon created another character, "the Evil One," that allowed him to stalk and terrify his customers.[56]

The imagery of Satan and eternal damnation proved powerful for an America seized with religious enthusiasm. Powers and Dorfeullie had their greatest success in the midst of Finney's revivals. At the same time, the use of such imagery for entertainment purposes suggests that the devil was becoming a less serious figure, at least in some quarters. The Prince of Darkness, for some Americans, represented funhouse horror, rather than a real, diabolical voice speaking within the soul.

This became true even for many active American Protestants, in both the pews and the pulpit. The devil's power, so strong at the beginning of the century, appeared to go into eclipse by the latter half of that century. Rather than a powerful being that could possess souls, urge them to suicide, and drive them into hell, he had become for many evangelicals of the late antebellum period less a supernatural warlord and more of a sneaky criminal working in darkness. He and his minions tempted souls to sin, but they could not drag them against their will into an abyss as they had Martha Roberson. Meanwhile, in the world of sawdust, the dime museum, and the traveling magic show, the devil represented little more than one prop among others, invoked primarily to entertain in a way that underscored his unimportance. Middle-class Protestants, who often looked in disdain on working-class culture, were unimpressed by the exotic devil of the dime museum and the magic show. Satan had fallen on hard times, as the evangelical message failed to appeal to Victorian audiences whose strong sense of sentimentality and notions of respectability kept the devil at bay.

The work of Dwight L. Moody in the post–Civil War era exemplified this trend. Beginning as a local evangelist in Chicago, Moody soon became America's most prominent preacher from the early 1870s until his death in 1899. Traveling the country with his popular song leader Ira

Sankey, Moody had enormous success with his simple message of personal conversion. Almost never touching on questions of social justice, larger cultural issues, or even theology, he became a unifying figure and a religious celebrity not unlike Billy Graham in the post-1950 era. Moody emphasized the supernatural in the individual's personal salvation but seldom mentioned Satan or even the terrors of hell. His straightforward and easily understood message combined calls for conversion with what George Marsden refers to as "the conventional moralism of middle class Victorian Protestantism." This message had great appeal for his conservative, conformist urban audiences. Colorful tales of the devil and his work had little attraction for post–Civil War middle-class Americans seeking social harmony and religious certainty, and Moody avoided these subjects.[57]

Moody's popularity symbolized how the devil's role changed with a changing American Protestantism. The Victorian era saw the beginnings of a "mainline Protestantism" that took a much more moderate approach to questions of the supernatural than their forebears. As we will see in a later chapter, mainline Protestant theology in the twentieth century would even call into question the metaphysical existence of the devil. The clergy of the downtown Presbyterian, Lutheran, Episcopalian, and Methodist churches in most cities kept quiet about their beliefs regarding the devil, if they held any such beliefs at all.

Changing patterns in belief would seem to describe the late nineteenth century as a moment when the American devil went into certain decline, indeed the first moment in American history when beliefs about his influence seem truly on the wane. The convulsion of the American Civil War had some influence on the devil's difficulties. This was not because of a decline in religious belief or theological interest. To the contrary, America emerged as a much more deeply religious place in response to the loss of life and personal hardship the war occasioned. In the American South, this became a moment when evangelical religious emotion reached fever pitch and church membership became an expected part of any respectable life. Both in the South and the rest of the nation, a period of deep mourning for the more than 600,000 dead promoted a sentimental religiosity that emphasized the peacefulness of the afterlife. No one wanted to imagine their young son, dead at the battle of Shiloh, burning in an endless hell and being tormented by a powerful and psychopathic supernatural being.[58]

The tone of evangelical preaching by Moody and his many imitators reflected this cultural shift. Four years of America's bloodiest conflict had made the language of "spiritual warfare" unattractive. Few Americans, whatever their relationship to their faith tradition, would have denied a belief in the devil, but at the same time, most did not want to hear about him and his den of torment. This cultural moment, a hangover from the crisis of the Civil War, would not last.

The strong American revivalist tradition soon reasserted itself. As America moved beyond its mourning for the Civil War dead, a new cultural mood emerged. The death of Dwight L. Moody coincided with the birth of the twentieth century and the appearance of a new cultural ethos. In this new century, one that would later be called "the American century," cultural dislocation and massive worldwide change, much of it violent and even genocidal, would awaken questions about the nature of evil. Meanwhile, American progressivism's challenges to some traditional mores about gender roles and sexuality would lead conservative forces in American society to reshape their conceptions of the demonic. In American culture, belief in Satan has always been much more than a gauge for belief in paranormal activity. The devil has been as much a powerful metaphor for cultural hatreds and anxieties as an expression of belief in the supernatural. Now the forces unleashed by social change in American society would help to give the devil new life.

American religion registered the move from a nation in mourning to a nation flexing its imperial muscles. The passing of Moody brought a new kind of evangelist into American life. Billy Sunday bridged the gap between D. L. Moody, the birth of Christian fundamentalism in America, and the modern evangelical movement. Preaching a "masculine Christianity" that derided liberalism as effeminate and useless, he borrowed as much from P. T. Barnum as from the apostle Paul in his public campaigns. In fact, no evangelist in American history had managed to link religious belief with American popular culture the way Billy Sunday succeeded in doing. Sunday, a former major league baseball player, brought together carnivalesque showmanship, the emerging American obsession with professional athletics, and a profound religious and cultural conservatism into a brew that intoxicated many of his hearers. In strong contrast to revival figures from the earlier evangelical awakenings and from Moody, Sunday made no effort to provide his hearers with a reasoned case for the message of the new birth. Instead, he relied on a combination of personal charisma, onstage acrobatics, and aggressive rhetoric delivered as if they represented homespun wisdom.

Billy Sunday's devil evinced all of the concerns of fin de siècle America. In the early twentieth century, Christian theologians were beginning to question the metaphysical reality of Satan, an upsetting notion for many traditionalists. Using a menagerie of metaphors, Sunday declared the devil to be both very real and very personal. He also suggested that those who questioned his existence might, in reality, be his best servants. Billy Sunday's devil was, however, more than a metaphysical tempter. He corrupted the best of American life; he was a traitor to the American way. This idea found expression in Sunday's view of the direction taken by American society. At a time when many middle-class Americans worried about the influence of socialism over labor unions, Sunday put God firmly on the side of capital and in opposition to what he called "the radical element." In one sermon, Sunday mocked those who, if they had their way, would change things so that "the laws of nature would be repealed . . . oil and water would mix; the turtle dove would marry the turkey buzzard . . . chickens would bark and dogs would crow; the least would be the greatest." Neither Sunday nor his hearers showed any awareness that the last phrase came, not from the writings of some socialist labor leader, but from the New Testament, words spoken by Jesus himself describing the reward of the humble and the compassionate.[59]

The desire for a greater knowledge of the Bible was not high on the list of reasons for Sunday's appeal. In fact, the great evangelical showman frequently showed limited knowledge of the Bible's most basic contents. Rather than rely on careful exegesis, Billy Sunday slid, jumped, and cavorted in front of audiences at a time when the American nation passed through enormous social changes accentuated by World War I. Sunday's simplistic sermons reflected anxieties over these changes, especially over gender roles. His ideal Christian, and ideal American, was a male who had "rich, red blood in his veins instead of pink tea and ice water." America's entrance into World War I impelled Sunday to urge a "hundred percent Americanism." He connected Germany with satanic influence, saying that "if you turn Germany upside down you will find 'made in hell' on the bottom." Sunday further labeled resistance to U.S. policy in the war as "treason," yet another propensity he described as inspired by the devil.[60]

Sunday managed to use his own image as an example of strapping, athletic, American masculinity in creating his demonology. He heavily favored the imagery of spiritual warfare in his sermons, telling the crowds that God desired "men who could stand up and do battle with the devil." Christians fought, in his words, as "Gospel grenadiers" on the front lines of the battle. At a time when mainline Protestantism tacked away from the concept of struggling with Satan, or at least made it metaphorical of struggles for social reform, Billy Sunday brought it back into the popular discourse in a powerful and vibrant fashion, allowing it to feed on his audience's anxieties about a rapidly changing culture. Sunday's popularity would draw from the same wells as the emerging Pentecostal movement and the rise of Christian Fundamentalism (both explored in chapter 4).[61]

Along with the idea of spiritual warfare, Sunday turned time and again to the imagery of boxing and baseball to describe the Christian soul's struggle with the devil, linking the pastimes of popular culture to his demonology. Satan, he once said, was a deadly foe who "could pitch with the best of them." He warned Christians that the devil would strike them out every time unless they prepared themselves spiritually. He described Satan as a cosmic pugilist who had "knocked out more men than all the boxing champions put together." Worse, he fought in a "tricky, treacherous and sneaky way."[62]

Sunday took this physical sense of a struggle with the devil and made it a part of his show. At least part of his acrobatic antics involved "fighting the devil," pugilistic moves against the Prince of Darkness that made an enormous impression on the audience. In the fall of 1916, the front page of the *Detroit News Tribune* featured images of Sunday in direct combat with Satan and apparently winning.[63]

A thousand imitators copied Billy Sunday's antics. Throughout the twentieth century, evangelists struck in his mold preached thousands of sermons that combined calls for conversion with general denunciations of American culture. The devil would always be present in these jeremiads, doing double duty as a threat to the individual soul and a source of moral corruption in the larger culture. Christians, when they converted, became warriors, "God's grenadiers," to use Sunday's term. Popular culture, these preachers declared, belonged to Satan, even as, ironically, their language and views became inextricably bound up in American popular culture and remain so in the present.

Sunday presaged the beginnings of a kind of reverse social gospel. Any efforts by liberal churchmen to find social and political expression for faith would be labeled "do-goodism," irrelevant at best and doing Satan's work of obscuring the gospel at worst. In a 1964 sermon, given during the heart of the civil rights struggle, Jerry Falwell would assert, "Ministers are not called to be politicians, but to be soul winners." The statement may seem ironic given Falwell's role in shaping the Christian Right's entrance into politics, but in some sense it is consistent. What Falwell meant is that a Christian should play no role in trying to make progressive improvement in society. He or she could, however, engage in "spiritual warfare," confronting Satan in American culture.[64]

In this sense, twentieth-century right-wing movements that define the "culture wars" as ultimately a struggle with the devil are not all that far removed from their evangelical precursors. While it is not easy to see Jonathan Edwards shaping a political movement out of the Massachusetts and Connecticut revivals of the 1730s and 1740s, his vision of spiritual warfare did become a central tenet of American evangelicalism. The war for souls, from Northampton to Cane Ridge to Upstate New York to the Big Tents of Billy Sunday, remained a war against Satan. Time and again, the Dark Lord took the form of opponents who had to be challenged, cultural phenomena that had to be destroyed. Throughout the nineteenth and into the early twentieth century, Americans discovered the devil in the politics of moral reform.

NOTES

1. Robert Jewett and John Shelton Lawrence, *Captain America and the Crusade against Evil* (Grand Rapids, MI: William B. Eerdmans Publishing Company, 2003), 3.

2. Campbell also sees similar patterns emerging in both seventeenth- and eighteenth-century Catholicism and Judaism. See Ted A. Campbell, *The Religion of the Heart: A Study of European Religious Life in the Seventeenth and Eighteenth Centuries* (Columbia: University of South Carolina Press, 1991).

3. Thomas S. Kidd, *The Great Awakening* (New Haven, CT: Yale University Press, 2007), 16–23.

4. Kidd, *The Great Awakening*, 19.

5. Jonathan Edwards, *A Narrative of Surprising Conversions* (Carlisle, PA: Banner of Truth Publishers, 1991), 25.

6. Kidd, *The Great Awakening*, 21.

7. Frank Lambert, *Inventing the Great Awakening* (Princeton, NJ: Princeton University Press, 1999), 9, 143–50.

8. George Marsden, *Religion and American Culture* (San Diego, CA: HBJ Publishers, 1990), 27–29.

9. Some historians no longer view "The Great Awakening" as a discrete historical event but rather as a phenomenon "invented" in print culture and institutional memory. A short description of this view can be found in Lambert, *Inventing the Great Awakening*, 3–6.

10. Gilbert Tennent, "The Danger of an Unconverted Ministry," in *The Great Awakening*, ed. Richard L. Bushman (Chapel Hill and London: University of North Carolina Press, 1989), 89.

11. Lambert, *Inventing the Great Awakening*, 211.

12. Quoted in Kenneth P. Minkema, "The Devil Will Roar in Me Anon': The Possession of Martha Roberson, Boston, 1741," in *Spellbound: Women and Witchcraft in America*, ed. Elizabeth Reis (Lanham, MD: Rowman & Littlefield, 1998), 111.

13. Minkema, "The Devil Will Roar," 114.

14. Kidd, *The Great Awakening*, 306, 307.

15. Kidd, *The Great Awakening*, 308–10.

16. Kidd, *The Great Awakening*, 316.

17. There are several good sources for the changes in this era. First, the massive and sometimes controversial work by Charles Sellers, *The Market Revolution: Jacksonian America, 1815–1846* (New York: Oxford University Press, 1991). A smaller work that ties these changes to the revivals is Paul E. Johnson, *A Shopkeeper's Millennium: Society and Revivals in Rochester, New York, 1815–1837* (New York: Hill and Wang, 1978). See also the highly readable Jack Larkin, *The Reshaping of Everyday Life: 1790–1840* (New York: HarperPerennial, 1989).

18. A social history of the revivals in this region appears in Johnson, *A Shopkeeper's Millennium*.

19. Sydney Ahlstrom, *A Religious History of the American People* (New Haven, CT: Yale University Press, 1972), 432–35.

20. The best introduction to the Second Great Awakening is Nathan O. Hatch, *The Democratization of American Christianity* (New Haven, CT: Yale University Press, 1989).

21. Neil Forsyth, *The Old Enemy: Satan and the Combat Myth* (Princeton, NJ: Princeton University Press, 1989), 298–99; Harry E. Wedeck, *The Triumph of Satan* (New Hyde Park, NY: University Books Inc., 1970), 78, 84–86.

22. Updated versions of the Puritan classic are in plentiful supply. See William Gurnall, *The Christian in Complete Armor: The Ultimate Book on Spiritual Warfare* (Diggory Press, 2007). *Pilgrim's Progress* is, of course, a Western classic and has been brought out by numerous publishers.

23. Samuel Stebbins, *The Policy of the Devil* (Hartford, CT: Hudson and Good-win, 1806), 12–13.

24. Nathan O. Hatch, *The Democratization of American Christianity* (New Haven, CT: Yale University Press, 1989), 7–9 and 49–66.

25. Frances Hill, *A Delusion of Satan: The Full Story of the Salem Witch Trials* (Cambridge, MA: Da Capo Press, 2002), 116.

26. Christine L. Heyrman, *Southern Cross: The Beginnings of the Bible Belt* (New York: Alfred A. Knopf Inc., 1997), 57.

27. Caleb Jarvis Taylor, *News from the Infernal Regions* (New York: John C. Totten, 1813). The American Antiquarian Society holds an 1803 edition of this work but Totten's version is far more legible.

28. Taylor, *News from the Infernal Regions*, 10, 26.

29. Isaac Watts, *A Wonderful Dream: With a Surprising and Visionary Account of His Triumph over Satan* (Greenwich, MA, 1804), 4.

30. Watts, *A Wonderful Dream*, 11.

31. *Jesus Camp*, DVD, directed by Heidi Ewing and Rachel Grady (New York: Magnolia Pictures, 2006).

32. Andrew Delbanco, *The Death of Satan: How Americans Have Lost the Sense of Evil* (New York: Farrar, Straus and Giroux, 1995), 71–76.

33. Heyrman, *Southern Cross*, 26–27.

34. *The Devil Let Loose, or a Wonderful Instance of the Goodness of God* (New York, 1805), unnumbered page.

35. *The Devil Let Loose*, 14.

36. *The Devil Let Loose*, 24.

37. Gerald Messadie, *A History of the Devil* (New York: Kodashna International, 1993), 191.

38. Eugene D. Genovese, *Roll, Jordan, Roll: The World the Slaves Made* (New York: Vintage Books, 1976).

39. Charles Grandison Finney, *Lectures on the Revival of Religion* (New York, 1835), 12.

40. Charles E. Hambrick, *Charles G. Finney and the Spirit of American Evangelicalism* (Grand Rapids, MI: William B. Eerdmans Publishing Company, 1996), 135.

41. Paul Conkin, *American Originals: Homemade Varieties of Christianity* (Chapel Hill: University of North Carolina Press, 1997), 162–64.

42. Ahlstrom, *A Religious History of the American People*, 501–4.

43. David Britton, ed. *Historical Dictionary of Mormonism*, 2nd ed. (Lanham, MD: Scarecrow Press, 2000), 171.

44. Paul Conkin, *American Originals*, 169–71.

45. Barbara Weisberg, *Talking to the Dead: Kate and Maggie Fox and the Rise of Spiritualism* (San Francisco, CA: HarperOne, 2004), 4; John Butler, *Awash in a Sea of Faith: Christianizing the American People* (Cambridge, MA: Harvard University Press, 1990) 252–53.

46. Clinton Colgrove, *The European Sphynx: Or, Satan's Masterpiece* (Philadelphia, 1866), 26–27.

47. Leigh Eric Schmidt, *Restless Souls: The Making of American Spirituality from Emerson to Oprah* (New York: HarperCollins, 2005), 158–59.

48. H. P. Blavatsky, *Isis Unveiled: A Master-Key to the Ancient and Modern Science and Theology*, Volume II (Pasadena CA: Theosophical University Press, 1988), 480.

49. Kathryn Teresa Long, *The Revival of 1857–58: Interpreting an American Religious Awakening* (New York: Oxford University Press, 1998), 38.

50. Long, *The Revival of 1857–58*, 111, 112.

51. Milbourne Christopher and Maurine Christopher, *An Illustrated History of Magic* (New York: Carol and Graf Publishers, 2006), 50–60.

52. Leigh Eric Schmidt, "From Demon Possession to Magic Show: Ventriloquism, Religion, and the Enlightenment," *Church History* (June 1998): 12.

53. Leigh Eric Schmidt, "From Demon Possession to Magic Show," 13 and n42.

54. Lewis O. Saum, *The Popular Mood in Pre–Civil War America* (Westport, CT: Greenwood Press, 1980), 35.

55. Andrea Stulman Dennet, *Weird and Wonderful: The Dime Museum in America* (New York: New York University Press, 1997), 110–13.

56. Dennet, *Weird and Wonderful*, 111.

57. Marsden, *Religion and American Culture*, 115–16.

58. The best discussion of how religious belief was influenced by the Civil War can be found in Drew Gilpin Faust, *This Republic of Suffering: Death and the American Civil War* (New York: Alfred A. Knopf, 2008), chap. 6.

59. Marsden, *Religion and American Culture*, 167.

60. Winthrop S. Hudson and John Corrigan, *Religion in America* (Upper Saddle River, NJ: Prentice Hall, 1992), 351.

61. Robert Francis Martin, *Hero of the Heartland: Billy Sunday and the Transformation of American Christianity* (Bloomington: Indiana University Press, 2002), 88.

62. Martin, *Hero of the Heartland*, 70.

63. "Billy Sunday Fighting the Devil," *Detroit News Tribune*, October 29, 1916, 1.

64. Quoted in Peter Applebome, "Jerry Falwell, Moral Majority Founder, Dies at 71," *New York Times*, May 16, 2007.

3

The Devils of Daniel Webster: Satanic Cultural Politics through World War I

Satan found a new ally in the nineteenth-century American middle class. The politics of nineteenth-century moral reform assigned Satan a role that laid the groundwork for his continued significance in twentieth-century America. Just as evangelical Christianity assigned him pride of place in the spiritual path of millions of Americans, the new social realities of nineteenth century America gave him a wider sphere of influence. His emergence as a figure in American politics and moral reform coincided with the rise of a powerful, prosperous, white middle class. The diverse forces that shaped this group, and the conception of American identity they created, depended heavily on a belief in America's moral innocence and, consequently, the need to literally demonize the enemies of that innocence.

In 1937, Stephen Vincent Benét published his prize-winning short story "The Devil and Daniel Webster." This story, better known for the 1941 film, took the concept of the Faustian bargain and located it in mid-nineteenth-century New Hampshire, using it to trace the lineaments of what America had become over the first 150 years of its existence. Inevitably, the narrative led Benét to raise questions about America's complex relationship with the notion of evil. Benét saw America's relation to evil as crucial to its identity, especially in its troubled partnership with violence. He created, as literary critic Robert Combs has written, "a vision of the violence that history, politics and religion involve, together with their attendant ironies."[1]

"The Devil and Daniel Webster" narrates the story of Jabez Stone, a New Hampshire farmer who strikes a deal with the devil in an effort to escape his endemic bad luck. Seven years of good fortune give him a dubious return on the deal. Eventually his "mortgage falls due" and the devil appears to claim his soul. Luckily for Stone, the great American political figure, orator, and New England folk hero Daniel Webster agrees to take his case and convinces the devil that a trial must be held. Benét's Satan chooses a jury that represents a rogue's gallery of American history, complete with Tory loyalists, pirates, and witch hunters. The devil puts not only Stone on trial but the entire American national narrative. Benét raises the possibility that at every moment in the national story, Satan has been the tutelary deity in America's mercenary struggle for land, gold, slaves, and imperial domination. Stone was not the only American to make a pact with the devil. The nation itself, Benét suggests, made a similar deal to ensure its success.[2]

Benét's short story found so much resonance among its readers because he explored a dark side of America's first 150 years that only a few cultural critics had been willing to examine. The market revolution, the rise of the middle class, moral reform, the national agony over slavery, the convulsion of the Civil War, the growth of industry had all come together to create modern America. These diverse influences shaped American identity. The market revolution created a powerful middle class at the same moment that a religious awakening made most of that class into evangelical Protestants. A "Protestant establishment" had been created that, by the 1830s, used its influence to define the parameters of American identity. The first experiments in American imperialism had occurred in the 1840s with the Mexican American War. This adventure had been followed by a half century of wars of extermination fought against Amerindian peoples. The Civil War represented a profound test, not only of America's political nationalism, but also of its cultural identity. The years following the conflict brought the failure and broken promises of Reconstruction and the rise of the economic engine that would make unbridled capitalism and a consequent imperialism the basic dynamics of twentieth-century America.

Cultural nationalism is always an ongoing work in progress guided by a variety of movements and social classes. Emigrants from Catholic Europe posed the central challenge to any restrictive definition of American identity, and dissident voices throughout the nineteenth century offered alternative religious and cultural visions. Writers and activists, too, offered an often lonely critique of dominant ideas about religion, race, gender, and sexuality. But by the twentieth century, middle-class Protestants, the holders of cultural, social, and political capital, had shaped and defined the mainstream understanding of American identity.[3]

Satan, Benét suggests, had appeared at each moment in this struggle to define American identity. His influence touched the core of the American experience. The American middle class and its clergy, on the other hand, saw evil on the margins of American society, threatening to corrupt the nation's innocence. The fashioning of an American nationalism and cultural ethos required the defense of the boundaries of American identity and the literal demonization of the cultural Other. A wide spectrum of cultural voices, from proslavery apologists to temperance advocates, saw Satan at work in their opponents and the social evils for which they held them responsible. By the late nineteenth century, the witch hunter's fervor to destroy evil had become central to American political experience.

Satan used as a metaphor for the cultural Other might seem like a devil bled of his theological power, shorthand for the social ills of American civilization. After all, can the Prince of Darkness as a simple trope for societal failings have the same power that is attributed to him by evangelicals who believed they struggled in hand-to-hand combat with the devil for their souls? He can in American history, because the devil of the evangelical revivals and the devil of moral reform are the same devil. The America that saw the devil at work in its cultural politics was the same America that saw him lurking about the edges of the camp meeting. The idea of demonically inspired individuals masterminding social evils represented more than a thin metaphor at a time when hundreds of thousands of Americans experienced powerful conversion experiences that taught them that they had become targets for the devil. The reform movements that impelled antebellum Americans to try to create a Protestant Christian commonwealth saw their fight as an extension of their spiritual struggle with Satan. The national mood in the aftermath of the Civil War weakened the use of demonic language in the church and camp meeting, and still Satan remained a fixture of political and ideological rhetoric.

Nineteenth-century discourse about the devil was a contested discourse. The emerging American literary tradition in New England engaged the demons of America, both past and present, and challenged the regnant idea of America's innocence and its alleged struggle against evil. Meanwhile, an alternative demonology developed in the slave quarters and in the writings of early feminist intellectuals. While using the image of Satan, these voices contested dominant discourses that attempted to shield Americans from the darker truths about themselves that their beliefs in the devil legitimized. These cultural conflicts, which carried over into the twentieth century, ensured that Satan would experience a powerful reemergence in American culture on every front, from pop culture to popular religion.

Powerful currents of social change unsettled early nineteenth-century America. Religious enthusiasm was not the only dynamic energy unleashed in the early Republic. The tradition of the American Revolution embodied in it certain egalitarian principles that helped give rise to the birth of fervent reform efforts. Indeed, the revivals themselves gave impetus to many of these efforts, especially in the northeast and the newly opened Midwest. In the South, where the issue of moral reform inevitably raised questions about the nature and practice of slavery, reform efforts remained notably quiescent. White Southerners, in this era, eschewed reform in favor of a profoundly conservative social system.[4]

Moral crusades of various kinds seized the imagination of much of the rest of the country. While small efforts appeared in this period toward the reform of labor laws and even a few small societies who dedicated themselves to the pursuit of world peace, no reform effort received more attention and garnered more participation than the temperance movement. Temperance societies often emerged in the aftermath of revivals, with many converts simultaneously taking various "cold water" pledges. While the temperance movement looked at from a contemporary perspective might appear to be an example of crabbed moralism, nineteenth-century America's consumption of alcohol can be viewed as a larger social evil rather than a matter of individual self-indulgence. Americans in 1800 consumed, per capita, twice as much alcohol as they do today. Public drinking served a recreational role in a society with little in the way of a popular entertainment culture. Women and children often bore the brunt of much of this recreational drunkenness, explaining in part why calls for women's rights and for temperance reform frequently went hand in glove.[5]

The temperance movement, perhaps more than any other reform effort, put the devil to good rhetorical use. "Demon liquor" and "demon rum" became shorthand for alcohol of any kind for the strict, "cold water" temperance advocates. While it is true that nineteenth-century reformers saw alcohol abuse primarily as a problem of the depraved will, they also saw their struggle against it in terms of spiritual warfare. This would continue to be true throughout the nineteenth century. A political party dedicated to agricultural reform in the 1890s, the Grange Movement, included in its platform a statement against alcoholic beverages that suggested both a satanic design behind the liquor industry and the idea that spiritual combat should be the response. "We have pledged ourselves to labor for the development of a better manhood and womanhood among us, but how can we hope to succeed if we allow Satan's stronghold to flourish?"[6]

Fighting demon liquor became a symbolic struggle on behalf of a host of values, as well as an expression of a host of social anxieties. One of the most influential temperance tracts, and indeed one of the more popular fictional stories in antebellum America, used the devil and his angels as a trope for anxieties about the religious hypocrisy, the emerging market, and the evils of alcohol consumption. The 1835 booklet *The Dream: Or, the True Story of Deacon Giles Distillery*, written by temperance reformer George B. Cheever, told the story of a Salem, Massachusetts, church deacon who made a deal with Satan that gave him a demon workforce to run a rum distillery. Deacon Giles also made a living selling Bibles and gave Satan a cut of this profitable commerce in exchange for his help. Controversy boosted the popularity of this story, as Cheever based his deacon on an actual Salem church leader who both sold Bibles and ran a brewery. Family, friends, and supporters of the real-life deacon actually destroyed the press that produced some of the original copies and a foreman at the distillery assaulted Cheever on the street. A local judge fined Cheever for libel and slander, and he spent a month in prison.

In the original tale, all of Deacon Giles's workers walk out of the distillery, forcing him to make a deal with the devil and employ demons as replacements. His demonic brewers, who will only work at night, inscribe their barrels of malt with various secret, diabolical inscriptions. A revised version, published by the fearless Cheever after his release from prison, drew even more heavily on the fantastic. His demon workers become an army of imps dancing around the vats of brewing beer and throwing in "the most noxious and poisonous of drugs." One published version of the story came sumptuously illustrated with skeletal demons and other phantasms.[7]

Temperance far exceeded every reform movement in nineteenth-century America in terms of popularity and successes. The contemporary abolition movement was, by comparison, tiny and ineffective. Beer and whiskey became symbols of diabolical evil for many Americans and brought together disparate groups into common cause. Temperance, by constructing individual self-control (and legislation that would encourage such control) as *the* premier virtue, fit perfectly into the emerging American ideal of disciplined workers and frugal managers. Emerging in a context in which many middle-class Americans believed that material success depended on the practice of the virtues of temperance, anything that seemed to threaten these values represented evil and chaos. By the Victorian era, the cliché of "the demon in the bottle" had entered the new national vocabulary of moralism and restraint.

Concern about the demons of alcohol functioned as more than a metaphor. The temperance crusade produced its own hymnology, and one example clearly reveals how, for many middle-class Americans, beliefs about lack of self-control and restraint shaded naturally into concerns about demonic influence. "The Temperance Plea," a hymn reproduced even into the early twentieth century, described alcohol as "the demon that threatens the soul" and "the robber who breaks in the home." A threat to the individual soul and to the domestic sphere, this devil could destroy the American experiment itself:

> Away with the Demon that Threatens our Land!
> If you are a man, vote it down!
> Thus lessen our prisons, make happy the poor;
> And yours is a heavenly crown[8]

The devil did not only live in a bottle. White Protestant America conflated its belief in the demonic power of alcohol with the belief that liquor represented only one of the vices coming ashore with the massive waves of mid-nineteenth-century immigrants from Italy and Ireland. Beginning in 1820, 4.5 million people emigrated from Ireland alone. Middle-class white America looked on in horror as these mostly poor and uneducated Roman Catholics became a major voting bloc in all the major northeastern cities. Large numbers of southern Germans and Jews from Central Europe followed. In just the 1840s alone, 3 million immigrants came to the United States, almost all of them Roman Catholics. By 1860, one in seven Americans had been born outside of the United States.[9]

"Native" America viewed the new Americans as a great mob exhibiting vices that contradicted Protestant cultural values, vices that included violence, laziness, and religious error. Even reformers, in fact especially reformers, tended to view the immigrants as a great obdurate mass of evil in the midst of the purity of the American experiment. Lydia Maria Childe, an important voice of conscience when it came to the struggle against slavery, wrote that "their [immigrants] moral and intellectual state is such that one might as well attempt to call the dogs together for reform."[10]

Drinking habits at odds with the temperance movement's objectives account for much of the concern about immigrants. In Germany, Italy, and Ireland, wine, liquor, and beer was seen as part of the culture of sociability and a basic staple at the family dinner table, rather than a male vice associated only with the tavern and domestic discord. German immigrants brought to the United States the craftsmanship of brewing that stretched back to the medieval era with both Anheuser-Busch and Miller representing nineteenth-century American breweries started by immigrant German brewing dynasties. Protestant leaders in America viewed these practices with a baleful eye. James King, a late nineteenth-century temperance advocate and pamphleteer, claimed that, due to alcohol, a significant number of Catholics in America found themselves in a downward spiral that took them "to the prison and almhouse, to reformatory and orphanage, to dive and brothel."[11]

Anti-immigrant rhetoric did not stop with the effort to assign moral depravity to the new Americans. Middle-class Protestants revitalized Timothy

Dwight's rhetoric of satanic conspiracy and applied it to the Roman Catholic Church. In doing this, they drew on a long tradition dating to the Protestant Reformation that connected the Church, especially the papacy to the power of the Antichrist. Eighteenth-century America had further strengthened this connection by viewing Catholicism as part of the "conspiracy against liberty" that threatened the very birth of America. At least some American patriots were convinced that their mother country's détente with Catholic Canada meant that Catholicism influenced the court of George III. In Charleston, South Carolina, a local rumor in 1775 had it that a British warship in the harbor held "14,000 stands of arms" that would be used to arm not only rebellious slaves but also "Roman Catholics, Indians, and Canadians."[12]

Anti-Catholic sentiment in the United States had strong links to the idea of satanic conspiracy, especially in New England. Puritan hatred of all things "Popish" had been a major force in English politics since the seventeenth century. The French and Indian War (1754–1763) strengthened this connection, with the enemies of the colonies seen as emissaries of the devil. The captain of one group of New England militia told them that they fought on the side of both King George and "King Jesus" against the "incendiaries of Hell and Rome." The conquest of Catholic Canada, according to Patriot leader Jonathan Mayhew, represented a conquest of "the seat of Satan." The celebration of November 5 as "Pope's Day" (Guy Fawkes Day in England) solidified a clear iconography of evil in the New England mind. As part of these rowdy celebrations, a mock trial for the pope and the devil would be held, and both were burned or hanged in effigy.[13]

The alleged connection between satanic evil and the Catholic Church grew in the nineteenth century, as Roman Catholics became a substantial part of the demography of America. The ancient enemy no longer simply ruled from Rome or Canada. Suddenly, the seat of Satan had moved to Boston, New York, and Philadelphia. A flood of anti-Catholic literature included some of the best-selling books in nineteenth-century America, literature described by historian Richard Hofstadter as "the pornography of the puritan."[14]

The most popular book of this type, Maria Monk's 1832 *The Awful Disclosures of Maria Monk* presented itself as a firsthand testimony of life inside a Catholic convent. Convents, Monk claimed, functioned as little more than harems for the priests who used the power of the confessional to have "criminal intercourse" with young women. Children born of these unions, she insisted, were strangled and buried by the elderly nuns, who acted as procuresses for the priests. Maria Monk's book, even after suspicious Protestant ministers proved its fraudulent, became the best-selling book in American history before the publication of *Uncle Tom's Cabin*.[15]

Numerous imitators followed the success of Monk's work, and the idea of forbidden, uninhibited sexuality taking place behind convent walls became part of the lore of anti-Catholicism in America. The Jesuit order, a favorite target for conspiratorial thinking since the seventeenth century, came in for special abuse. One Protestant writer in the 1850s called the monasteries under the control of Jesuits "vast sodoms." It made little difference to the writer or to his readers that the Jesuit order did not actually operate monasteries.[16]

James A. Morone has noted that much of this sensationalist literature about female religious and male priests replicates aspects of the European and American witch-hunting tradition and the demonology that accompanied it. American misogyny functioned as fertile soil for these fantasies. Women, unable to control their lusts or to protect their virtue are at the heart of this narrative of evil, not unlike the witches of Puritan New England. They are portrayed, in the anti-Catholic accounts, as having sexual congress with the priests, just as witches in the fevered Puritan imagination had sexual intercourse with the devil. Young women like Maria Monk hurled accusations, just as in the seventeenth-century witch hunts the young and "innocent" had been the first to accuse. Protestant clergy such as Lyman Beecher followed in the footsteps of Cotton Mather and laid the theological and diabological groundwork for widespread panic and persecution.[17]

The Civil War took the emphasis off of the nativist political movement for only a short time. In the 1880s, the idea of Satan's work in America through the "popish church" flourished once again. The American Protective Association, founded in 1887, soon had a membership of almost 2.5 million. All took an oath to oppose "the diabolical work of the Roman Catholic Church." Robert C. Fuller notes that such efforts received increased impetus from Josiah Strong's hugely popular *Our Country: Its Possible Future and Present Crisis*, which suggested that "America was uniquely vulnerable to the devil's strategies."[18]

Satan cloaked in the red robes of the Catholic Church became a permanent part of Protestant America's conception of demonic evil. Reborn in the 1920s, fear of Satan's work through Catholicism would find new life in a renewed nativism. A supposed connection between the Catholic Church and the work of the Antichrist made end-time speculation an especially virulent discourse. As late as 2008, these views affected a presidential election as critics forced Republican candidate John McCain to reject the endorsement of Texas evangelical leader John Hagee. Hagee had described Catholicism as part of a larger satanic conspiracy and connected its influence to the end of days.[19]

While being accused of bringing the devil's advance agents, Catholic immigrants from Ireland, Italy, and Central Europe brought their own, very powerful, sense of Satan to American shores. Nineteenth-century Catholic devotionalism included a strong sense of the spiritual life as a struggle with

Satan, whose influence corrupted the soul and could even bring physical misfortune. Devotion to St. Michael the archangel proved especially strong among Irish immigrants, a devotion that included a strong conception of spiritual warfare. Michael had, according to scripture and church tradition, driven Lucifer and his fellow rebels from heaven. St. Michael's present concern was to aid believers in their struggle against both temptation to sin and the tragic aspects of human life that much of folk Catholicism attributed to Satan. A popular prayer to St. Michael, introduced by Pope Leo XIII in the late nineteenth century, asked the warrior angel to "defend us in battle. Be our protection against the wickedness and snares of the devil . . . cast into hell Satan, and all evil spirits who roam throughout the world seeking to ruin souls." A story that became popular in American and European folk Catholicism described Pope Leo as having composed the prayer after receiving a vision of "the misleading powers and the ravings of the devil against the church in all countries." The prayer to St. Michael remained a standard way to end Mass in most Catholic parishes in America until the Second Vatican Council of the 1960s.[20]

These devotional practices never situated Satan in the institutional and cultural politics of nineteenth-century America. However, Satan did become a potent force within the immigrant households and the confines of the parishes. Fear of his power policed the boundaries of sexuality and identity. Among Italian immigrants in New York, children were warned of the satanic evil that threatened them if they betrayed the values of the *domus*, or the household. Over the decades, young men found ways to escape the smothering intimacy of these households, often through close friendships or street gangs (or both). The options for young women, their lives carefully guarded by an almost impossible weight of expectations, proved much more limited.[21]

Young women who sought to escape the control of the *domus* found themselves regarded as agents of the devil, even progenitors of the devil. Jane Addams, the reformer who founded Chicago's famous Hull House, wrote an article for the 1914 *American Journal of Sociology* that reported a strange incident in which "three Italian women" came into Hull House and demanded to see "the devil-baby." Addams, full of WASPish scorn, connected this strange occurrence to the recent birth of a deformed newborn and to a genre of "devil-baby" tales she had heard from her Italian neighbors. At least one version of this story featured "an Italian girl married to an atheist who vehemently tore a holy picture from the bedroom wall" saying he'd prefer to have the devil in his house than a picture of a saint. Satan promptly incarnated himself into a child sleeping in the mother's womb. The monstrous birth was, like the Jersey Devil, horribly deformed, but the devil escaped when the atheist father, suddenly a God-fearing man, sought to have the child baptized.[22]

This story obviously served as a cautionary tale about the dangers of women marrying outside of the faith and betraying the Italian *domus*. In fact, Addams herself reported that "mothers threatened their daughters that if they went to dance halls . . . they would be eternally disgraced by devil-babies." Such beliefs, borrowing from the tradition of monstrous births, patrolled the boundaries of gendered expectations, in a way not dissimilar to the New England tales of "the Jersey Devil." The devil, as always, proved a handy instrument with which to draw lines and make distinctions.

The devil of the Catholic immigrants remained a potent force in American ethnic life well into the twentieth century. Over time, the public voice of Catholicism would bring the devil of devotionalism into the public discourse. By the twentieth century, as the posterity of the first Catholic immigrants secured a strong economic, social, and political tradition within the United States, they joined their Protestant brethren in attacking various aspects of modern life and culture as "demonic" and part of "the wiles of Satan." By the 1950s, everything from precode Hollywood films to Communism had been described by Catholic leaders as part of a larger satanic conspiracy. Just as Satan and his wiles could darken a human soul with mortal sin, he could blot an entire culture.

The new Americans who had entered the country in the mid-nineteenth century came to a country divided. Slavery, since the 1820s, had become the most pressing moral and political issue confronting the nation. Both North and South had profited from the toil of enslaved black people; indeed, a small number of slaves had been held in the North before the Revolutionary period. Since the late eighteenth century, the economic and social development of the country had created a sharp divide between slave and free states. White Southern planters had become the elite class in their region and had created an economy that rested on the backs of its slaves. By the 1820s, some Southerners increasingly viewed their slaveholding economy and culture as a superior way of life and argued that slavery was not simply a "necessary evil" but represented "a positive good."

The reformist impulse in the North helped to produce first a number of antislavery associations and, by the 1830s, abolitionist societies that called for the immediate end of the South's "peculiar institution." In Congress, the conflict over slavery became the defining issue in the discussion of admitting new territories as states in the American west. Southern politicians viewed any effort to halt the spread of slavery as a challenge to their property rights, while Northern politicians spoke increasingly of "the slave power" that threatened free American institutions. By 1860, the almost 4 million enslaved black people in the United States were pressing for their freedom through various forms of resistance. Former slaves such as Frederick Douglass became outspoken advocates of abolition.[23]

The clash over slavery inevitably included satanic imagery, especially after the 1830s when both sides began to perceive the conflict as a moral struggle. Southern apologists became convinced that the Northern abolitionist movement represented a larger spiritual malady in the region, a tendency toward religious experimentalism that suggested satanic influence. Southern conservative writers saw the North as embodying the devil's desire to overturn traditional mores and subvert the divinely ordained social order that slavery represented. Methodist leader Augustus Baldwin Longstreet responded to the abolitionist use of the religious argument by comparing it to the incident in the gospels when "Satan quoted scripture" to Christ as part of an effort to tempt him.[24]

Many white Southerners viewed the Civil War itself as a struggle against satanic evil. Ministers increasingly described secession as a sacred duty, withdrawal from the Union as a kind of religious purification. White Southerners saw their social order as legitimized by God and thus interpreted any challenge to it as the device of the devil. Late in 1863, the *Confederate Baptist*, a denominational paper in South Carolina, insisted that the North had "chosen Lucifer for their patron divinity and [were] seeking to reinstate him to his lost dignity and honor." Local newspapers sometimes reflected this theme. A writer for the *Keowee Courier* in upcountry South Carolina referred to Satan as "the first abolitionist." Like the devil, the writer believed, modern abolitionists sought to subvert God's ordinances, to overturn the very nature of things.[25]

A few Northern writers at the time of the coming of the Civil War also speculated about the satanic influences on their enemies. L. S. Weed, a Brooklyn clergyman, saw in the conflict the fulfillment of Revelation chapter 12, in which the true Israel, embodied in the American North, struggled against the Dragon with the help of St. Michael. The fall of "a third of the stars of heaven" described in that passage promised the defeat of those Southern states that had rebelled against the federal government. Late in the war, a pamphlet distributed by the Ladies Christian Commission, described the North as working for "the downfall of the antichrist."[26]

Northern public opinion after the war continued to view the former Confederacy as being in the thrall of the devil. Presbyterian minister Charles Robinson in Brooklyn responded to talk of Northerners and Southerners being of the "same race" by reminding his listeners that "Satan was of the same race as Gabriel . . . but one became a rebel." Edward J. Blum, in his outstanding book *Reforging the White Republic*, comments that, in Robinson's eyes, "Like Lucifer, Confederates had earned expulsion from the sacred community. . . . They now belonged to the netherworld of spiritual, racial and national otherness."[27]

The former slaves, many of whom helped to transform the war for the Union into a war for emancipation, also viewed the Civil War as a theological and moral struggle against satanic evil. Running away to take up arms for the Union cause (or, in the case of women, to serve as spies, scouts, and nurses) became the most powerful symbol of resistance. Enslaved people freed themselves by the tens of thousands during the Civil War, escaping into Union lines by foot, by boat, and by stolen horse. Some fought the Southern slave masters with the weapons of the spirit. Historian Albert Raboteau has pointed out that prayer for the defeat of the Confederacy represented a powerful means of resistance in a place and time when both slaves and masters believed heartily in the power of prayer.[28]

Folklore about the devil blended, as it always had in the enslaved black's experience, with the struggle against slavery. One of the most common tales of deadly encounters with the devil reads more like an attempt to run away from a cruel master than a supernatural encounter. In this folktale, the devil appears as a rider on a great black horse, wielding a sword or pitchfork. The imagery recalls the slave patrols fugitives had to contend with as they made their flight to freedom. This devil was both the overseer and the slave patrol, described in one account as "sitting in the middle of the smoke of hell with his eyes wide open, staring at his prey." Devil imagery also found its way into the slave conversion narrative. Storytellers employed the language of fugitive and runaway to describe the soul coming to Christ, with the devil "hotly pursuing the candidate for salvation" or "throwing metal balls at the fugitive." Riggins R. Earl Jr., in his comprehensive study of religious imagery in the slave community, notes that these examples never make explicit the identity of Satan as the white master. Yet they clearly encoded the experience of becoming a fugitive with salvation and escape from demonic horrors.[29]

Almost 200,000 African American men joined the Union army during the Civil War, often taking up arms against their former masters. Many of these saw themselves as fighting to destroy the power of Satan over themselves and their community. In the South Carolina low country, the First South Carolina African regiment (later mustered formally into the Union army as the Thirty-third United States Colored Troops) went into battle singing "Oh Mary, Don't You Weep," a song that promised the former slaves God's deliverance. Satan would be confounded and the white South (compared to Pharaoh in the Exodus account) would be destroyed;

> Old Mister Satan, he got mad
> Missed that Soul that he thought he had
> Pharaoh's army got drowned
> Oh Mary, don't you weep!

Following the end of the war, the effort to reconstruct the nation and preserve the freedoms won by African Americans faltered on institutionalized racism and the white South's refusal to stomach democracy. In 1867, a Congress controlled by Radical Republicans passed the Reconstruction Acts. For a brief time, experiments in participatory democracy appeared across the aristocratic Southern landscape. In Mississippi, Hiram Revels became the first African American to enter the U.S. Senate, taking a seat once belonging to rebel leader Jefferson Davis. In South Carolina, Joseph H. Rainey took the oath of office in 1870 and became the first African American congressman in the state's history. For a ten-year period, African Americans held real political power in the South, with a majority of congressmen and senators (reflecting the makeup of the population) in some state legislatures.

Northern public opinion, shaped by a deeply conservative vision of race, could not stomach some of the changes their own victory had wrought.. Gradually, North and South coalesced around a white ethnic nationalism. The collapse of Reconstruction in the late 1870s brought a wave of violence against African Americans and the restructuring of Southern society. White leaders, often former Confederates, used intimidation and voter fraud to overthrow Reconstruction governments. The restored white leadership, with no interference from the federal government, actively worked to disenfranchise the free people, stripping them of their hard-won gains. By the 1880s, Southern states violated the Fifteenth Amendment with impunity and employed a bewildering array of voter registration requirements that kept African Americans from the polls. Southern state legislatures, often affirming county ordinances, segregated Southern society.

This period in American history is often thought of as the nadir of the African American experience. The end of the hopes inspired by Reconstruction had come with an overwhelming white backlash. Public lynchings of African American men accused of crimes or simply believed to have violated Southern racial etiquette became epidemic. Historians have estimated that a little over 5,000 lynchings occurred in America between the end of the Civil War and 1968. A number of writers and historians have noted that these public, communal events had all the elements of religious ritual. Ralph Ellison wrote that it was odd that Hemingway had chosen the bullfight to describe ritualized violence, since "he might have studied that ritual of violence closer to home, that ritual in which the victim is the human scapegoat, the lynching bee."[30]

Religion did play a role in the extraordinary violence that white Southerners inflicted on their black neighbors. The freed slaves came to be viewed in the minds of white Christians as agents of Satan among them. Southern ministers viewed Confederate defeat as the apocalypse or at least a sign of the apocalypse. Thus, the struggle to end Reconstruction and then secure the stability of the social order became a struggle against the Antichrist. The former Confederate referred to African American women who took part in political action during Reconstruction as "female demons" and "polluted wretches." A writer for the *Southern Review* suggested that Reconstruction "had its beginnings in heaven when Lucifer raised the standard of revolt." Such beliefs transformed the American South into a nightmare for African Americans in the years following Reconstruction's collapse.[31]

Satan clearly played an important role in the way many Americans perceived their Civil War. The titanic nature of the struggle and the moral force with which both sides attempted to invest their cause allowed for a true demonization of the enemy. More than any other American crisis up to that time, speculation about the devil's role in American history helped to shape an apocalyptic sense of that history. Michael Northcott suggests that the Civil War, along with the American Revolution, gave Americans a nationalism born of "a unique combination of apocalyptic violence and religious fervor."[32]

Diabolical imagery in the nineteenth century provided the majority of white Americans with a boundary line beyond which waited evil and the Other, symbolism that patrolled the boundaries of respectability and purity. But throughout that century, dissident voices sought to challenge this understanding of evil. Literary currents in nineteenth-century America often reflected a desire to untangle the devil from the American conception of evil, to force Americans to rethink their use of demonic imagery and even turn it around on them. Thus, many American writers attempted to exorcise the devil by invoking him, using the traditional imagery of the devil and even of spiritual warfare to critique the moral state of nineteenth-century America.

Nathanial Hawthorne's work returned again and again to the problem of evil, not only for the individual but for the whole social order. Hawthorne saw evil not in the visage of a supernatural Satan but rather in his own Puritan heritage of intolerance and violence (Judge John Hathorne was a distant relative) and in the unbridled growth of capitalist individualism. Hawthorne concluded that the problem of sin and moral guilt, conceived by Puritan America as an individual's pact with Satan, actually existed within a complex web of social conventions, ideological commitments, and national ambitions. This did not mean that Hawthorne ignored the Calvinist conviction that sin painted the human soul with the darkest of hues. On the contrary, his conception of sin and human depravity allowed him to reject the tendency of his audience, the emerging American middle class, to draw sharp lines of distinction and disgrace around what they found morally objectionable and to justify violence against anyone outside those lines. Every face wore a black veil, to paraphrase his conclusion to the famous short story "The Minister's Black Veil," and the veil drew darkness over the hubris of nineteenth-century America.

The images of Satan as a cold-blooded tempter appear frequently in Hawthorne's work, drawing on the author's obsession with the themes of sin and guilt. Human characters can embody satanic attributes, though Hawthorne defines them not as truly satanic but rather as human beings corrupted by turning inward. The best example is Roger Chillingworth, the husband of Hester Prynne in *The Scarlet Letter*, who attempts to destroy his wife and the Puritan minister who is secretly her lover and father to her illegitimate child. Satanic imagery is used to describe even Chillingworth's features. His face, contorted with rage, is a "writhing horror" reminiscent of a serpent. He tempts Hester to reveal the secret name of her lover, causing her to compare him "to the Black Man that haunts the forest round about us." Chillingworth does the devil's work by being a connoisseur of sin in much the same way that Puritan moral theology seemed to take delight in a voyeuristic examination of moral failure. When he finally discovers that Arthur Dimmesdale had been his wife's lover, Hawthorne writes that "had a man seen old Roger Chillingworth, at that moment of ecstasy, he would have no need to ask how Satan comports himself, when a precious human soul is lost to heaven, and won into his kingdom."[33]

Chillingworth embodies the rising American middle class, convinced of its own moral power and able to justify the destruction of sinners. Notably, Hawthorne makes Chillingworth into a prosperous Boston physician, a symbol for the emerging professional and business classes of nineteenth-century America who became the center of the country's social and economic gravity. His death is marked by a seemingly respectable act, that of leaving a financial legacy for young Pearl. While this could be read as a redeeming act, even this is morally complicated for Hawthorne, who tended to view the transfer of funds as an assertion of pride and power rather than an act of moral heroism. His final comment on Chillingworth is that he died "when there was no more devil's work on earth for him to do."[34]

Hawthorne perceived a link between the inability to face one's own moral failures and lack of compassion for those marginalized in American society. Moreover, he saw the closing of the national heart as far more than a set of corrupted attitudes. At best, such a naive ethical system led to cynicism, but at worst, such a belief in one's own moral innocence goes hand in hand with a willingness to inflict violence on those outside the circle of virtue. Hawthorne's short story "Young Goodman Brown" portrays a young, newly married Puritan's nightmarish vision in which he discovers that his whole village, including his supposedly innocent young wife, takes part in depraved rites of satanic worship. He withdraws within himself and dies a gloomy old man. The reader is left to wonder whether or not his dark visions simply emerged out of the young Puritan's own heart, a heart where the meaning of good and evil was simple, uncomplicated, and unforgiving. Hawthorne extended this analysis in stories such as "Earth's Holocaust" and "Egotism, or, the Bosom Serpent." In both tales, reformers and moralists attempt to destroy the evil in society or within themselves by violence, and in both cases they only evoke powerful, and ultimately evil, forces that they cannot control.[35]

Nathanial Hawthorne believed that his young country's absolute faith in its own goodness and innocence only served to further underscore the point, since pride had been the devil's sin. The "benevolent empire of reform," drawing on the well of religious enthusiasm of the nineteenth-century religious awakenings, had created a flurry of moral activity among the American middle class. In the heat of moral fervor, few recognized the seeds of hubris that would bear bitter fruit in the years following the Civil War, the birth of an imperial American consciousness convinced of its own moral uprightness. Hawthorne's work can be read as a critique of this tendency. The heir of witch hunters found Satan not outside the parameters marked by the morality of the middle class but writhing like a serpent within the American experience itself. America was, in some sense, the living embodiment of Satan's pride.[36]

American writers of the nineteenth century also used the devil to discuss the changing realities of class and economics in America. These changes reverberated into America's Victorian era and on into the twentieth century. Anxieties over the market helped to shape what became the most predominant image of Satan outside of religious circles, the idea of the devil as malevolent salesman. Edgar Allan Poe's 1839 short story "The Devil in the Belfry" tells the tale of a stranger who interrupts the economic and social life of a village by causing the town clock to strike thirteen. This simple prank destroys the life of the town since commerce cannot exist without proper timekeeping and, the story suggests, the American town can no longer maintain a cohesive life without commerce. The devil, Poe intimates, deceives in a world of deceit. Herman Melville's *The Confidence Man* expands on this idea. Melville tells the story of a fair-haired "deaf-mute" who boards the ship *Fidele*, a kind of ship of fools whose passengers are warned to expect "a confidence man" who will try to trick and betray them. Satan becomes a figure of the American market in this context, a diabolical con artist whose business is business. As critic Thomas McHaney notes, "He [Satan] is both the Puritan devil ready to sign up the willing or unsuspecting, and a particularly modern devil, too, who sells stock in the Black Rapids Coal Company."[37]

The devil, for these American writers, had become a way to express anxieties about the voracious nature of American capitalism. Louisa May Alcott made a contribution to this genre in her 1877 *The Modern Mephistopheles*. Referred to by literary critic Madeleine B. Stern as "an exotic in the Alcott canon," a first draft of *Modern Mephistopheles* was rejected by her publisher for being too long and "too sensational." In Alcott's novel, the satanic Jasper Helwyz exerts a kind of mesmeric control over Felix Canaris. Offering him power and liberation, Helwyz binds to himself Canaris's soul. Canaris's ambition and desire for fame, his ruling passion, allows him to become tamed by Helwyz and turned into his "Greek slave." Canaris's wife, Gladys, challenges the patriarchal assumptions of both her husband and his tempter/enslaver, helping Canaris overcome his hellish ambition. Canaris is released from the devil when he becomes free from ambition, but, like Goethe's *Faust*, he must watch the death of the feminine soul who freed him. Alcott's Satan, a representation of America's lust for power on the cusp of the Gilded Age, is left alone at the end of the novel, his prey lost to him. This ending could be read as Alcott's assertion that human relationships could overcome the predations of the market, an idea very much in line with the general trend of her work.[38]

The manifestations of Satan that appear in Hawthorne, Melville, Alcott, and Poe have a number of similarities. All embody certain repugnant aspects of America's nineteenth-century "go-ahead" spirit that reduced the totality of the human experience to getting and spending, a lack of true human feeling hiding behind either a mask of piety or entrepreneurial spirit (or both). These American devils are not tricked out with horns and pitchforks but are the greedy entrepreneur, the crabbed and bitter Puritan, the seducer whose only desire is the heated pursuit of desire itself. Andrew Delbanco describes the Satan of nineteenth-century American literature as "priapic, engorged with the desire to hoard other people's lives and fortunes for his own use. Yet he is also one's neighbor, one's colleague, one's self." Some of America's literary lights understood Satan, in some basic sense, as the American spirit, the spirit of gain constructed as progress. Satan became in their work America's doppelganger, her secret self.[39]

The work of Mark Twain dealt more extensively with the Satan mythos than any writer in nineteenth-century America. Twain used variant expressions of the devil in his short fiction to ask basic questions about the nature of evil, the nature of the universe, and the nature of America. This obsession of Twain's, well-known to scholars but little known to the popular American consciousness that connects Twain primarily to *Huckleberry Finn* and the steamboats on the Mississippi, helped produced some of the author's best writing. His Satans become the mouthpiece for some of the most vituperative writing about religion to ever come from an American pen by the late nineteenth century, a full-throated critique of the Protestant America that had been built on the ruins of the Civil War.[40]

Perhaps the most infamous vision of Satan in the Twain canon appears in his *Letters from the Earth* in which the devil, rather than being a sinister tempter, acts as ironic observer of the creation and fall of the human race. In a series of secret letters to the angels Michael and Gabriel, he makes light of God's refusal to allow the first human access to the "Tree of Knowledge." At the same time, Satan turns an ironic eye on the human race itself, viewing it as primarily an absurdity. Literary critic Coleman O. Parsons notes that here, and in much of the rest of his corpus, Satan becomes for Twain "a daring, free, and inquisitive spirit, in opposition to factitious theologies and illusory realities." He is no god of evil but rather a creative rebel. Parsons sees Twain using this Satan to critique the author's own hatred of racial violence and American imperialism, an evocation of a powerful, chthonic spirit that can laugh bitterly at America's dark, hidden self.[41]

Twain's most complex Satan appears in his unfinished work "The Mysterious Stranger." Building on certain aspects of his earlier satire of Christian beliefs about the devil and original sin, the Satan of this work is truly an original invention. Satan embodies the spirit of unleashed creativity, the genius of the arts. But he is not simply the spirit of liberation that appears in Blake's *Marriage of Heaven and Hell*. Like the devil of the *Letters from the Earth*, he mocks the human race for its destructive wars and violence but goes even further, mocking the nature of existence itself. "What does it all amount to?" said Satan with his evil chuckle, "nothing at all."[42]

Twain created an American Satan that would have little to do with the popular image of God and humanity's enemy. His Satan puts humanity, and indeed God, on trial, rather than the other way around. Putting Satan in the dock, Twain showed again and again in his work, has been a replacement for placing ourselves in the dock. In one of the most memorable passages from "The Mysterious Stranger," Satan ridicules human beings for their intense hypocrisy, their willingness to cloak their warlike and greedy nature under a patina of religion. "Two or three centuries from now," he bitterly comments, "it will be recognized that all the competent killers are Christians." The progress of civilization has been little more than a refinement of the arts of murder. Human beings are the true devils.[43]

Twain could also see America itself as the devil, especially in its fascination with violence and greed for economic gain. Twain, as he neared the end of his life, became increasingly gloomy, a kind of avatar of Hawthorne's "Young Goodman Brown." This attitude came in part from personal struggles but also from a dark view of the American experience at the end of the Gilded Age. Twain famously critiqued the late nineteenth-century obsession with business and the technology of death in *A Connecticut Yankee in King Arthur's Court.* Twain's prototypical American brings a big-business mentality and the machine gun to Camelot, irrevocably destroying it. The devil as American entrepreneur also appears in his short story "Sold to Satan." Drawing inspiration from Madame Curie's discovery of radium, the short story has Satan "as a courteous successful Tempter who is made of radium worth millions on the market." A special shield keeps him from destroying the world, while the narrator, an American businessman, seeks to kidnap him and tap the source of his power. If only, he fantasizes, it were possible "to kidnap Satan, and stock him, and incorporate him, and water the stock up to ten billions—just three times its actual value—and blanket the world with it!"[44]

Literary critic Stanley Brodwin notes that the devil in *Sold to Satan* appears as pure, and possibility destructive power, is an "eerie foreshadowing" of the destructive power of nuclear weapons. In the context of Twain's story, Satan is the potency behind American innovation, complicating and ultimately dehumanizing human life. Satan represents the power that will run America's "machines and railways for a hundred million years." Satan is the tempter but he is also the temptation. He is for Twain the secret power behind American business, the truth about American progress. Twain found a fertile metaphor in Satan. He was an ironic voice critiquing American religion; the temptation for an America increasingly turning toward inhumane values; and, in some sense, America itself, expressed as pure power driving the technological advance of the industrial age. In Twain's dark vision, we certainly see the seared shadows of Hiroshima, the deathly symbol of Yankee know-how.[45]

The popularity of these American writers in no way means that their publics responded to this basic critique of their values. Few, even today, know of Twain's copious writing on Satan or, as an adjunct to those reflections, his probing attacks on emerging American imperialism (especially American atrocities in the Philippines). In the commercial boom of turn-of-the-century America, few wished to apply the brakes and reconsider the nation's understanding of evil.

The writers of the American literary renaissance were not alone in critiquing America's concept of the demonic and raising questions about the American understanding of evil. Elizabeth Cady Stanton, the powerful voice for women's rights in nineteenth-century America, attempted to revise traditional beliefs about Satan and place them in the service of human liberation. Stanton's 1895 project *The Woman's Bible* subverted the popular understanding of Satan, especially as tempter of weak souls, and transformed him into a symbolic argument for the liberation of women.

Stanton firmly believed that religion had long been a primary partner in the patriarchy's denigration and oppression of women. She notes in the preface to *The Woman's Bible* that when nineteenth-century women first raised questions about the nature of their oppression they had been "referred to the Bible for the answer." Stanton argued that only by challenging the august authority of the allegedly sacred book, thus challenging religious patriarchy on its own field of battle, could women emancipate themselves from the hold of religion.

In *The Woman's Bible*, chapters 1–3 of the book of Genesis receive special attention from Stanton and her collaborators, in large part because of the biblical passage's status as most favored by misogynists through the ages. The "sin of Eve" had been regarded as the origin of male domination in the world, with childbirth and subservience part of the first woman's punishment for listening to the devil's temptation. Some commentators had even seen Adam's decision to partake of the forbidden fruit as the result of being seduced by his wife to do so, absolving him of responsibility for "original sin." Thus, even the opening chapters of the Bible had become what feminist theologian Phyllis Trible would later call "a text of terror."[46]

Stanton read the tale quite differently. The serpent who speaks to Eve, traditionally rendered by Christian interpreters as the devil, is described by Stanton as a "seraphim" who offers the gift of Knowledge, promising that "if the mortal body does perish, the immortal part will live forever." The serpent, then, is a beautiful, angelic creature, only later imagined as a devil. The woman's action, in partnership with the serpent, is read as an act of bravery. Eve is "fearless of death if she can gain wisdom." Meanwhile, "the conduct of Adam was to the last degree dastardly." He "whines" to the angry god in the garden about his wife's behavior, using her as a shield for his own irresponsibility. Eve, in *The Woman's Bible*, is not deceived by Satan. Instead, she makes a choice in partnership with the beautiful angelic creature later cursed by the patriarchy as "a serpent."[47]

Stanton's efforts to redact the theological history of patriarchy proved futile in late nineteenth-century America, although later, post-Christian feminist theologians such as Mary Daly would make use of some of her ideas. In Victorian-era America, however, powerful cultural forces constructed every effort by American women to exercise agency outside of traditional marriage and family as the devil's work. The tragic case of Victoria Woodhull illustrates this point. Woodhull became the first woman to run for president in 1872, sharing a ticket with Frederick Douglass, and in 1871, the first woman to address a congressional committee. Characterized by her many enemies as a "free love" advocate, Woodhull criticized what she described as the "legalized prostitution" of marriage that often bound women for life in abusive and unfulfilling legal contracts. She called for a massive overhaul of divorce laws that would take away the husband's "right of property in the wife."[48]

Woodhull found herself lambasted in the press, constructed as a demonic temptress who sought to destroy holy matrimony. In 1872, a Thomas Nast cartoon that appeared in *Harper's Weekly* portrayed Woodhull with long, leathery wings, urging a much-abused wife to leave her drunken husband. Later, in the 1870s, Anthony Comstock convicted Woodhull of violating the antiobscenity laws he had worked to implement across the country, effectively silencing her calls for reform (after this, Elizabeth Cady Stanton ceased discussing the topic in her public lectures). By the 1880s, individual states actually put further restrictions on divorce laws that had been briefly liberalized following the Civil War.[49]

The Comstock laws represented a larger wave of moral panic that washed over the country at the end of the nineteenth century, a cultural movement that differed from the concerns of earlier reformers in that it seemed to focus less on reform of social ills and more on the restriction of personal behavior. According to Gaines Foster, even the white American South, traditionally anxious about reform given its connection with abolition, "focused their efforts on forcing the government to legislate strict definitions of pure and pious behavior." This trend throughout the nation can be explained in part by the triumph of the American middle class, politically and economically powerful, and anxious that newly freed slaves, immigrants, and the working classes conform to their standards of propriety.[50]

The Comstock laws represented more than the latest wave of sexual prudery. Andrea Tone notes that obscenity laws in this period included, for the first time, efforts to limit women's access to reproductive control. Since the 1830s, a flourishing trade in condoms, "womb veils" (diaphragms), and intrauterine devices provided numerous options (of uncertain reliability) for women and men seeking to limit family size. These new technologies gave birth control a very public presence, and moralists worried that it created a cultural environment where sexual pleasure could thrive independent of both reproduction and domesticity.[51]

In 1870, physician Nicholas Francis Cooke linked women's rights, sexual liberation, and family limitation with the wiles of Satan. Cooke's *Satan in Society* became the definitive anti–birth control text of the period, linking reproductive choice with "immoralities, indecencies and crimes" that, in Cooke's view, represented a demonic attack on the American experiment. "The hosts of Satan are mustering for the contest which shall decide the possession of our vast domain," Cooke declared. He went on to detail how everything from birth control to excessive masturbation among American men threatened the foundations of the republic. Birth control, in particular, represented a satanic threat because it promised, in his view, to loosen the bonds of the American family. Cooke referred to these "mechanical contrivances" as "inventions of hell" that led to debauchery and ruin.[52]

Developments in the early antiabortion crusade in nineteenth-century America reveal the motivating anxieties and the role played by demonic imagery in them. Abortion had previously been largely a private, domestic affair. Some early antiabortion efforts originally focused as much on the life of the mother as of the child she carried. State legislatures as early as the 1840s made procuring an abortion a misdemeanor, based on the logic that abortion presented a danger to the life of the mother. These efforts were restricted to the northeast, with no real attempts in other parts of the country to limit the practice at all. In the late nineteenth century, however, the increasing professionalization of medicine and the emergence of the commercial drug industry transformed abortion from a private affair within a household or within networks of female neighbors into a public issue amid the swirl of market forces and political and cultural rhetoric.[53]

Some of the most vituperative opponents of abortion quickly removed all moral nuance out of public discussions of the issue and deployed the imagery of satanic evil in attacking their opponents. While the emerging pharmaceutical industry brought abortion into the world of commerce, a generation of self-appointed moral crusaders were not going to allow it to remain there, branding both abortion providers and women seeking their help as demonic monsters. The folk tradition of the monstrous birth, a tradition that had long encoded anxieties about gender and sexuality, emerged in a new form to castigate women who sought to end their pregnancies. Various "true crime" journals in urban America reported on dead women and deformed births as the result of abortion. The *New York Police Gazette* focused frequently on stories of botched abortions and the ruined lives and health of the women who attempted to receive them. One infamous issue of the *Gazette* featured "The Female Abortionist" as a bourgeois white woman with a monstrous demon devouring her womb. Carol Smith-Rosenberg notes that such imagery encapsulated bourgeois fears and anxieties perfectly, reviving ancient imagery of demonic female sexuality and the rebellion of "the Good Wife" who steps out of the bounds of a middle-class marriage.[54]

Summoning this powerful imagery, antiabortion forces managed to convince thirty state legislatures to prohibit abortion between 1866 and 1877. The American Medical Association joined in efforts to stamp out what they called the "unwarranted practice." The motives of those driving this debate were mixed. Horatio Storer, perhaps the first important antiabortion crusader in the country, called abortion "a crime against life." But he also seems to have believed, through a tortured logic, that the easy availability of abortion would mean the death of the Anglo-Saxon race. Storer, noting that native Protestant women had more frequent abortions than Catholics, worried that this would lead to "the low, the ignorant and the alien" overwhelming the WASP population. The portrayal of women and their desires as demonic had a long history in America, stretching back to the witch trials of New England. The abortion debate now made it a prominent part of the history of American moralism. The effects of unforgiving abortion laws would prove to be disastrous for women. In 1964 alone, 10,000 women were admitted to New York City public hospitals due to complications from "underground abortions."[55]

The American middle-class crusade against the devil at the end of the nineteenth century, with all its destructive effects, proved an even greater human disaster when it went abroad. At the beginning of the twentieth century, America took up its role as redeemer-nation. This is the other side of the diminution of the devil's role after the Civil War, discussed in the previous chapter. A mournful America wanted a more optimistic picture of the supernatural than the idea the devil presented. At the same time, a new, more optimistic public culture found in America's military and religious ascendancy a chance to defeat the devil.

Evil remained a threat to American innocence, but like Billy Sunday, Protestant, Victorian America seemed ready to challenge the Evil One to a bout. In the minds of many Americans, the struggle against evil embodied in the antebellum efforts to create a "Christian commonwealth" combined with a sense that the Civil War had created a "purified nation," one ready to assume a messianic role on the world stage. Josiah Strong, who worried about the demonic influences of immigrants, came to see the Anglo-Saxon race as the bearer of civilization and American imperial expansion as "the coming of Christ's kingdom in the world."[56]

Diabolical imagery frequently influenced the use of race in the fashioning of U.S. foreign policy. The concept of race as a defining characteristic, the philosopher's stone that explained the "success" of the white peoples of the world, held allure for a culture coming to grips with Darwinian theory (and using it for its own ends). Race became a primary site to construct conceptions of the demonic. White Christianity transferred all things apocalyptic and diabolical onto the male African American body in the outbreak of lynching at the turn of the century. The "purified nation" could now struggle against the devil in the world at large. In 1898, the United States launched a war of aggression in the Caribbean, seizing the island of Cuba from Spain and putting a pro-American regime in its place. This adventure would also lead to the seizure of the Philippines in 1899, which in turn opened up China to American commerce (one year later, American troops would help put down the Boxer Rebellion). These imperial adventures would be constructed as a struggle against the demonic on the world stage. Rudyard Kipling's infamous poem and phrase "White Man's Burden" first appeared in an 1899 issue of *McClure's Magazine*, bearing the subtitle "The United States and the Philippine islands." Voicing the views of many Americans, he described the people of the islands as

> *Your new-caught sullen peoples*
> *Half-devil and half-child*

The belief in the devilish nature of the Philippines found expression in America during the efforts to crush native resistance in the first decade of the century. Albert J. Beveridge, Indiana senator and strong believer in American exceptionalism, proclaimed that God had prepared the white race over thousands of years to civilize the "savage peoples" of the world. Major Edwin Glen of the U.S. Army put these beliefs into practice when he forced forty-seven imprisoned guerrilla fighters to "kneel and repent of their sins" before he had his troops bayonet them to death. Over a decade, the U.S. occupation of the Philippines and its war against savagery there resulted in the deaths of a quarter of a million of the native population.[57]

American mission organizations joined in this rhetoric, justifying American imperialism with references to Satan's influence over the pagan multitudes. One leader in the student mission's movement of the 1890s (inspired in part by the work of Dwight Moody) proclaimed that "the kingdoms of heathenism are the kingdoms of Satan." Africa in particular was designated by the America of lynching and Jim Crow as the center of Satan's kingdom on Earth and "the land of the blackness of darkness forever."[58]

America, by the twentieth century, had settled on a definition of evil that legitimized its own worst tendencies. Satan's work, it had learned from the antebellum religious awakening, primarily focused on corrupting the individual soul by preventing the spread of the gospel or surfeiting it on the pleasures of the flesh. Satan's supposed attempts to undermine American morals allowed evangelicals to paint any critique of Victorian-era gender and sexual norms as demonic. The new missionary zeal to conquer the world with American Christianity, indeed the identification of American influence with "Christ's kingdom," meant that any critique of American imperialism had its source in hell. By extension of this logic, expanding American influence meant the decline of the devil's power.

World War I became a coming-out ball for America's sense of its providential destiny. Billy Sunday's unremitting support for U.S. intervention in the European conflict and castigation of the kaiser as a pawn of the devil drew on a strong sense of America's messianic purpose. Ironically, mainline Protestants echoed a similar theme in more sophisticated language. Randolph H. McKim, from his influential Washington pulpit told his congregation, "This conflict is indeed a crusade. The greatest in history—the holiest . . . it is Christ, the King of Righteousness who calls us to grapple in deadly strife with this unholy and blasphemous power."[59]

America's emerging popular culture would abet this tendency through the popular and powerful medium of film. Metro Productions *To Hell with the Kaiser* (1918), one of the earliest cinematic portrayals of Satan in the United States, followed Billy Sunday's script about the meaning of the war almost exactly. The German emperor, we learn, achieved military success through an infernal pact with Satan. In an effort to emphasize the depravity of the German foe, the film shows the kaiser appearing to rape a young girl in a church. The hero of the story, an American pilot, captures the kaiser who, in despair, commits suicide and sends his soul to hell. But the enemies of American civilization are more satanic than Satan himself. The devil gives up his throne, confessing that the kaiser is far more sinister than he could ever hope to be. *To Hell with the Kaiser* may have come across to many Americans as tongue-in-cheek. For many, however, the short film surely had the force of a moral parable, a cinematic representation of what their favorite evangelist or even local pastor had told them about America's role in the world.[60]

The nineteenth century saw the transformation of America from an agricultural society hugging the Atlantic coast of North America to a market-driven world power able to flex its imperial muscles around the globe. A strong belief that its innocence could not be tarnished by its actions remained an ideological constant along with a concomitant belief in the demonic nature of threats from without and within. Dissenting voices from within American society, raising questions about how their society interpreted the nature of evil and made use of the imagery of Satan, were either ignored or quieted. Acting as Europe's "Savior" during World War I placed the United States on a trajectory to become the great power of the twentieth century, what some would call "the American Century."

The twentieth century, examined from the perspective of American religious belief and popular culture, raises the possibility that another term might be in order. While the shapers of American foreign policy helped forge an empire, popular religious movements and popular culture showed an increasing fascination with the Prince of Darkness. In the United States, the twentieth century became the satanic century.

NOTES

1. Robert Combs, "Waking from Nightmares: Stephen Vincent Benét's Faustian America," in *Stephen Vincent Benét: Essays on His Life and Work*, ed. David Garret Izzo and Lincoln Konkle (Jefferson, NC: McFarland and Company Publishers, 2003), 158.

2. Stephen Vincent Benét, *The Devil and Daniel Webster and Other Writings* (New York: Penguin Books, 1999).

3. On the shaping of the American middle class, see Mary P. Ryan, *Cradle of the Middle Class: The Family in Oneida County, New York, 1790–1865* (Cambridge: Cambridge University Press, 1981). See also Charles Sellers, *The Market Revolution: Jacksonian America, 1815–1846* (New York: Oxford University Press, 1991), especially 237–38.

4. Sean Wilentz describes this as the rise of "the politics of moral improvement" in *The Rise of American Democracy: Jefferson to Lincoln* (New York: W.W. Norton, 2005), 265-282.

5. W. J. Rorabaugh, *The Alcoholic Republic: An American Tradition* (New York: Oxford University Press, 1979).

6. Robert C. Fuller, *Naming the Antichrist: The History of an American Obsession* (New York: Oxford University Press, 1995), 88.

7. John Granville Wooley, *Temperance Progress in the Century* (Linscott Publishing Company, 1903), 83.

8. "A Temperance Plea" (Pittsburgh, PA: The Co-Operative Association, n.d.). Author's Collection.

9. James A. Morone, *Hellfire Nation: The Politics of Sin in American History* (New Haven, CT: Yale University Press, 2003), 191.

10. Quoted in Morone, *Hellfire Nation*, 191.

11. Morone, *Hellfire Nation*, 193.

12. Robert Olwell, *Masters, Slaves, and Subjects* (Ithaca, NY: Cornell University Press, 1998), 229.

13. Francis D. Cogliano, *No King, No Popery: Anti-Catholicism in Revolutionary New England* (Westport, CT: Greenwood Press, 1995), 15–17, 24, 25.

14. Richard Hofstadter, "The Paranoid Style of American Politics," *Harper's*, November 1964, 77–86.

15. James T. Fisher, *Communion of Immigrants: A History of Catholics in America* (New York: Oxford University Press, 2002), 46.

16. Morone, *Hellfire Nation*, 194.

17. Morone, *Hellfire Nation*, 195.

18. Fuller, *Naming the Antichrist*, 99.

19. Holly Bailey, "A Turbulent Pastor," *Newsweek*, May 8, 2008.

20. Carl Vogl, *Begone Satan! A True Account of a 23-Day Exorcism in Earling, Iowa, in 1928* (Rockford, IL: TAN Publishers), 1973.

21. Robert Anthony Orsi, *The Madonna of 115th Street: Faith and Community in Italian Harlem, 1880–1950* (New Haven, CT: Yale University Press, 1985), 122–23.

22. Jane Addams, "The Modern Devil-Baby," *American Journal of Sociology* (July 1914), 117–18.

23. One of the finest political histories of the sectional crisis is William W. Freehling's *The Road to Disunion: Secessionists at Bay, 1776–1854* (New York: Oxford University Press, 1990).

24. James O. Farmer, *The Metaphysical Confederacy* (Macon, GA: Mercer University Press, 1999), 208–9.

25. "Yankee Heresy," *Confederate Baptist*, November 11, 1863; *Keowee Courier*, January 26, 1861.

26. Fuller, *Naming the Antichrist*, 89–91.

27. Edward J. Blum, *Reforging the White Republic: Race, Religion, and American Nationalism, 1865–1898*. (Baton Rouge: Louisiana State University Press, 2005), 28.

28. Albert Raboteau, *Slave Religion: The Invisible Institution in the Antebellum South* (New York: Oxford University Press, 1978), 308.

29. Riggins R. Earl, Jr., *Dark Symbols, Obscure Signs: God, Self, and Community in the Slave Mind* (Maryknoll, NY: Orbis Books, 1993), 62.

30. Ralph Ellison quoted in Orlando Patterson, *Rituals of Blood: Consequences of Slavery in Two American Centuries* (New York: Civitas Books, 1998), 173. See also W. Scott Poole, "Confederate Apocalypse," in *Vale of Tears: New Essays in Religion and Reconstruction* (Macon, GA: Mercer University Press), 36–52.

31. See Poole, "Confederate Apocalypse," 44–45.

32. Michael Northcott, *An Angel Directs the Storm: Apocalyptic Religion and American Empire* (London: I.B. Tauris Books, 2004), 9.

33. Nathaniel Hawthorne, *The Scarlet Letter*, in *Novels* (The Library of America, 1983), 169, 184, 237.

34. Hawthorne, *The Scarlet Letter*, 342–43.

35. Otto Bird and Catherine Bird, *From Witchery to Sanctity: The Religious Vicissitudes of the Hawthornes* (South Bend, IN: St. Augustine's Press, 2005), 61–66.

36. Hawthorne, according to John R. May, is "the American master of the romance concerned with exposing the demon's lasting influence." Works such as "Ethan Brand" and "The Celestial Railroad" raise the possibility that evil feeds on the vitals of what appears to be innocence. See "American Literary Variations on the Demonic," in *Disguises of the Demonic: Contemporary Perspectives on the Power of Evil*, ed. Alan M. Olson (New York: Association Press, 1975), 36–37.

37. Thomas L. McHaney, "*The Confidence Man* and Satan's Disguises in Paradise Lost," *Nineteenth Century Fiction* 30, no. 2 (September 1975): 200–6.

38. Louisa May Alcott, *A Modern Mephistopheles and Taming a Tartar* (New York: Praeger Press, 1987), vii, xxxiii.

39. Andrew Delbanco, *The Death of Satan: How Americans Have Lost the Sense of Evil* (New York: Farrar, Straus and Giroux, 1995), 101.

40. A full discussion of Twain's fascination with the figure of Satan appears in Stanley Brodwin, "Mark Twain's Masks of Satan: The Final Phase," *American Literature* 45, no. 2 (May 1973): 206–27.

41. Coleman O. Parsons, "The Devil and Samuel Clemens," in *Mark Twain's Mysterious Stranger and the Critics*, ed. John S. Tuckey (Belmont, CA: Wadsworth Publishing Company, 1968), 155–68.

42. Mark Twain, "The Mysterious Stranger," in *Mark Twain's Best* (New York: Scholastic, Inc., 1962), 229.

43. Twain, "The Mysterious Stranger," 228–29.

44. Stanley Brodwin, "The Masks of Satan: The Final Phase," *American Literature* 45, no. 2 (May 1973): 216–17.

45. Stanley Brodwin, "The Masks of Satan: The Final Phase," *American Literature* 45, no. 2 (May 1973): 216–17.

46. Phyllis Trible, *Texts of Terror: Literary-Feminist Readings of Biblical Narratives* (Minneapolis, MN: Augsburg Fortress, 1984).

47. Elizabeth Cady Stanton, *The Woman's Bible*, Part 1, Reprint Edition (Salem, NH: Ayer Company Publishers, 1988), 26–27.

48. Morone, *Hellfire Nation*, 234–35, 237.

49. Morone, *Hellfire Nation*, 237.

50. Gaines Foster, "The End of Slavery and the Origins of the Bible Belt," in *Vale of Tears: New Essays in Religion and Reconstruction* (Macon, GA: Mercer University Press, 2005), 162–63. For a full discussion, see his outstanding work *Moral Reconstruction: Christian Lobbyists and the Federal Legislation of Morality, 1865–1920* (Chapel Hill: University of North Carolina Press, 2002).

51. Andrea Tone, *Devices and Desires: A History of Contraceptives in America* (New York: Hill and Wang, 2001), 14, 15.

52. Nicholas Francis Cooke, *Satan in Society* (Chicago: C.F. Vent, 1873), 90–92, 218, 256.

53. Morone, *Hellfire Nation*, 254.

54. Carol Smith-Rosenberg, *Disorderly Conduct: Visions of Gender in Victorian America* (New York: Alfred A. Knopf, 1985), 226–28.

55. Morone, *Hellfire Nation*, 253; Smith-Rosenberg, *Disorderly Conduct*, 223. The number included by Smith-Rosenberg does not, as she notes, include the thousands who, out of fear of prosecution or other barriers, never made it into the hospital system's files.

56. Robert Jewett and John Shelton Lawrence, *Captain America and the Crusade against Evil* (Grand Rapids, MI: William B. Eerdmans Publishing Company, 2003), 68–71.

57. John Bellamy Foster, Harry Magdoff, and Robert W. McChesney, "Kipling, the 'White Man's Burden,' and U.S. Imperialism," in *Pox Americana: Exposing the American Empire*, ed. John Bellamy Foster and Robert W. McChesney (New York: Monthly Review Press, 2004), 12–21.

58. Blum, *Reforging the White Republic*, 223; the best history of Protestant conceptions of a world mission is William R. Hutchinson, *Errand to the World: American Protestant Thought and Foreign Missions* (Chicago: University of Chicago Press, 1987).

59. Jewett and Lawrence, *Captain America*, 73.

60. Nikolas Schreck, *The Satanic Screen: An Illustrated Guide to the Devil in Cinema* (London: Creation Books, 2001), 29–30.

Puritan conceptions of sexuality and gender informed their notions of the Devil and of witchcraft. This image provides an artistic portrayal of the search for a "witches mark" on an unfortunate Salem woman. Women accounted for all but one of those executed for witchcraft in the Salem trials. Courtesy Peabody Essex Museum, 134, 536 "Examination of a Witch" (1853) by T. H. Matteson.

THE PROVIDENTIAL DETECTION

Thomas Jefferson's Enlightenment conceptions of religious truth made him the target of numerous scurrilous attacks. Some of his critics even accused him of being in league with the Devil. Here, Satan encourages him to destroy American liberty and spread "French infidelity." The Reverend Timothy Dwight went further, seeing Jefferson as the harbinger of the Antichrist. "A Providential Detection" (1797–1800). Courtesy American Antiquarian Society.

IN THE MONSTER'S CLUTCHES.
Body and Brain on Fire.

By the mid-nineteenth century, American Protestants perceived alcohol, literally, as "the demon in the bottle." Here, a temperance image connects drinking alcohol, not only with personal and domestic ruin, but with demonic forces of darkness. "Grappling with the Monster; or, The curse and the cure of strong drink," by T. S. Arthur. Courtesy of the University of Michigan Library.

Opponents of women's rights advocate Victoria Woodhull referred to her as "Mrs. Satan" for her advocacy of divorce laws that would allow women some control over their personal and financial destinies. Conservatives viewed this as advocacy for "free love." Here, Thomas Nast portrays Woodhull as the Devil tempting a wife (portrayed by a long-suffering Christ figure) away from a loveless marriage. Thomas Nast, "Get Thee Behind Me (Mrs.) Satan," *Harper's Weekly*, 1872.

Satan played a role in the politics of abortion as early as the nineteenth century. This image from a Victorian scandal sheet borrowed on the long tradition of the monstrous birth and misogynous notions of women's alliances with the Devil. "The Female Abortionist," *National Police Gazette*, March 13, 1847. Courtesy of Rare Book Division, The New York Public Library, Astor, Lenox and Tilden Foundations.

II

THE SATANIC CENTURY

4

Casting Out Devils: American Theology and Popular Religion Meets the Devil

Memphis Pentecostal minister L. P. Adams believed the devil interfered with every aspect of human life. Adams reminded his congregation that the New Testament describes the devil as "the prince and power of the air." Building on this image, Adams suggested that Satan occupied a throne that literally floated in the earth's atmosphere. The devil used this dais to issue commands to legions of demons on Earth. Adams was not alone in this belief. Other early Pentecostals described demons as "swarming like asteroids" around the human soul and living off of human beings "like ticks on cattle" in the very "juices of their blood." Satan could even come to church and disrupt camp meetings. Only the power of the Holy Spirit could cast him out and, even then, it was a life or death struggle, often over matters that an unbeliever might find trivial. In 1908, for example, a Pentecostal camp meeting included an "exorcism" of a family pet whose possession by evil spirits had led to incessant barking, as well a child who was controlled by a "whining demon."[1]

The Pentecostal belief in the actions of the devil in everyday life provides one example of how the twentieth century became the satanic century in both American religion and popular culture. American religious leaders and major American religious movements, more than at any other time since the seventeenth century, became obsessed with the work of the devil on Earth. Two powerful American religious movements born in the early twentieth century, Pentecostalism and fundamentalism, gave the devil a special role in both their worldview and understanding of personal spiritual experience. Roman Catholicism also remained convinced that Satan's influence represented a threat to the lives and souls of its adherents.

Ironically, the powerful twentieth-century devil of popular belief took his throne at a time when some of the most sophisticated thought about the meaning of evil and the significance of the image of the devil was being produced by the best theological minds of America's oldest religious traditions. The Satan of the twentieth century's American theologians owed little to the devil who had come down in great wrath among the Puritans or the soul-, home-, and nation-wrecking devil of the nineteenth-century reformers. Instead he became a symbol, but a powerful symbol, of the insidious nature of evil and the myth of American innocence. Few outside of America's best seminaries had the opportunity to hear these new reflections on the meaning of evil. For most religious Americans, the devil remained a literal being that embodied all they hated and feared in a supernatural force, rather than a deep-rooted mechanism within the human person and in human culture.

The brief, but very real, decline of fascination with the devil in American Victorian culture quickly passed. At least part of Satan's newfound strength, the growth of simplistic beliefs in his power, can be explained by a major realignment in Protestant Christianity. This realignment came about at a time of manifest change in American society. Between 1900 and 1930, American society was embroiled in a series of cultural conflicts that profoundly altered the cultural and religious landscape. Economic change in the late nineteenth century created a new urban working class and a rural underclass. Industrialization fueled these changes, transforming American cities. The rise of Jim Crow in the aftermath of slavery placed African Americans in the South in the double bind of social and economic marginalization. Meanwhile, the influence of new patterns of thought among the country's cultural elites helped to shape what Lynn Dumenil calls "the modern temper." Intellectuals, artists, and writers, alienated from traditionalist concepts of religion and community, helped to shape a new ethos. In turn, a conservative backlash erupted with the 1919 Red Scare and continued through the 1920s with the rise of fundamentalism and the reemergence of the Ku Klux Klan.[2]

These conflicts eventually led to the decline of the Protestant establishment, the death of the cultural hegemony of mainline Protestantism, and the cultural consensus it represented. Seemingly, this powerful cultural ethos had remained strong in the late nineteenth century. Dwight L. Moody had represented the embodiment of a Protestant consensus. Although deeply conservative in his own theological beliefs, he preached a generalized message of Christian conversion that had little sectarian edge. He and other theological conservatives, of many denominational labels, worked with liberal Christian leaders on a variety of social causes, most especially prohibition. The death of Moody and the popularity of Billy Sunday signaled the beginning of a new religious era in which the devil would play a vital role and the mainline churches—the Episcopal Church, the Methodist Church, the Presbyterian Church, and the large northern Baptist denominations—would see their numbers shrink precipitously. Meanwhile, the Southern Baptist Convention, a deeply and self-consciously conservative denomination became the largest Protestant denomination in the United States.

The background to this religious crisis lay in the Victorian era. In the late nineteenth century, a significant shift had occurred within the leadership of America's major Protestant denominations. Theological liberalism had become the regnant tradition in most of America's mainline seminaries and molded some of America's most popular mainline pastors. Historian of religion William R. Hutchinson estimates that by 1920 liberal leaders controlled about half of America's seminaries and Protestant pulpits. New currents in theological and biblical studies accounted for much of this realignment. Since the early nineteenth century, major European thinkers, especially in German universities such as the University of Berlin, had reexamined the study of the Bible, employing the emerging discipline of literary criticism and the assumptions of naturalism that viewed historical institutions, movements, and even sacred texts as products of social and cultural forces. The Bible became not simply (and perhaps not primarily) a sacred document but rather a historical document open to criticism. These efforts produced a revolution in the study of the scriptures, giving the Christian church a much deeper understanding of issues ranging from authorship of the biblical books to the historical context of the Near East in which its authors wrote. Transmitted into the American context by Union Theological Seminary professor Charles E. Briggs, this new way of reading the Bible proved both influential and highly controversial among religious conservatives.[3]

But something even more revolutionary than higher criticism had entered American Protestant thought. Given their naturalistic assumptions, some "higher critics" disregarded the miraculous aspects of both the Hebrew and Christian scriptures, viewing them as historical artifacts that tell us more about the belief systems of ancient peoples than the work of God in the world. Many European biblical scholars went one step further and challenged the particularity of Christianity, taking what was called "the history of religions" approach to the study of the Bible and the Christian faith. These scholars suggested that the entire belief structure should be studied as a cultural construction, no different from any other religious tradition. For some of the more radical of these historians of religion, Christian doctrine became little more than a set of cultural artifacts with little or no meaning in the modern world.[4]

Another major reorientation of Protestant thought in the early twentieth century concerned the applicability of the Christian message to modern American society. The liberal theological impulse that informed mainline Protestantism tended to emphasize morality, the teachings of Jesus,
over against a simple adherence to "correct" doctrine. Urban Protestant
leaders often followed their congregations in reacting against the older
Protestant notion that restricted ethical behavior to individual choice, an
attitude that had frequently defined morality as the avoidance of specific
behaviors. The transformation of America's social and economic life
discussed in the previous chapter helped to push many American theologians toward what would be known as "the social gospel."

The work of two thinkers, Washington Gladden and Walter Rauschenbusch, defined the social gospel. Gladden, the more moderate of the pair,
was a Congregationalist minister in Ohio moved to concern himself with
the politics of America's white working class after watching the social disorder brought about by the Hocking Valley coal strikes of the mid-1880s.
His views have been described as a "mild progressivism" that made the
"Golden Rule" into a central social principle. Baptist theologian Walter
Rauschenbusch took a more radical approach. His 1907 *Christianity and
Social Crisis* challenged some of the central assumptions of American
capitalism and counterposed to it the ethics of the Sermon on the Mount.
Rauschenbusch sometimes referred to himself as "Christian socialist,"
having been heavily influenced by nineteenth-century Christian socialism from Europe. Like those European thinkers, the New Testament
concept of the "Kingdom of God" provided the organizing principle of
his thought. Rather than viewing "the Kingdom" as an abstract, largely
transcendent concept, he situated the Kingdom of God in the midst of
human history and society.[5]

These new ways of imagining the Christian message had little room
for the devil. The combined influences of the social gospel and the new
way of reading and understanding scriptures undercut, and in some cases
entirely negated, mainline Protestantism's interest in the supernatural.
Liberal theology in the first half of the twentieth century raised critical
questions about biblical miracles, the nature of creation, and whether a
"literal" interpretation of doctrines such as the Trinity or the divinity of
Christ had any contemporary meaning. In this new intellectual milieu,
many Protestant preachers and professors refined, or defined out of existence, the traditional concept of Satan, tossing him onto the scrap heap
of premodern ideas. The concept of a "personal devil" seemed to belong
to the childhood of human history, especially for those whose belief in
progress led them to see themselves in the adulthood of humanity.

These attitudes found expression in the pages of *The Christian Century*,
the flagship publication of mainline, liberal, urban Protestantism. The

Century had been founded in Chicago in 1884 as the *Christian Oracle* but was renamed in 1900 to suggest the idea that, in the twentieth century, Protestant Christianity would exert an enormous influence over society and culture through a partnership with the latest advances in science and technology. In 1908, Charles Clayton Morrison, a devotee of the social gospel who hoped to see mainline Christianity advocate issues ranging from pacifism to women's suffrage, purchased the magazine.[6]

In the following decades, the *Christian Century* became a listening post for liberal Protestants in America. The publication maintained a kind of theological advice column for its readers in the 1930s entitled "The Question Box." In 1934, the *Century* answered a reader's question about whether there is "any authority for a belief in a personal devil" by writing that the frequent scriptural references to such a being are evidence that ancient Palestine found in the devil "an easy explanation of the evils, physical, mental and religious, which afflicted the world." Jesus may have accepted such a belief, but only because it was the prevailing "superstition" of the age. The writer goes on to explain that the devil provides "an easy and superficial explanation" for the problem of evil. Increasingly, the writer assured the liberal readership of the *Century*, biblical scholars are learning to "distinguish between the essentials and incidentals of the scripture and it is among the latter it would seem the idea of a personal devil belongs."[7]

This dismissal of the devil from the Christian tradition caused some consternation in the mainline pews. Around the time the *Christian Century* fielded the above question about the existence of a personal devil, a minister wrote in for instructions on how to deal with a problematic layman who insisted "that to deny the existence of a personal devil is to impute the origin of evil to God." "The Question Box" reminded the minister that conceptions of angelic and demonic hierarchies had encrusted biblical theology, but, it asserted authoritatively, "these ideas have passed away with the growth of an intelligent psychological interpretation of the facts." The column advised the pastor to explain to the troubled layperson that "the devil is not the source of evil. "Evil comes from the mind of man, seduced by the lesser good."[8]

The profound optimism displayed by the *Century*, the idea that the human mind had somehow exorcised belief in the devil and his works, had no basis in the social and religious reality of the times. Moreover, the tendency on the part of Protestant liberals to see in the devil a metaphor of human psychological maladjustments showed, in some cases, a refusal to confront the realities of structural evil in human society, the potential for violence inherent in the state or embodied in the corporation. Meanwhile, proponents of the social gospel tended to view evil as purely structural, such that a proper realignment of the gears and wheels of human society could bring about a millennial order. Christian liberalism failed to confront the fact that the devil was alive and well in American religious life in the 1930s and having a far greater impact on the American religious experience than anything occurring in the seminary classroom or within range of respectable downtown pulpits.[9]

In fact, while mainline Protestant theology questioned the reality of the devil's existence, the Prince of Darkness orchestrated a major comeback in twentieth-century popular religion. The explosion of Pentecostalism in the early part of the century, with its emphasis on "Signs and Wonders" and apocalyptic thought, gave the devil a more important place in their mythology than any other Christian movement in America had ever done. Meanwhile, the birth of Protestant Fundamentalism in the 1920s, a loosely organized movement formed largely around a rejection of certain selected aspects of modernity, put a heavy emphasis on the devil and his work.

The Azusa Street revivals of 1906 inaugurated the modern Pentecostal movement. Pentecostalism emerged out of a late nineteenth-century interdenominational movement known as "Holiness." Holiness adherents believed in a "second experience" after the experience of conversion that brought about greater personal moral purity, or "sanctification." Modern Pentecostalism further emphasized personal purity, especially in matters related to sexuality, but also the idea that the "second experience" would include "signs and wonders," especially glossolalia (speaking in other tongues), healing, and deliverance from demonic spirits. The 1906 revivals in Los Angeles became a training ground for evangelists who spread the message throughout the country. Although originally a para-church movement, Pentecostals created new denominations that flourished throughout the twentieth century. The Assemblies of God numbered over 1.2 million members by 1989. The Church of God would include about half a million members by the same time.[10]

Pentecostalism teaches that "life in the Spirit" (sometimes called "the Spirit-filled life") represents a continuous and powerful religious experience, a life lived in almost constant contact with the world of the supernatural. While the Pentecostal message emphasizes spiritual joy, it also proclaims the reality of the devil and demons. In fact, the Pentecostal tradition in America has, over the last century, created an elaborate demonology that rivals anything produced in the demonological texts of early modern Europe. It is a demonology with links to both personal behavior and the social order. Historian Damien Thompson describes how Pentecostalism fashioned a cosmology "infested by demons of abortions and masturbation and witchcraft, which supposedly have the ability to enter fetuses or cling to the back of a person's head."[11]

Pentecostal writers created catalogs of demonic spirits, legions of demons under Satan's command that seemed to involve themselves in almost every aspect of human life and culture. Charles Parham, one of the earliest leaders of the Pentecostal movement, claimed that a greater diversity existed in the world of demons than in human beings and that each type sought to possess individuals who shared their characteristics. This belief led to the creation of elaborate taxonomies of diabolical beings. Historian of religion Grant Wacker notes that this meant "that there were demons of witchcraft, of fortune-telling, of insanity, of gluttony, of idleness and of wonder-working." For many Pentecostal believers, no human foible or misfortune appeared without its attendant evil spirit.[12]

The role of Satan and his army of demons in Pentecostal belief remained closely connected to the powerfully eschatological orientation of the movement. In the American experience, Pentecostalism began with the faith of what David Martin calls "the culturally despised," who found in the "baptism of the Spirit" a new significance for their lives. Pentecostals viewed all of the "gifts of the Spirit," from healing to glossolalia to deliverance from demons, as eschatological gifts, a special outpouring of the Holy Spirit that signaled the end of time. Along with Fundamentalists, Pentecostals generally adopted a premillennial understanding of history. They believed in the imminent coming of Christ but also in the imminent coming of the Antichrist. In the understanding of premillennial thinkers, a time of darkness would come when the earth itself would convulse and Satan would be given free reign. During this period of time, the Antichrist would rule the earth and persecute the faithful. At the end of this period (often referred to as the Tribulation) Christ would come to set up a "millennial Kingdom" on earth in which believers would reign along side him. This kingdom would last 1,000 years, followed by a final battle and the last judgment, when Satan would finally be consigned forever to the Lake of Fire. A "new heaven and a new earth" would be born. James Barr, a historian of American Fundamentalism, has called this schema "a remarkable achievement of mythopoeic fantasy." Nevertheless, since the early twentieth century, premillennial belief has exerted a powerful hold on American Pentecostals, Fundamentalists, and evangelicals.[13]

The Antichrist played a central role in this understanding of history. Regarded as either the child of Satan or even the incarnation of Satan himself, the Antichrist has been seen as a demonic human being able to seduce the world into giving him absolute political and social power. A number of obscure passages in the New Testament suggest the concept of the Antichrist and it has been a frequent trope in Christian history, but the idea has played an especially powerful role in twentieth-century Protestant Christianity. Robert C. Fuller in *Naming the Antichrist* describes this as an American obsession, placing "doubts and uncertainties on a demonic Other." For both Pentecostals and Fundamentalists, the literal meaning of the Antichrist has been that Satan will invade the geopolitical history of their world and Christians must be on guard against Satan's manifestations in society, culture, and politics.[14]

Pentecostalism perceived itself to be at war with the emerging forces of the Antichrist in the world. Pentecostal believers in the early twentieth century believed that demonic activity would increase, heralding the appearance of the Antichrist even as the gifts of the Spirit prepared the way for the Second Coming of Christ. Satan and his hierarchy of demons had, according to early Pentecostals, unleashed their full assault against true believers and the world as a kind of warm-up session for the End of Days. A strong belief in the power of the miraculous informed their spiritual experience, and Pentecostal preachers asserted that Satan was almost as active as God in the supernatural milieu. Individual Pentecostal preachers, who often exercised "healing gifts" in the context of both church services and tent revivals, sometimes saw the devil at the root of physical illness. Sickness, according to one Pentecostal leader, was the result of a "demonic assault." Healing came to the body through "a process of driving out evil spirits through the greater power of the Holy Spirit." The same was true of everything from psychological difficulty to problems of addiction (that sometimes could be remedied by driving out "an alcohol demon"). Spiritual warfare became a daily, almost quotidian, affair.[15]

Fundamentalists had demons of their own to cast out, demons they believed resided within America's popular culture and in its perceived enemies. The Fundamentalist revolt against the liberalization of mainline Protestantism put a renewed emphasis on the devil's work within American culture. Fundamentalism became, along with the Pentecostal movement, a true American grassroots movement. Although numerous denominational leaders represented the movement at the national level, Fundamentalism flourished in a network of regional leaders, local churches, national conferences, traveling evangelists, and Bible colleges. Fundamentalism received its name from a series of books published between 1909 and 1915, essay collections by conservative Protestants writing about theological issues. These essays insisted on a literal reading of the Bible and, in fact, a belief in the "inerrancy" of scripture. This concept became a rallying cry for Fundamentalist Christians throughout the twentieth century, who insisted that the Bible provided an accurate historic and scientific record of events as well as accurate teaching about theology and morals. Fundamentalism, previously strong in the rural south and Midwest, also emerged in the urban north as conservative leaders challenged northern Presbyterian and Baptist denominations for the control of seminaries, mission organizations, and publishing houses.[16]

Fundamentalists, over against their liberal opponents, insisted in the literal reality of the devil. Moreover, they saw him active within American culture. Satan stood behind the heresy of the liberal mainline churches, the theory of evolution, and new attitudes toward sexuality. In this belief, Fundamentalism continued to follow the path blazed by the preaching of Billy Sunday. Satan was an active supernatural force, a real entity who struggled against God. This very same Satan could be embodied in their cultural enemies. The cultural Other functioned as his agent on Earth.

American Jews and their influence in American cultural life became one of Fundamentalists' preferred targets. Gerald B. Winrod, a Baptist evangelist who published the highly influential *Defender* magazine, became convinced that the Antichrist himself would be Jewish and that the New Deal was part of a worldwide Jewish conspiracy to prepare for Satan's last struggle against God at the end of time. Winrod, whose magazine went to hundreds of thousands of Fundamentalist households, visited Nazi Germany in the mid-1930s and returned home praising Hitler's policies toward the Jews. Another Fundamentalist leader, Gerald L. K. Smith, believed that, in his words, FDR and "his Jew advisors" were working to bring about the rule of Satan.[17]

Fundamentalist preachers believed the devil to be far more ubiquitous and insidious than the reforming Protestants of the nineteenth century had ever imagined. Isaac M. Haldeman, the pastor of New York City's highly conservative First Baptist Church, called into question the whole concept of "benevolent reform" so important to American Christians in the previous century. Haldeman believed that such efforts rested on the false premise that human beings could actually bring reform to sinful society. What America really needed, rather than social reform, was a powerful religious revival. Haldeman, an influential if singular voice, went so far as to claim that "the Devil would be glad to see prohibition successful. Nothing would please him more than to be able to shut up every saloon and house of shame." The devil willingly allowed social and moral reform, as long as the human soul could be damned.[18]

Not all of the early Fundamentalists saw moral reform as inherently satanic (though all gave pride of place to "soul saving" in their understanding of the Christian church's mission). Fundamentalism came to be defined in part as being in embittered conflict with all aspects of modernity. This state of conflict created significant ironies in the Fundamentalist understanding of American society. Early twentieth-century American Fundamentalists could both damn American culture and praise the American nation. John Roach Stratton, an influential Fundamentalist minister at New York City's Calvary Baptist Church, insisted that the struggle with Satan was, in part, a struggle against vice and against political radicalism. In his *Fighting the Devil in Modern Babylon* (1929), Stratton portrayed the Church in America as locked in a death struggle with a combination of theological heresy and moral ruin. The United States was, ultimately, "Christian America," a chosen nation that Satan sought to ruin through a vast conspiracy of evil. George Marsden has noted that Stratton's ideas embody the Fundamentalist confusion over whether the United States is "The New Israel" or "The Great Whore, Babylon," a confusion that remains in Fundamentalist rhetoric about the United States into the present day. Despite this confusing rhetoric, few Fundamentalists fully renounced the notion of America's "original innocence," preferring to suggest that the social and cultural changes of the early twentieth century represented a threat to the Christian soul of a Christian America.[19]

Fundamentalists wove the disparate strands of their beliefs into a single narrative about their combat with the devil. Satan represented the real enemy, and thus they could turn their sights on a variety of cultural opponents who fought at his side. Texas Baptist J. Frank Norris, for example, combined the desire to save the world from moral ruin (always part of the American Protestant experience) with the willingness to damn it all as belonging to the devil. One of Norris's most popular sermons was his 1926 "The 10 Worst Devils in Ft. Worth, Names Given." In it, as promised, he named ten local leaders he believed had sought to further Satan's agenda in the Fort Worth area. Norris included in his list the Roman Catholic mayor, H. C. Meachem, whom Norris accused of being inspired by Satan to divert municipal funds to Catholic institutions. This incident set off a chain of events that brought much disapprobation to Fundamentalism. A friend of Mayor Meachem's, D. E. Chipps, threatened Norris by phone and then came to his church. A scuffle ensued that ended with Norris pulling a gun and shooting Chipps. A jury ruled that Norris had acted in self-defense and the Texas pastor was free to continue his war on Satan.[20]

While it often contemplated on the evils of modern society, Fundamentalism believed that the devil's work in the larger American culture had as its ultimate goal the destruction of the individual human soul. The harvesting of souls remained a powerful aspect of the devil's fearsomeness among the evangelized well into the twentieth century, and it frequently motivated the Fundamentalist grass roots to new commitment. Minor, regional evangelists such as J. Harold Smith of Tennessee built a career around the notion that even those who believed themselves "saved" had been deceived by the devil and would soon face an eternity in hell. Smith's "Radio Bible Hour," established in 1935, carried this message until the evangelist's death in 2001.

"God's Three Deadlines," a sermon given by Smith literally thousands of times both to radio and live audiences, became a true classic in the genre of theological fearmongering. Smith wove a colorful and emotionally harrowing tale of murder, automobile accidents, and assorted human tragedy to assure his hearers that, unless they made sure they had been "saved," they would become part of the throng "screaming, dying, doomed and damned" in hell. Most terrifying of all, a "saved" Christian could, Smith claimed, commit so much sin that God would turn them over to the devil. According to Smith, "God says to Satan, 'take him, kill him.'" Smith warned his hearers that they could face the terror of "Satan's slaughterhouse" unless they repented, tithed to their congregations, and studied the Bible regularly. "I don't want the Devil to kill me. Do you?" he would ask.[21]

New varieties of Protestantism were not alone in giving Satan a special role to play in the Christian experience. The Roman Catholic tradition in America had, in both theology and popular belief, long put a heavy emphasis on the power of the devil. By the early twentieth century, these ideas could begin to reach a larger American audience. American Catholics, in the two decades between the world wars, began to become more a part of the American mainstream than ever before, while also strongly asserting their separate identity through their own institutions and traditions. Frequently coming under attack by Fundamentalists, the Church remained a very conservative institution fighting its own rearguard action against modernity. George Marsden notes that during this period the Catholic Church managed to be both "victims of conservatism and reaction" and to disseminate "its own brand of political fundamentalism." Like Protestant Fundamentalists, the culturally conservative hierarchy of the Church in America sought to shield the faithful from the dangers of modernity. Also, much as in Protestant Fundamentalism, the devil played a significant role in their worldview.[22]

In fact, while Pentecostal preachers cast out hundreds of devils in revivals across the country, a Roman Catholic monk performed the most celebrated exorcism of the first half of the twentieth century in 1928. *Begone Satan! A True Account of a 23-Day Exorcism in Earling, Iowa in 1928* purports to tell the story of the exorcism of a young girl that took place over a twenty-three-day struggle. Sixty-year-old Capuchin Father Theophilus Riesinger, who had preached "missions" throughout the country and been involved in a number of supposedly successful exorcisms, received permission from the bishop to perform the exorcism on an unnamed woman who, since the age of fourteen, had struggled with the combination of spiritual despair, blasphemous thoughts, sexual confusion, and auditory phenomena. Once a devout young girl, since the age of fourteen Anna had heard "sinister inner voices" that called her to "unmentionable acts." She could not find comfort in the sacraments, and medical treatment had failed even though, according to Fr. Vogel's account, she had been taken to "the best specialists in the profession."[23]

The exorcism itself, taking place in an Iowa convent, entered powerfully into the American consciousness and became a template for later descriptions of the effects of demonic possession. In fact, many of the descriptions of the possessed are recognizable in the infamous film *The Exorcist*. As with the 1949 exorcism that directly inspired *The Exorcist*, mysterious circumstances swirled around the case of a woman who first met the devil as a young teenager. At one point, the many devils roiling about in the victim responded to Father Riesinger's invocation of the Trinity by levitating the body. In this "hair-raising scene," the victim "landed high above the door of the room and clung to the wall with tenacious grip." Like *Exorcist* director William Friedkin's Regan, the woman's "whole body became horribly disfigured . . . the woman's face became so distorted that no one could recognize her features."[24]

Begone Satan! offers the reader a tour of how popular Catholic devotionalism lived in close harmony with concepts of the demonic. A number of references to the devotional piety that swept nineteenth-century Europe and came to America from Ireland and Italy played a central role in the account. Vogl describes the devil's reactions to a priest entering the room with a relic of St. Therese, the Little Flower, in his pocket. Therese, destined to become one of the most popular saints of the twentieth century, had only recently been canonized in 1925. The story of the young French nun, one that combined the personal sufferings of a tubercular young woman with a moving and complex spiritual message, had a compelling effect on Catholics throughout the century. Not only did her relics cause the devils of Earling, Iowa, special pain, but also the Little Flower herself made visionary appearances to the possessed, assuring her that the ordeal had almost passed. Vogl also notes the power of the prayer of St. Michael, the immigrant's invocation against evil given by the beloved turn-of-the-century pope, Leo XIII.[25]

Perhaps the most striking aspect of the account concerns the source of the woman's possession and the identity of the devils within her. According to Vogl, one of the demonic spirits claimed to be Jacob, the name of her long-dead father, who had a reputation for "a passionately unchaste and debased life." This evil spirit claimed that in its earthly life it had attempted to "force his own daughter to commit incest with him" and cursed her when he failed. Another spirit, Mina, is described by Vogl as Jacob's earthly concubine, a child murderer. As with the witch trials of the past, uncontrolled and unnatural sexuality had provided the devil a gateway into the young girl's soul, a gateway opened against her will. Like the "satanic panics" that later emerged in 1980s America, the devil was seen as at work in incestuous sexual abuse, parents offering their children to Satan and forcing them to take part in unnatural acts.[26]

The devils infesting young Anna are encoded anxieties about womanhood, the nature of the family, adolescent sexuality, and the dangers of religious apostasy. The Catholic tradition says nothing about the possibility of being possessed by the demonic ghosts of the evil dead (although it is not specifically denied either). Instead, like most of the assertions in Vogl's account, these are ideas that emerged out of the beliefs of the Catholic folk tradition. And yet the account of Anna's struggles received the official imprimatur of Bishop John Busch of Minnesota in 1935. The pamphlet has been republished in numerous editions since 1928, most recently by Tan Books, a traditionalist Catholic publishing house.

The popularity of this account forced leaders in mainline Protestantism to take notice after its first publication in 1935. In fact, The *Christian Century* wrote a response to *Begone Satan!* that tells us much about the attitude of Protestant liberalism in the middle of the twentieth century. *The Century* asserted in a March 1938 column that "modern intelligence has learned to explain many puzzling facts that were once referred to demons and spirits." Although the *Century* carefully noted that "in times past Protestants had been as credulous as Catholics in regard to demons and witches," it also noted, rightly, that Catholicism had tended to claim "a monopoly on the means of defense against occult power." In the 1930s, on the eve of World War II, *The Christian Century* wrote with all the rosy optimism of the nineteenth century that "rational science and sane religion support each other in bidding us believe that, beneath the distracting and unpredictable whimsies of weather and human behavior, there are some underlying stabilities."[27]

The *Century's* happy assertions aside, the Western world encountered evil in a new way during the 1930s, evil that called into question any "underlying stabilities." By 1935, the liberal apotheosis in mainline Protestantism, buffeted by Fundamentalist assaults, anxiety in the pews, and rapid intellectual and cultural change, had begun a long and slow period of decline that, by the 1960s, would end in a collapse. Protestantism in America, after World War II, would be a highly variegated phenomenon with hundreds of new religious movements exploding out of both the evangelical and Pentecostal traditions. Scholars have noted that this period would see the decline and arguably the death of the "Protestant establishment" in America. The downtown, mainline churches hemorrhaged members in the decades following World War II, while more conservative denominations and Pentecostal sects exploded. Studies of the mainline churches between the 1960s and the 1980s found a 14.5 percent decline in the membership of the United Methodist Church, a 15.4 percent decline in the Presbyterian, U.S.A. denomination, and a 14 percent decline in the Episcopal Church. In 1972, the United Methodist Church alone posted a decline of over a half million members in the previous four years.[28]

During the years that mainline Protestantism crested and then began a rapid decline, some Christian thinkers within that tradition made an effort to better explore their tradition's understanding of Satan and evil.

A new mainline Protestant theological tradition emerged beginning in the years after World War I and coming to full maturity by the end of World War II. Known as neo-orthodoxy, this movement drew heavily on European currents of thought, especially the German theologians Karl Barth and Emil Brunner. Neo-orthodoxy accepted many of the premises regarding supernatural manifestations that had shaped Protestant liberalism. But this new movement utterly rejected liberalism's roseate view of human nature and belief in evolutionary progress. The catastrophes of the twentieth century and a new intellectual confrontation with what German theologian Karl Barth called "the world of the Bible" forced them to reconsider some of Christianity's older themes.[29]

Reinhold Niebuhr became the primary American representative of this movement. The Yale-educated Niebuhr, the son of immigrant parents, became a pastor in the booming industrial center of Detroit in 1915. Detroit in 1915 witnessed the beginnings of the automobile industry, and Niebuhr became deeply concerned at the treatment at the new Ford plants of the working-class members of his congregation. Equally disturbing was the state of race relations in a city whose population had grown from 10,000 to 80,000 in the period between the time of Niebuhr's arrival and 1925, a growth largely caused by the in-migration of African Americans fleeing the South. But in the city they had come to for refuge, a brutally racist police force patrolled African American neighborhoods. Public services for these same neighborhoods were inadequate or nonexistent.

Influenced by these dark realities, Niebuhr came to believe that Christianity needed a much tougher edge than what was offered by liberalism and the social gospel. The problem of evil, its origin and power, would deeply concern him. In 1928, when he left his pastorate to teach at Union Theological Seminary in New York, his thought had changed definitively and he had rejected much of his liberal Protestant worldview. The groundwork had been laid for Niebuhr to become one of America's greatest theologians and social critics.[30]

Niebuhr examined the problem of evil with a sophistication and prophetic power seldom seen in American religious thought. Niebuhr hauled in both Christian theology and American society for a thorough analysis. In a challenge to the optimistic rationalism of liberalism, Niebuhr demanded a reexamination of, and a reemphasis on, the notion of "original sin," pointing out the evidence of radical evil in human experience. Against Fundamentalism and the rising evangelical movement, Niebuhr warned against the tendency of these groups to define the Christian experience as a private, individualistic experience within the human soul.[31]

Niebuhr brought his own experience as a pastor to his position teaching theology at Union seminary. Not only had the social crisis confronting America's city's moved him, but he had also been appalled by how quickly Christian leaders, himself included, had allowed their notions of progress and civilization to be hijacked by the war effort during World War I. The death of Wilsonian hopes for the postwar world further disillusion him. The Christian concept of evil had to be tougher and more durable than the optimistic liberalism of much of mainline Protestantism. "Modern liberalism," he warned, "is steeped in a religious optimism that is true to the facts of neither the world of nature nor the world of history."[32]

The social gospel, according to Niebuhr (and a larger group of American theologians sometimes referred to as "Christian realists"), had been too quick to see the teachings of Jesus as a tonic for modern social problems. Proponents of the social gospel had forgotten how extraordinarily complex is the relationship of evil to the human soul. Rather than seeing evil as simply the result of unjust social structures, Niebuhr also saw it bound up in the depths of the human personality, the result of humanity's attempts to escape its anxiety about the meaning of existence by asserting power over the world or escaping into a self-induced coma of natural desires. Thus, while championing a radical social activism, Niebuhr also warned about the dangers inherent in any social crusade, any effort to reform. This insight called into question the entire "benevolent empire" of nineteenth-century American Protestantism. It also opened a new line of inquiry into the nature of the devil.[33]

Niebuhr's interpretation of the meaning of Satan showed both his theological heritage and his willingness to critique and rethink that heritage. This does not mean he embraced the devil of Fundamentalism as an antidote to liberal optimism. He inherited from the tradition of American Christian liberalism the tendency to reject the idea of the devil as a literal entity, a personality actively working from his headquarters in hell to corrupt souls. Instead, he saw in the idea of Satan the basic existential quandary of the human race. Human beings are natural creatures, bound by the circumstances of their history and their birth. But they also have a profound spiritual freedom that calls them out of their environment and that invites them to see their limitations as temporary. The tension produced by this conundrum leads to profound existential anxiety. Human beings misinterpret their situation, and this misinterpretation, this tendency to use evil means to escape the tension, is the devil. Niebuhr reinterpreted the myth of the Garden of Eden along these lines, seeing it as a parable of the human misuse of freedom. The combination of stubborn pride and misunderstanding of the proper uses of our spiritual nature is the serpent in the garden. The devil is very real and many times worse than a frightening supernatural apparition. He does not appear with cloven hooves and a pitchfork, indeed he is not a personal consciousness at all. The devil is the misuse of our freedom, the search for transcendence that becomes transmuted into political ideologies and social experiments that leave thousands, even millions, of corpses in its wake. Or, equally, the attempt to escape our angst and retreat into ennui, ignoring our responsibilities to our neighbor.[34]

Niebuhr's understanding of the meaning of Satan and the nature of evil had profound implications for the persistent belief in American exceptionalism, the notion that the actions of the United States, no matter how arbitrary or imperialistic, could be justified by the prima facie reality of American innocence. Niebuhr noted in *The Irony of American History* that America has always had a strong sense of its own innocence but these have been "early illusions" that lived on from the first founding. In fact, Americans held to this belief in their own innocence, this unwillingness to confront the nature of evil, even after the young nation's "surge of infant strength" on the frontier had completed its "imperial expansion over the continent." It is worth noting that some of the conclusions Niebuhr draws from his analysis would later be criticized by a new wave of radical theologians in the post-1960s era who noted that his views could easily be used to justify a theological realpolitik. These theologians would point out that, despite its belief in its own innocence, the United States had always been willing to dirty its hands, a point Niebuhr sometimes failed to make.[35]

Satan, as understood by most traditional Christians, did not play a substantial role in Niebuhr's writings. Satan, Niebuhr believed, could not be rendered as a literal creature if American theology was to find a new and more complex way for Americans to understand evil and the Christian faith's response to it. Niebuhr, like most serious American theologians at mid-century, tacked away from any literalistic rendering of the devil even when they rejected many of the premises of the earlier liberal theology. Some even believed that the full force of the Christian message would be missed as long as it came packaged in a premodern worldview. German theologian Rudolf Bultmann, whose writing became highly influential in American seminaries, believed that the Christian faith could only become relevant when fully purged of all mythological elements. "Demythologizing," as he called it, would free the Christian proclamation from the cosmology of the first century CE that included supernatural events and angelic powers, fallen and otherwise. "It is impossible," Bultmann insisted, "to use electric light and wireless and to avail ourselves of modern medical and surgical discoveries and at the same time believe in the New Testament world of spirits and miracles." Belief in "Satan and his demons," he wrote, belonged to a passé mythical worldview.[36]

But not all of America's postwar theologians rejected the literal language of the Christian tradition when discussing evil. In fact, they often broadened and deepened that language in order to examine both personal and structural evil in American society. German theologian Paul Tillich, fleeing persecution by National Socialism, came to the United States in 1933. Reinhold Niebuhr (and his brother H. Richard Niebuhr) paved the way for Tillich to teach at Union Theological Seminary. He would later hold chairs at both Harvard and the University of Chicago. Tillich, during his long career in America, joined Niebuhr in thinking and writing profoundly about the problem of evil and what Tillich called "the demonic."[37]

Tillich's definition of "the demonic" would not have pleased any evangelical thinker or satisfied Pentecostal believers. Tillich recognized that demons belonged to the realm of religious mythology and embodied the ambiguous nature of evil. Tillich's thought separated these dark realities from what he called "the profane," or the world outside of the boundaries of the transcendent (the everyday, mundane world). The demonic represented a power in human life and cultural experience directly related to the transcendent realm. Indeed, they were essentially dark energies in human culture, politics, or religion that made absolute claims. Fascism, from Tillich's own experience, functioned as one such demonic force in the world. So would religious Fundamentalism, since it distorts spiritual experience by making absolutist claims for limited realities. Tillich linked the demonic to the idolatrous. Religion was especially prone to embodying these demonic energies. In his words, Christian churches often found themselves in danger of serving "a demonic absolutism which throws the truth like stones at the heads of people, not caring whether they accept it or not." Such fanaticism was the devil.[38]

Niebuhr and Tillich formulated their ideas in an America increasingly moving in a religiously conservative direction, a direction that seemed almost hungry for the literal devil of an earlier age. The Pentecostal movement functioned as a response to modern critiques of the supernatural, a "remythologization" of Christianity that continued to grow in strength in the years after World War II. A revitalized Fundamentalist movement, often called the evangelical movement, experienced its own "new birth" that challenged and eventually displaced mainline, liberal Protestantism. Both of these movements proved less interested in the structural or philosophical nature of evil but gave Satan a crucial role to play in their understanding of the Christian faith, as well as the history of America and of the world.

In the postwar era, Americans seemed to choose the more literalist rendering of the Christian message, as they left the mainline denominations in large numbers, either for the theological certainties of the evangelicals or the religious pyrotechnics of the Pentecostal movement. Few believers in the pews found the new theology attractive, as it seemed to divorce religious experience from mystery and leave little more than social activism and moral concern, both of which could be found in plenitude outside the churches. Even if they were not always clear on the content of traditional doctrinal language, American Christians basked in the safety and comfort such language offered.

The longing for the traditional imagery of evil, powerfully expressed, led to the growth and transformation of American Pentecostalism between the end of World War II and the early 1960s. Michael Cuneo describes how Pentecostalism, by 1960, had left the "storefront missions and creaky country churches" to become a much more middle-class movement. Many former mainline Christians, those who did not join one of the Fundamentalist denominations, entered the Assembly of God and other classical Pentecostal churches. Meanwhile, the movement began to affect members of confessions whose theological and liturgical orientation are far from the Pentecostal ethos. A small but vibrant group within the Protestant Episcopal Church and the Roman Catholic Church emphasized the "gifts of the Spirit" while remaining, often uneasily, within their own traditions.[39]

By the 1960s, American Christians who accepted speaking in tongues, the gifts of healing, deliverance from demons, and an affective and enthusiastic style of worship characterized themselves as "Charismatics" (taken from the Greek word for "gifts" or *charisma* in the New Testament). Representatives of this movement could be found in every American denomination. Frequently, they overlapped identities with Christian Fundamentalists (although the latter often made a point of trying to create discreet differences between the two movements). They were no longer drawn primarily from the ranks of the poor and the marginalized but rather had a solid, middle-American and middle-class constituency.

Ironically, this new, middle-class version of the Pentecostal outpouring ushered in a golden age of the deliverance from demons. Beginning in the 1930s, as Pentecostals went from being the "culturally despised" to one of America's most powerful religious movements, the longing for respectability sometimes led to a tamped-down belief in demonic possession and satanic influence. Particularly in the primarily white denominations that emerged from the Pentecostal movement (such as the Assemblies of God) the emotional fervor that accompanied public exorcism proved an embarrassment. Historian of Pentecostalism Vinson Synan, in an interview with Michael Cuneo, says that exorcism went through a brief "state of dormancy" after World War II but reemerged in the early 1960s more powerful than it ever had been. At the end of that decade, the American charismatic movement had a full panoply of so-called deliverance ministries that brought back, with even greater force, the Pentecostal movement's emphasis on the power of the devil and the necessity of spiritual warfare.[40]

The devil emerged on other fronts as well, a literal devil working within the souls of human beings to prevent their salvation. The Prince of Darkness found new life in the emerging evangelical movement that borrowed many of the concerns of the Fundamentalist movement while creating a much more popular style that gave it a broad appeal. In 1942, Harold John Ockenga formed the National Association of Evangelicals in an effort to revitalize conservative Protestants and clean up their provincial, angry Fundamentalist imagery. The postwar Youth for Christ organization gave evangelicalism an almost bohemian feeling, with young missionaries dressed in the latest styles touring the country in brightly painted buses. Billy Graham had his start as a YFC evangelist. His better-known municipal crusades made him a national celebrity in 1949–1950 and gave evangelicalism its first national face. Graham became the most influential American evangelist since Billy Sunday, the public face of evangelicalism's newfound cultural cachet.

The new evangelical theology that emerged after World War II refused to accept the reformulations of the problem of Satan offered by Niebuhr or Tillich. Evangelical theologians believed that those thinkers had not come far enough in revaluating the alleged naïveté of liberal thinkers. A literal belief in a literal devil was essential. Carl F. H. Henry argued in the magnum opus of evangelical theological writing, the six-volume *God, Revelation, and Authority*, that the supernatural, including the belief Satan, could not be separated from the Christian faith. In a 1987 interview with the *New York Times*, Henry noted that "Jesus affirmed the personal reality of the devil as a rebellious, angelic creature" and that "if the moral principle of 'the good' can be grounded in a personal, invisible spirit—that is, God—why cannot the principle of evil likewise be grounded in a personal demonic spirit?"[41]

The evangelical interest in the personal devil accounts for the enormous popularity of the British writer C. S. Lewis. Lewis's published work in the 1940s and 1950s would have far more influence than the writings of Niebuhr and Tillich. Lewis became, as Robert S. Ellwood notes, virtually a cult figure among evangelicals and one of the top-selling Christian authors in America. Lewis was known both for his thinly veiled Christian allegories called the *Chronicles of Narnia* and his apologetic works such as *Mere Christianity*. The Oxford medievalist who loved his pipe and pint, and who converted to Christianity under the influence of his close friend (and Roman Catholic) the fantasy writer J. R. R. Tolkien, seems an unlikely candidate to become an American evangelical icon. Much of his status can be attributed to a best-selling foray into demonology for the modern evangelical reader in his enormously influential *Screwtape Letters*.[42]

Lewis imagined *Screwtape* as a senior devil giving advice to his nephew, a young tempter named Wormwood. Demons literally swarmed around Christian believers and attacked their spiritual well-being, just as much as American Christianity had long believed. Demons were parasitic spiritual beings, vampires who fed off of souls corrupted by sin (meanwhile, saintly deeds, and saints themselves, make the devils sick to their spiritual stomachs). The popularity of *The Screwtape Letters* among evangelicals (but also among many mainline Protestants and even Roman Catholics) grew in part from the book's nearly pitch-perfect ability to blend humor with a close examination of the foibles of humanity and real spiritual insight. *Screwtape* spoke of the "lowerarchy" of hell and gave praise to "Our Father Below." God, meanwhile, was referred to as "the Enemy." In powerful narrative form, Lewis gave form and content to the deeply held American notion of spiritual warfare.[43]

Despite the popularity of C. S. Lewis, Billy Graham's strongly literal beliefs about the devil and demonic influence became the most public expression of evangelicalism's ideas about the nature of the devil. Graham gave new life to the concerns of America's earlier "great awakenings." The devil, in his view, worked overtime to prevent conversions to the Christian faith. He also sought to bring moral ruin to America. Notably, Graham's criticisms of American culture amounted to an expression of anxieties about outward dangers and devils, particularly communism.

Graham's most extended, and influential, discussion of Satan appeared in his book *Angels: God's Secret Agents*. The book, first published in 1975 and appearing in three subsequent editions, purported to detail the work of angelic beings in the world, with special emphasis on the services they perform on behalf of evangelical Christians. A significant part of the book also focuses on fallen angels, asserting repeatedly that "Satan is a real being who is at work in the world, together with his emissaries the demons." Graham's thoughts on the work of Satan would be read by millions. By 1978, the book had gone through fifteen printings and sold 1.2 million hardback copies. A new edition of the work appeared as late as 1994.[44]

Millennialism has always played an important role in Graham's thought, the belief that that world is moving to an apocalyptic end and the Second Coming of Jesus Christ. He spells out the significance of this theme in *Angels*. Graham warns of "a significant increase in satanic activity against people on the planet today [that] may indicate the Second Coming of Jesus Christ is close at hand." Graham suggests that such activity takes the form of an increased interest in satanic themes in popular culture (he specifically mentions *The Exorcist*) and a "renewed interest in the occult and Satanism."[45]

Graham's views on angels and demons reflected evangelical concerns about conversion and the human soul's relationship to New Testament cosmology that date back to the great awakenings of the eighteenth century. The devil's primary interest is preventing human beings from finding salvation and, in the twentieth century, "the devil is alive and at work more than at any other time" to further this end. Angels, on the other hand, are in the vanguard of the struggle to help save the souls of the human race. Graham even raised the possibility, though he admits that it is "speculation at best," that increased sightings of UFOs might be a sign of increased angelic activity, efforts by angels to defeat the devil's stratagems.[46]

Graham's belief in demonic spirits is, for him and for millions of evangelical believers in America, part of a much larger sense that the Christian experience can be best understood through the metaphor of warfare. This view would help galvanize the evangelical movement in American politics by the 1980s and, at times, serve as a legitimation of American foreign policy. Graham notes in *Angels* that nations prominent in early history (he mentions Israel, Egypt, Syria, and Iran) have become part of the geopolitical struggle for supremacy in the Middle East today. This, he says, points to the fact that "under the command of God, Michael the Archangel is now organizing his forces for the last battle." While Graham does not suggest that this calls the United States to a specific Middle East policy, other evangelical leaders would not be so reticent. By the 1980s, the premillennial views of evangelical leaders would inform evangelicals' (and recent presidents') ideas about the role of America in the world.[47]

Graham was not the only evangelical voice pointing to the increased work of Satan in the modern world. The sense of Satan as profoundly active in the world appeared again and again in evangelical writings of the late twentieth century. *Christianity Today*, the most significant periodical in the evangelical world by the 1970s, consistently argued for the power of the devil at work in the world. In a series run by the magazine on "Basic Christian Doctrine," Satan and demonology received thorough treatment. The author, G. C. Berkouwer, insisted that the true evangelical must speak about "the powers of darkness" with "the language of the Bible." This effort did not represent an abstract consideration of the problem of evil, but rather authoritative writing and proclamation about a real, and highly dangerous, supernatural force. Berkouwer noted that "it is not our concern to pursue an academic curiosity about evil." This lack of interest in the nature of evil is replaced by an insistence that Christians recognize the reality of the devil in the contemporary world, a reality that he and other evangelicals saw as insinuated into every aspect of modern life. The author reminded his readers that Satan can appear as "an angel of light" and thus masquerade behind what might appear to be legitimate social concerns. "The antichrist shall appear to be *for* many things. He shall be for culture, for human religions, for the earth." Berkouwer's comments fit a pattern of postwar evangelicals who tended to view efforts at religious tolerance or environmental concern as the snares of Satan. Such ideas drew on the long Fundamentalist war with modernity that viewed any effort at reform as, at least potentially, the devil's gambit.[48]

Christianity Today consistently repeated the themes of the devil's personal reality and growing strength throughout the latter half of the twentieth century. A 1974 article, in part a response to the popular fascination with demon possession inspired by the film *The Exorcist*, John Warwick Montgomery wrote that both "scripture and experiential evidence" for the reality of the devil "is simply too powerful to ignore." Montgomery noted that the twentieth century had been a century of "world holocausts" that seemed to argue for the work of the devil in the world. In the end, he simply asserts the scriptural evidence of Jesus and the early Christians battling with demonic forces as proof enough for evangelical believers that Satan fought them at every turn. A 1994 article in the same publication, written by popular evangelical writer and theologian J. I. Packer, accepted the premise of Satan's reality and went further by insisting that the devil had almost absolute control over the earth. Christians are engaged in "spiritual warfare" with a being "unimaginably malicious, mean, ugly and cruel." Moreover, this being "controls all this rebel world apart from the church and the Christians who constitute it."[49]

The devil continued to haunt Roman Catholicism in the postwar years. By the 1950s, the Roman Catholic Church represented, by far, the largest Christian tradition in the United States. Until that era, American Catholics had, in many respects, remained sequestered within their own world of ethnic neighborhoods, parishes, and parochial schools. A strong devotional piety flourished and, along with it, a powerful belief in the power of Satan. Numerous folk beliefs of European origin remained strong, passed down to children from family members and parish priests.

Beginning in 1962, the Second Vatican Council, known as Vatican II, proposed by Pope John XXIII and completed by his successor, Paul VI, sought to bring the Roman Catholic Church into a closer dialogue with the modern world. Pope John XXIII had referred to this as a moment to bring the Church *aggiornamento* ("up to date," or "with the times"). He would, he said, open the windows of the Church to the modern world and let in "some fresh air." It seemed a new day for the American Catholic Church. As the council met in Rome, America had its first Catholic president in John Fitzgerald Kennedy, a startlingly fashionable face for American Catholicism. The Church's relationship with American culture had changed forever.[50]

Observers, depending on their place along the spectrum of American Catholic opinion, viewed the Council in distinct ways. Progressive voices within the Church saw the worldwide Council as a way to revise

Catholicism, erasing some of its medievalism and reaching back to the early centuries of the Christian church for a more authentic expression of the faith. Most saw it as an effort to better articulate the teachings of the Church in the modern age, part of the Church's ongoing efforts at reform. But some of the American Church's most traditional elements saw it as a betrayal. Michael Cuneo, who has closely examined the wide spectrum of right-wing Catholic groups in his book *The Smoke of Satan*, notes that "extremist voices" on the right saw Vatican II as "a liberal abomination." Mel Gibson, actor-director behind the controversial 2004 film *The Passion of the Christ*, and his father, Hutton Gibson, belong to one such traditionalist sect known as "the Holy Family."[51]

A small number of the traditionalist movements that emerged after the Council believe that Vatican II represented something even more sinister than increased liberalization. Conspiracy theorists on the extreme right, Catholic separatists known as sedevacantists ("the Chair is empty"), believe that there has been no true pope since the death of Pius XII in 1958. Some believe that left-wing radicals in the Church killed or imprisoned the true pope. A few combine this belief with the idea that Soviet Communism survived the collapse of the Soviet Union in 1991 and lives on in an underground alliance with Freemasons and a worldwide Jewish financial cabal. This brew of paranoia and anti-Semitism is fueled by the belief that Satan has orchestrated the current calamity. They believe, in the words of one of their spokespeople, that in Vatican II "Satan has overseen the communistic takeover of the Church."[52]

A firm belief in the devil's influence on Earth for traditionalist American Catholics included a belief in the devil's influence over geopolitics. Monsignor Leon Cristini's *Evidence of Satan in the Modern World*, written in 1959, became the most influential of these works. Cristini combines close and detailed descriptions of possessions and exorcisms, mostly in a European context, with a steady insistence that Satan wields enormous influence over the politics and culture of the twentieth century. Although much of the work functions as a kind of catalog of exorcism cases in both the nineteenth and twentieth century, Cristini asserts that "the spectacular episodes we have recorded here are not the essence of Satan's work among men." Possession of an individual soul might interest us as a phenomenon, he writes, but the real work of Satan "in institutions and customs, in human, individual, family, national and internal life, is something infinitely vaster."[53]

Nations in the late twentieth century, Cristini claims, have suffered from a "collective possession," complete control by the power of the devil. Notably, and of great comfort to traditionalist Catholics in both Western Europe and the United States, both The People's Republic of China and the Soviet Union represented the two nations clearly under the sway of

Satan. Because of their "atheistic communism" (and the role played by what Cristini calls "ancestor worship" in China) these two nations fought at the vanguard of Satan's invasion of Earth. The Cold War, then, was ultimately a holy war against national states under Satan's command. Cristini did not let the West entirely off the hook but commented mainly on Satan's influence on certain cultural practices in the United States and Europe, primarily the growing interest among the young in the occult and paranormal, "the erotic atmosphere exuded by our novels and plays" and "the degradation of modern art."[54]

Cristini's work has been reprinted a number of times in the United States by conservative TAN Books & Publishers (who also have brought out new editions of Vogl's *Begone Satan!*). It would, however, be false to see traditionalists in American Catholicism as the only theological defenders of a firm belief in Satan. The extremist elements in the Roman Catholic Church have no monopoly on belief in the devil. Despite traditionalist claims, the American Catholic bishops have remained firmly tied to a generally conservative view of the role of the supernatural in Christian life. The changes brought about by Vatican II in no way eliminated, or really even truncated, the Church's traditional beliefs about Satan. In 1990, John Cardinal O'Connor of New York announced his belief in the devil and his work in modern American culture, especially in demon possession, Satanism, and heavy metal music. His comments caused a brief stir when Ozzy Osbourne, former lead singer of Black Sabbath and the godfather of the metal movement, responded with an open letter that insisted that the Cardinal had "insulted the intelligence" of heavy metal fans throughout the nation. Of course, the official teaching of the Church has been less colorful than some of its spokespeople's public comments. An updated *Catechism of the Catholic Church*, appearing in English in 1994, made only a handful of references to the devil and, generally, used restrained language in describing his work. Nevertheless, it clearly asserted his reality and his activity, including the possibility of demonic possession and the belief that, through sin, "the devil has acquired a certain domination over man."[55]

Despite powerful conservative claims on the concept of the devil, some theological thinkers in the 1960s and 1970s attempted to examine the nature of evil without resorting to Fundamentalism or liberal optimism. The devil for some in American society was not necessarily a "literal" concept, but it was concrete. New currents in theological thought, currents moved by the tides of social revolution in the late 1950s and early 1960s, dissented heavily from the reigning middle-class conceptions of the meaning of ultimate evil. Pentecostalism cast the devil out and evangelicalism identified him as a cultural opponent. Marginalized Christian thinkers and movements, meanwhile, identified evil in the very constitutive fabric of American society. This was especially true in the work of feminist/ womanist thinkers and the new black liberation theology.

The civil rights movement (explored more fully in chapter 6) helped shape black liberation theology, especially in its post-1965 form that emphasized calls for "Black Power." James H. Cone, a native of Arkansas, was raised in the rich tradition of the African Methodist Episcopal Church. Cone brought his strong sense of African American spirituality to his teaching career in Michigan where, in the summer of 1967, he found himself pondering the religious meaning of the insurrection in Watts, especially in relation to the bromides he heard from many white religious leaders. In two important books, *Black Theology and Black Power* (1969) and *A Black Theology of Liberation* (1970), he argued that American Christianity had disregarded the message of social justice in the scriptures, particularly the idea that God fights on the side of the oppressed rather than the powerful. White theologians had betrayed the gospel by insisting that its message be read through the lens of the white historical experience. In the American context, Cone asserted, "Jesus is Black," since "Christ *really* enters into this world where the poor, the despised and the black are [emphasis in original]."[56]

Cone's work had special implication for black Christians seeking to understand the meaning of Satan and the nature of evil. Christianity, according to Cone, must be interpreted within and through the experience of oppressed people. In this light, the life of Jesus takes on a new meaning. The exorcisms of Jesus, for example, are not simply elements of first-century mythological beliefs that encrust the real gospel message. Interpreted within the life of the African American faith community, Jesus' acts of challenging and defeating demons are signs of a new age coming, "disrupting the order of injustice."[57]

Women also rethought the meaning of the demonic in the 1960s. The emergence of feminist theology in this period drew on many of the insights formulated by the work of Elizabeth Cady Stanton and other "religious feminists" of the nineteenth century. As with black liberation theology, feminist religious reflection refused to accept traditional beliefs and readings of scripture as absolute, given that masculine modes of thought had influenced their construction. Women's experience of the divine became part of the material for religious reflection, a lens through which to ponder the Christian message.

Feminist/womanist theology has tended to exclude the idea of a literal Satan from serious theological discussion. In this respect, theologians such as Rosemary Radford Ruether, Elizabeth Schussler-Fiorenza, and Elizabeth A. Johnson are not especially unique, as many in the tradition of Christian liberalism had done the same. What is truly powerful in the writing of feminist/womanist thinkers on this subject is their critique of the way satanic imagery has traditionally been used as a tool of patriarchal ideology. For example, the theme of "the devil as tempter" is viewed as especially useless to theological thinking about evil, as it has tended to be tied to a male conception of the moral universe in which the free exercise of female choice, all by itself, constitutes a fall into temptation.

The traditional reading of the story of the Fall comes in for special indictment. Misogynist readings of this story have tended to emphasize the insidious role played by Eve, rendering her almost a partner with the satanic serpent in bringing sin into the world. Feminist/womanist thought rejects this model, confronting the problem of moral and natural evil in a more direct way. Rather than asking oblique questions about evil's nature, these thinkers have tended to focus directly on the issue of the suffering produced by evil, evil embodied in "demonic" structures that oppress and destroy both human beings and the created universe. Elizabeth A. Johnson, one of the founding mothers of feminist theological thought, makes the idea of suffering as a result of evil a central part of her theological enterprise. Making little use of the concept of the demonic, Johnson focuses most of her attention on the idea that God (accessible through feminine as well as masculine metaphors) suffers profoundly alongside the human race.[58]

The examples of Cone and Johnson underscore that important efforts have been made in the United States to reflect theologically on the problem of evil without incarnating that evil in human scapegoats. Elements of American theological thought, at almost every stage of the catastrophic twentieth century, urged Christian believers to ponder the meaning of evil, to think about the larger implications of human sinfulness in the reality of American racism; physical, emotional, social, and symbolic violence against women; war as an instrument of foreign policy; and the despoliation of the environment and degradation of the climate.

Meanwhile, conservative theological voices, including those who had sought to popularize certain elements of evangelical theology, simply insisted, loudly and repeatedly, that the devil must be believed in. They made such a belief an essential part of the Christian confession. Moreover, they insisted that the devil bore responsibility for threats to individual happiness and to the nation. Evangelicalism in the latter half of the century, especially as it transmogrified into the Christian Right of the 1980s, focused heavily on the devil embodied in its cultural opponents. This mind-set, as historian Robert Ellwood notes, "tends to need an antichrist."[59]

This latter approach prefers to believe in an embodied devil rather than undertaking the complex task of pondering human suffering. Moreover, popular culture during the "satanic century" reveals that few Americans had any interest in questioning the myth of their nation's innocence or fighting demons within the national soul. Instead of pondering the problem of moral evil, millions accepted the supernatural solutions to human misery offered by the evangelical and Pentecostal movements in America. American popular culture became an odd kind of partner to these religious movements, a partnership that had its origins in the very roots of mass culture in America. For many Americans, the vast output of the American entertainment industry, in the form of films, music, books, comics, and public spectacles of diverse kinds, provided much of their education in the wiles of the devil. These two powerful forces—religious belief and Satan's public, popular iconography—helped propel the devil to celebrity status. This would have a powerful effect on the way Americans imagined not only the devil but also the world in which they lived, the enemies they hated and feared. This process began early in the satanic century. As early as the 1920s, America had a hellhound on its trail.

NOTES

1. Examples are taken from Grant Wacker's excellent study of early twentieth-century Pentecostalism. Wacker depended heavily on materials such as regional and state Pentecostal newsletters. *Heaven Below: Early Pentecostalism and American Culture* (Cambridge, MA: Harvard University Press, 2001), 91, 92.

2. One of the best social, cultural, economic, and intellectual histories of this era is Lynn Dumenil's concise *The Modern Temper: American Culture and Society in the 1920s* (New York: Hill and Wang, 1995).

3. A close description of the spread of these ideas appears in Gary Dorrien's *The Making of American Liberal Theology: Imagining Progressive Religion, 1805–1900* (Louisville, KY: Westminster John Knox Press, 2001), 335–58.

4. Ferenc Morton Szasz, *The Divided Mind of Protestant America, 1880–1930* (Tuscaloosa: University of Alabama Press, 1982), 10–14. Szasz suggests that mainline Protestantism managed to absorb this approach with "minimum" conflict, although it did play into the controversy over "higher criticism" that he sees as a decisive break within the Protestant establishment.

5. Strong, brief descriptions appear in Winthrop S. Hudson and John Corrigan, *Religion in America*, 5th ed. (New York: Macmillan Publishing Company, 1992), 300–301.

6. Linda-Marie Delloff, et al., *A Century of the Century* (Grand Rapids, MI: W.B. Eerdmans Publishing Company, 1987).

7. H.L.W., "The Question Box," *The Christian Century*, November 21, 1934, 1493.

8. H.L.W., "The Question Box," *The Christian Century*, October 25, 1933, 1340.

9. William R. Hutchison does note in "Liberal Protestantism and the End of Innocence," *American Quarterly* 15, no. 2, part 1 (Summer, 1963): 126–39 that many of the most sophisticated liberals of this era had a more complex view of evil in human society. He notes that Shailer Matthews saw in World War I a profound

turning point in his own thought that called any easy optimism about progress into question.

10. George M. Marsden, *Religion and American Culture* (Belmont, CA: Wadsworth Publishing, 2000), 258–59.

11. Damien Thompson, *Waiting for Antichrist: Charisma and Apocalypse in a Pentecostal Church* (New York: Oxford University Press, 2005), 44.

12. Grant Wacker, *Heaven Below: Early Pentecostals and American Culture* (Cambridge, MA: Harvard University Press, 2003), 92.

13. David Martin, *Pentecostalism: The World Their Parish* (Oxford: Blackwell, 2001), 5; James Barr, *Fundamentalism* (London: SCM Press, 1977), 195. A full discussion of the roots of "premillennialism" appears in George M. Marsden, *Fundamentalism and American Culture* (Oxford: Oxford University Press, 2006).

14. Robert C. Fuller, *Naming the Antichrist: The History of an American Obsession* (Oxford: Oxford University Press, 1996), 13.

15. Michael W. Cuneo, *American Exorcism: Expelling Demons in the Land of Plenty* (New York: Doubleday, 2001), 88.

16. Lynn Dumenil, *The Modern Temper* (New York: Hill and Wang, 1995), 185–87.

17. Fuller, *Naming the Antichrist*, 139–41.

18. Marsden, *Fundamentalism and American Culture*, 126.

19. Marsden, *Fundamentalism and American Culture*, 161–64.

20. Marsden, *Fundamentalism and American Culture*, 190.

21. A version of this sermon, preached for over fifty years, is available online at www.jesusclips/view_video.php?category+page (accessed July 28, 2008).

22. Marsden, *Religion and American Culture*, 193.

23. Carl Vogl, *Begone Satan! A True Account of a 23-Day Exorcism in Earling, Iowa in 1928*, trans. Celestine Kapsner, O.S.B. (Rockford, IL: Tan Books & Publishers, Inc, 1973).

24. Vogl, *Begone Satan!* 21.

25. Vogl, *Begone Satan!* 23, 24; on the growth of devotional practices to "the Little Flower," see Monica Furlong, *Therese of Lisieux* (Maryknoll, NY: Orbis Books, 1987), 126–28. She was often evoked in exorcisms even before her canonization in 1925.

26. Vogl, *Begone Satan!* 19, 20.

27. "The Devil in Iowa," *The Christian Century*, March 23, 1938.

28. Winthrop S. Hudson and John Corrigan, *Religion in America* (Upper Saddle River, NJ: Prentice Hall, 2003), 390, 391.

29. Hudson and Corrigan, *Religion in America*, 361–62; for a brief elaboration of some of the main themes of this new theological enterprise, see Karl Barth, *Evangelical Theology* (New York: Doubleday/Anchor Books, 1963).

30. Ronald H. Stone, *Reinhold Niebuhr: Prophet to Politicians* (Washington, DC: University Press of America, 1981), 23–34.

31. An example of Niebuhr's views on this point appears in Reinhold Niebuhr, *The Nature and Destiny of Man*, vol. I (New York: Charles Scribner's Sons, 1941).

32. Stone, *Reinhold Niebuhr*, 39, 40–43.

33. Robin W. Lovin, *Reinhold Niebuhr and Christian Realism* (New York: Cambridge University Press, 1995), 91–92.

34. Stone, *Reinhold Niebuhr*, 96–100.

35. Reinhold Niebuhr, *The Irony of American History* (New York: Charles Scribner's Sons, 1952), 28, 35.

36. Rudolf Bultmann, "New Testament and Mythology," in *Kerygma and Myth*, ed. Hans Werner Bartsch (New York: Harper and Row, 1961), 1, 5.

37. J. Heywood Thomas, *Paul Tillich* (Richmond, VA: John Knox Press, 1966), 4.

38. Paul Tillich, *Systematic Theology*, vol. 3 (Chicago: University of Chicago Press, 1963), 102, 186.

39. Cuneo, *American Exorcism*, 86–88.

40. Cuneo, *American Exorcism*, 89.

41. "TV Followers See the Devil's Hand in Bakker's Fall," *New York Times*, April 13, 1987. (Archive Accessed August 8, 2008).

42. Robert C. Ellwood, *1950: Crossroads of American Religious Life* (Louisville, KY: Westminster John Knox Press, 2000), 190.

43. C. S. Lewis, *The Screwtape Letters* (New York: Macmillan, 1961).

44. Billy Graham, *Angels: God's Secret Agents* (Nashville, TN: W Publishing Group), 1994, 8; Edwin McDowell, "Billy Graham a Bestseller Too," *New York Times*, June 24, 1978.

45. Graham, *Angels*, 9.

46. Graham, *Angels*, 12, 28.

47. Graham, *Angels*, 158–60.

48. G. C. Berkouwer, "Satan and the Demons," *Christianity Today*, June 5, 1961, 18–19.

49. John Warwick Montgomery, "Exorcism: Is It For Real?" *Christianity Today*, July 26, 1974, 5–8; J. I. Packer, "The Devil's Dossier," *Christianity Today*, June 21, 1993, 24.

50. Hudson and Corrigan, *Religion in America*, 385.

51. Michael Cuneo, *The Smoke of Satan: Conservative and Traditionalist Dissent in Contemporary American Catholicism* (New York: Oxford University Press, 1997), 23.

52. Cuneo, *Smoke of Satan*, 89.

53. Leon Cristini, *Evidence of Satan in the Modern World* (Rockford, IL: TAN Books & Publishers, 1974), 157.

54. Cristini, *Evidence of Satan*, 157, 165, 171, 180–81.

55. Michael G. Mauldin, "Satan Makes Headlines," *Christianity Today*, May 14, 1990, 15; *Catechism of the Catholic Church* (New York: Image Books, 1994), section 407.

56. James H. Cone, *God of the Oppressed* (San Francisco: Harper Books, 1975), 7–10, 136.

57. Cone, *God of the Oppressed*, 224.

58. Elizabeth A. Johnson, *She Who Is: The Mystery of God in Feminist Theological Discourse* (New York: Crossroad Publishing, 1992), 246–72.

59. Ellwood, *1950: Crossroads of American Religious Life*, 192.

5

Hellhound on My Trail: Satan and Twentieth-Century American Culture

The devil met Robert Johnson at a lonely Mississippi Delta crossroads and Johnson became one of the greatest guitarists of the twentieth century.

Before he made the infernal pact, Johnson, born in Mississippi in 1911, had attempted to learn the plaintive notes of the emerging blues style from virtuosos like Son House, Willie Brown, and Charlie Patton. He had mostly failed, and then, mysteriously, he disappeared. He returned with an inexplicable talent surging through his fingers and mysterious stanzas pouring out of his mouth. Out of this surprising turn of events the belief came that another force beyond native talent had been involved, a dark force. Son House later insisted that Johnson "sold his soul to the Devil to get to play like that" and this gave birth to a dark legend, a legend aided and abetted by the fact that, in the words of Southern historian Pete Daniel, Johnson's "lyrics overflow with references to Satan." In time, some would even claim they knew the exact spot where Johnson struck his demonic bargain.[1]

The devil may not have taught Johnson how to play, but dark themes certainly suffuse the bluesman's music. The delta impresario has been called America's "existential poet," whose vocals vibrate painfully "with a brooding sense of torment and despair." Although his music has become well known among blues and "roots music" aficionados (and in the larger world of rock through Cream's "Crossroads" and the Rolling Stones' "Love in Vain") the life of the delta bluesman remains a mystery. Johnson produced only a thin catalog of recordings and lived a nomadic life, playing his music from the delta to Chicago. He died in 1938, not yet thirty years old.[2]

What Johnson produced in his short life made him a legendary figure. Blues historian Francis Davis describes "his raw vocals and sophisticated guitar techniques" that later confused a young Keith Richards, who, on first hearing a Johnson recording, was convinced that he was hearing more than one guitar played at a time. The rediscovery of Robert Johnson in the postwar era created several new generations of fans, the 1990 *Complete Recordings* selling almost half a million copies within six weeks of its release.[3]

Beyond the seminal importance of his music, the role of the devil, and of the nature of evil, in Johnson's lyrics give his work a profound cultural significance. Robert Johnson's musical tour of hell tells us much about African American culture but also the trajectory of satanic imagery throughout the twentieth century. His talent may not have come from a meeting with the devil at a deserted crossroads in Mississippi twilight. But his lyrics did come from an encounter with personal and collective darkness, an encounter that all of American culture would soon face.

Americans coming of age in the 1920s, 1930s, and 1940s knew many faces of Satan. He was a central figure in many Americans' religious faith but also in the comic books they hid beneath their beds. After the trough of the Great Depression and the triumphalism of the period after World War II, a new sense of American purpose and identity emerged, and much of white, middle-class America believed in a devil that threatened the mores that buttressed this strong sense of identity. But just as in the nineteenth century, dissident voices proclaimed that they saw the devil where most Americans were afraid to look, possessing and controlling some of the very structures that strengthened the nation's conservative consensus.

The early twentieth century saw the apotheosis of a highly racialized religious nationalism in America. The United States had been moving in this direction since the end of Reconstruction, and American Protestantism played an integral role in the process. Edward J. Blum, in *Reforging the White Republic*, argues that American religion between the end of the Civil War and the Spanish-American War fashioned a new white unity grounded in racial terrorism and imperialistic, global ambition. Blum notes Arthur Bird's 1899 work entitled *Looking Forward* (an obvious play on Edward Bellamy's utopian novel *Looking Backward*) that imagined the next hundred years as truly an "American century" in which white, Anglo-Saxon Protestants gained global supremacy, a supremacy expressed by the triumph of American nationalism. "The power and stamina of the Anglo Saxon race," Bird claimed, would make America the "Light of the World."[4]

This religio-nationalist jingoism blossomed like dark flowers by the 1920s. Popular memory preserves this decade as "the Roaring Twenties," a time of bathtub gin, striking new fashion styles, and unbridled prosperity on the brink of the ruin of the Depression. The reality was much different. In truth, the decade evinced a powerful strain of conservatism with an ugly spirit of nativism. A resurgent Ku Klux Klan used violence against Jews, blacks, Catholics, and immigrants of all types in an effort to defend the boundaries of white American identity. An income gap yawned like a chasm in the middle of American life. Racial tensions seethed in the cities and resulted in a number of so-called race riots, really attacks by the white community on the emerging black wards of large cities. Most of the rural South, meanwhile, entered a "Great Depression" a full eight years before the stock market crash of 1929. A precipitous drop in cotton prices in 1921 combined with the coming of the boll weevil, a pest that actually consumed cotton bolls from the stalk, transformed the region into what FDR would later call "economic problem number one."[5]

Social upheaval meant for most white Americans that the boundaries of national identity needed to be maintenanced. The widespread membership in the Ku Klux Klan, and the group's respectability are witness to this impulse. Most Americans believed that the struggle to maintain this identity took place not only in the physical world but also on the equally real spiritual battleground. As white Christians in America sought to defend their cultural values against change, the theme of spiritual warfare remained central to their understanding of Christianity. The growing Fundamentalist and Pentecostal movements, as well as the highly conservative Roman Catholic hierarchy in America, found it easy to extend the metaphor of spiritual warfare to include America's enemies, both foreign and domestic.

Spiritual warfare remained central to religious beliefs, while many of its themes also made their appearance in film, radio, pulp magazines, and comics. Diabolical themes in popular culture strengthened and influenced religious views, often of a conservative bent. Popular culture and religion could, together, function for Americans as what Peter Berger calls "plausibility structures." Religious belief, no matter how firm, often depends on having the social and cultural structures necessary to support and maintain it.

By the 1930s, Christian believers found their belief in Satan confirmed at every turn by a vast system of plausibility structures, signs and symbols that mutually reinforced one another in creating a cultural and religious worldview. The young conservative Southern Baptist, for example, might slip away into town on a Saturday afternoon and watch guiltily in the dark Tod Browning's Mephistophelean images of *Dracula* as seducer of innocence, a force both beautiful and brutal. This imagery would remain in his mind on Sunday morning when his minister preached a sermon on Satan's wiles, the glamour of evil, and the need for the believer to engage in spiritual combat with the Enemy. Such imagery further influenced him the following week when one of his school pals handed him a grimy, rolled-up copy of the popular comic *Madam Satan*, which combined satanic imagery with a voluptuous feminine form and centuries-old misogyny. Out of these fragments of religious belief and popular culture are worldviews born, and from such do they grow into cultural obsessions.[6]

Marginalized communities in America were influenced by these dominant beliefs but also responded to them creatively. The devil of white America was not, at least univocally, the devil of the African American community. African American culture, marginalized by the white nationalistic paradigm, faced a number of profound changes by the end of World War I that resulted in new creative energies that transformed American and, eventually, global culture. African American writers, artists, and musicians unleashed these new energies in the midst of a reign of terror in which Jim Crow segregation solidly enveloped the states of the former Confederacy and lynching remained the common and accepted white response to real and perceived violations of racial etiquette. Following the end of World War I, African Americans by the tens of thousands fled the South in what would become known as "the Great Migration." The urban North, as well as the rural South, became a cauldron of suffering and creativity. This context of oppression gave birth to Blues, Gospel, and Jazz in both the American South and the cities of the American North.

Satan played a central role in this experience. The devil haunted the sharecropper shacks, logging camps, juke joints, and rural crossroads of the early twentieth-century South. He also made his appearance in the urban centers of the North, where storefront churches (many of them in the Pentecostal tradition) carried the beliefs of the rural South to New York, Detroit, and Chicago. African folklore continued to influence African American beliefs about Satan, but by the twentieth century, the devil's image had also been shaped by profound African American encounters with evil.

By the 1920s, gospel music, a more professionalized and stylized version of the "slave spirituals," allowed the black community to continue to sing about God, oppression, and deliverance, especially the possibility of deliverance from the devil. Lawrence Levine, in his seminal work on African American culture since slavery *Black Culture and Black Consciousness*, notes that in these songs "The Devil . . . often looked suspiciously like a surrogate for the white man." Levine cites many of the plaintive cries of early twentieth-century gospel that asked, "Why don't the Devil let me be?" and "What makes Satan hate me so?"[7]

Sometimes gospel explicitly linked the devil's work to race hatred and black oppression. Images of freedom from racial oppression blended with images of freedom from the devil. One gospel tune described how:

> *He got me once an' let me go*
> *Ol' Satan thought he held me fast*
> *Broke his chain and I'm free at last*

Others spoke with even greater clarity of the aftermath of emancipation and of Jim Crow as the work of the devil:

> *Just let me tell you how this world is fixed*
> *Satan has got it so full of tricks*
> *You can go from place to place*
> *Everybody's running down the colored race*

Robert Johnson symbolized the rise of secular music in the African American community and a different response to the black experience, in which religious themes, particularly a fascination with Satan, continued to predominate even as religious aspirations to salvation diminished. In Johnson, the music of Saturday night and Sunday morning, the twin polarities of the juke joint and the church, blended and cross-fertilized one another. This represents a larger phenomenon in the creative life of this oppressed community. Bessie Smith's 1927 recording "Preachin' the Blues" used religious imagery to sing of sexual salvation, and many observers noted that blues performances elicited ecstatic cries of "Amen!" and "preach it!" that seemed more at home in a revival meeting than at a Saturday night dance.[8]

Johnson's music represented the soundtrack of a kind of satanic religious revival, an evocation of the power and complexity of evil. Rudi Blesh's 1946 *Shining Trumpets* describes Johnson's lyrics as being "full of evil, surcharged with the terror of one alone among the moving, unseen shapes of the night. Wildly and terribly, the notes paint a dark wasteland." Johnson's wasteland was America at the beginning of the twentieth century, one that had made its own deal with the devil at a crossroads in its history.[9]

Robert Johnson's Satan owed less to the slave tradition than to his own personal vision of darkness, a vision shared by an increasing number of Americans, black and white, as the century unfolded. But this sense of darkness, of being hunted by evil and unable to escape, is only one of the complex images of Satan that appears in Johnson's work. "Me and the Devil Blues," for example, describes an encounter with the devil that brings about a sense of liberation. After greeting the devil at his door by saying "Hello, Satan, I believe it's time to go," Johnson chants, in an eerie presaging of the mystery surrounding his burial:

> *You may bury my body, oooh*
> *Down by the highway side*
> *So my old evil spirit*
> *Can catch a greyhound bus and ride*

Johnson almost always linked the devil with violence, sometimes the violence inherent in American society and other times violence he viewed as an adjunct to the lifestyle he lived and performed. Johnson sings of a walk with the devil in "Me and the Devil Blues," a walk ending with Johnson deciding, "And I'm gonna beat my woman until I get satisfied." But his personal encounters with Satan are usually about fear and flight rather than succumbing to the Devil's blandishments. Blues historian Francis Davis notes that Johnson sang his songs of fleeing for his life, running from the devil that had met him at the crossroads, during the time when many African Americans were fleeing the violent Southern landscape, trying to escape the violence that hounded them night and day. "Hellhound on My Trail" tells the listener in almost desperate tones that

> *I've got to keep moving*
> *I've got to keep moving*
> *Blues falling down like hail*
> *Blues falling down like hail.*
> *And the day keeps on worryin' me*
> *It's a hellhound on my trail*
> *Hellhound on my trail*
> *Hellhound on my trail.*

Johnson's vision came too early in the century to make a larger cultural imprint in his own lifetime. Nevertheless, in his short life Johnson became America's poet of decadence. His fascination with, and explication of, the dark shadows of the American experience shared with the decadent poets of the late nineteenth century (and his fellow bluesmen and women) the desire to look at an underground world that mainstream culture chose to ignore. This catalog of deviations is rehearsed by Ellis Hanson when he describes decadent poetry and story as a fascination with "all that was commonly perceived as unnatural or degenerate, with sexual perversity, nervous illness, crime and disease." Johnson's music added to these concerns a fascination with satanic themes, the devil as an aesthetic and moral reality eating at the vitals of modern American life. The devil for him became violence unleashed in a desperate search for liberation, a search ignited by demonic desires and driven forward by the hellhound's hot breath. Johnson's musical search constituted a flight from an America that could not truly be escaped. Some of his best music recognizes the fact of his American damnation. Johnson's "Crossroad Blues" registers his despair and his place of meeting with the devil becomes a Dantesque circle of hell in which "poor Bob" is forever condemned.[10]

The themes explored by Johnson, and indeed all of the concepts of the nature of evil explored by African American culture, seldom found purchase in twentieth-century America's public culture. In fact, Johnson's dark ponderings seemed out of place in the America that emerged out of World War I. Popular entertainment would, for the most part, eschew Robert Johnson's close exploration of his own, and his nation's, demonic tendencies. Instead, mass entertainment mirrored the obsessions of race and gender that were common to religion in America since colonial times and were especially pungent in a time of manifest social and cultural change. A stream of evil women, evil foreigners, and evil conspiracies defined the demonic in popular culture. The devil, just as he had done in nineteenth-century reform, took the shape of middle-class disapproval. Satan played an important role, one that would only grow in mainstream entertainment culture, largely because popular culture in America can never be severed from America's religious culture. Anxieties about the nature of evil found expression in the modern magic lantern show of American movies. Books and comics gave expression to the American tendency to project demonic evil on the Other. The concerns of American Fundamentalism, especially by the time of World War II, played an increasing role in the entertainment industry as conservative Christians slowly became consumers of the cultural mainstream. Only some very solitary voices suggested that the devil hid in America's own soul. Most saw him in America's cultural enemies.

American popular culture of the 1920s and 1930s stood on the verge of a new epoch. While a public culture of entertainment had always existed in the United States, cultural historian LeRoy Ashby describes its rise and dissemination as a process that increased in pace during the twentieth century, in which "assorted amusements" became "mainstream entertainment." In the late nineteenth century and early twentieth century, much of what would later be defined as popular culture existed as discrete islands of amusement, surrounded and sequestered by moral strictures and the disdain of the white middle class. De facto and de jure censorship limited access to entertainment along lines of age, gender, class, and race. By the 1940s, some of these strictures lifted in the face of cultural shifts and technological breakthroughs that led to a steady stream of books, films, comics, music, and magazines. By the latter half of the century, the stream would widen and become, in the present day, a flood tide of easily accessible sounds, sights, and experiences in movies, video games, sequential art, and numberless forms of expression.[11]

Film transformed popular culture forever. The ghostly images watched with strangers in the dark proved powerful enough to incite as well as to entertain. Very quickly in the history of the medium, Americans sought to use film to frame their history and identity, as well as to project, literally, their fears and anxieties. Race played a central role in this determination to secure the boundaries of American identity. Some of the most popular early silent films argued that whiteness ultimately grounded this American identity. D. W. Griffith's 1915 *Birth of a Nation* represents the most notorious example of this early trend. A masterpiece of filmmaking technique, it attempts to retell the story of the American founding, the Civil War, and Reconstruction from a white supremacist perspective. That same year, a revivified Ku Klux Klan emerged in a special ceremony at Stone Mountain, Georgia, in part inspired by the heroic picture of the Klan presented in Griffith's film. Local audiences could be affected by it even more immediately. A group of white farmers in Greenville, South Carolina, pulled their guns and peppered the screen with bullets during the infamous scene in which an African American soldier assaults a young white heroine.[12]

Along with creating a highly racialized image of American identity, films of the silent era sought to police the parameters of bourgeois respectability. The devil's appearances in the early silents testify to the American film industry's search for respectability in their effort to appeal to middle-class sensibilities. In an America where many liberal pastors and theologians questioned the devil's reality, his cinematic image became less a supernatural juggernaut and more an archetype of moral temptation. Director Thomas Ince's 1915 *The Devil* provides one example. In the film, a bohemian painter is visited by a suave, debonair Satan, shorn of his horns. This dapper devil urges the artist to woo a married woman and the painter wreaks havoc in his lover's marriage. The film ends with the screaming sinners being sent off to hell for their lack of respect for the married state.[13]

Two things are notable about this early effort to portray the devil on screen. First, this was primarily a moralistic tale about sexual purity and the sanctity of marriage (as well as perhaps a warning about the dangers of bohemianism and art). The supernatural trappings turn the lesson into a parable but are not essential for the didactic point. In fact, a 1920 remake of *The Devil* used both the title and tale of seduction but left out the supernatural element entirely. Second, the film traded heavily in the misogynistic tendencies that had long been a part of American understanding of Satan. The female object of desire in *The Devil* is shown as easily seduced, even willingly taking part in her own diabolical seduction. In twentieth-century popular culture, this deep misogyny became a part of almost all media concerned with satanic topics. American films about Satan in the twentieth century represent a catalog of patriarchal fear and anxiety, with women imagined as either the devil's easy marks or his willing partners. The Universal Pictures production *The Devil's Bondswoman* (1916) further illustrates how pop-culture Satanism could reflect gender anxieties. The female lead, Adele Farrington, plays a woman with such powerful sexual impulses that she draws Satan's attentions. The film ends with Farrington being dragged off to hell, punished for her desire. The film rendered female sexuality literally as a demonic lighting rod drawing evil and death into the lives of everyone around it (as we will see, this idea even becomes the subtext of the possession in *The Exorcist*).[14]

Rampant and unrestrained sexism in demonic pop entertainment reflects middle-class anxieties about the "new woman" of the early twentieth century. Janet Staiger argues convincingly that the beginnings of popular film in America coincided with the white middle class's "intense struggle . . . to define an appropriate version of and explanation for Woman and women's sexuality." At the very moment that powerful screen images first appeared, often shocking to the first audiences, American life passed through a profound upheaval that led William Marion Reedy, in a 1913 essay, to pronounce that it was "Sex O'clock in America." Public discussions about vice, the changing role of women in the economy, popular urban legends about "white slavery," and the possible results that women entering political life might have on marriage and family obsessed the American middle classes. If Victorianism had imagined woman as the angel of the household, early twentieth-century social change led conservatives to reimagine her image as the devil in the bedroom.[15]

The conservative cultural response, one that the emerging film industry readily expressed, was to create the image of the "vamp," or the female vampire. Filmmakers represented the vamp as a financially independent woman, free of male control, who used her overwhelming sexuality to bring men financial and domestic ruin. Actor Theda Bara appeared in several films playing, according to one reviewer, "the type of woman that made men uneasy, from St. Anthony to Rudyard Kipling." Nikolas Schreck notes that the idea of the vamp worked perfectly with the notion of demonic influence. The silent screen filled up with a number of Satan's female partners, the villainess who ignored all bounds of propriety. The emerging American film industry put new technology to very old uses, presenting a message about the wiles of the devil and the dangers of female sexuality that would have pleased the dourest Puritan divine.[16]

Numerous other satanic features were produced in the silent era, most of which are entirely forgettable. Many of the themes of nineteenth-century Protestant moral reform found their way onscreen, as the devil pushed various intemperate delights on the unwary. These efforts almost always presented themselves as moral parables that used the demonic for spice rather than to buttress, even unintentionally, an ideological viewpoint. In some cases, these films couldn't keep a straight face. The 1929 *Seven Footprints to Satan* created a fascinating screen villain in the form of a criminal warlord who loved satanic imagery and transformed his lair into a Dantesque inferno. Though based on a fairly dark and popular novel, the film version of *Seven Footprints to Satan* borrowed elements of screwball comedy and what would later become the standard Hollywood trick of creating a supernatural scenario later revealed to be a hoax perpetrated by a criminal mastermind. Introduced just as the first talkies appeared, the producers dubbed the film with a haunted-house-inspired musical score and overwrought sound effects that make it virtually unwatchable today.

Seven Footprints, while unimportant in film history, does show a willingness to use the devil as a source of fun, which is surprising since so many Americans saw him with deadly seriousness as their opponent in spiritual warfare. Most notably, the film appeared soon after many of these same Americans had discovered the devil active in Dayton, Tennessee, conspiring with Clarence Darrow to foist the teaching of evolution on America. But as the events of Dayton showed, strains and cracks had begun to show in the American Protestant consensus. *Seven Footprints* illustrated a real and growing divide in America between those who took Satan with deadly seriousness and those who took him, and the supernatural in general, with a grain of salt. Reimagining the devil as an entertaining, not altogether serious supervillain, rather than a moral and supernatural threat, suited at least one aspect of American culture in the 1920s. While America after World War I experienced a resurgence of conservatism in the form of the "Red Scare," the Ku Klux Klan, and the spread of Christian Fundamentalism, other influential voices challenged traditional verities, especially those associated with Victorianism.

America had its prophets of irony as well as its prophets of moralism. F. Scott Fitzgerald proclaimed irony as "the Holy Ghost of the new era," and he and other writers brought out a vibrancy that led to a critique of older, accepted values. Ernest Hemingway joined Fitzgerald in his cynicism with a style that celebrated a liberated modernity, his short sentences coming in machine gun bursts that seemed to mow down the old cosmologies. The poet Edna St. Vincent Millay attacked traditional mores both in her verse and in her lifestyle, and devotees memorized it until it became a kind of soundtrack for youthful hedonism.

The academic world joined this literary assault on the old verities. The emerging discipline of anthropology, especially in the work of Ruth Benedict and Margaret Mead, relativized cultural values. Refusing to view societies as simply either "primitive" or "civilized," they instead studied belief, ritual, and folkways as the result of specific cultural and historical traditions developed over time. The geography of the human soul had been remapped as well. Freudianism came to be applied to a wide range of cultural and social behaviors, suggesting that surface realities functioned as blinds for deep-seated, hidden impulses. Cultural critics, most famously H. L. Mencken in *The American Mercury*, attacked traditional American mores as artless, commercial, and hobbled by Puritanism.[17]

Andrew Delbanco describes these diverse phenomena as the birth of a "culture of irony." Variant voices definitively rejected the old certainties, finding in Darwinism and Freudianism an explanation for sin and Satan as well as for God and the soul. This reaction came with a powerful undertow of despair. In America, perhaps because the moral and religious strictures remained overwhelmingly powerful components of the national culture, the culture of irony quickly lost the liberating vibrancy it first exhibited. Quoting cultural historian George Steiner, Delbanco shows that for many intellectuals, the newfound sense of liberation from older verities led to "a world gone flat." Ennui, rather than ecstatic freedom, became the cultural mood. In some cases, this led to a repentant conservatism (T. S. Eliot and Ezra Pound). For others, it meant that they threw up barricades, becoming isolated voices in the midst of a generally conservative America.[18]

These changes in American intellectual and cultural life had a profound effect on America's future trajectory. In 1925, the so-called Scopes Monkey Trial in Dayton, Tennessee, became the opening salvo of the American culture wars, a conflict whose intensity would only grow with time. Clarence Darrow may have made William Jennings Bryan look rather foolish in his uncomplicated and unreflective faith. But millions of Americans shared both Bryan's horror of evolution and his simple faith. While few states, at least in 1925, passed measures against the teaching of evolution, local school boards did move to restrict it.[19]

These facts suggest that perhaps America was no "culture of irony" in the 1920s and 1930s. Instead, an isolated culture of irony existed as an island in a much larger sea of traditionalism, a traditionalism finding renewed strength from religious dynamism. We have already seen that the period between the two world wars marked the explosion of the Pentecostal movement, the dramatic rise of Protestant Fundamentalism, and the continuing conservatism of American Catholics, all groups who, in different ways, challenged the "modern temper" to hand-to-hand combat. F. Scott Fitzgerald may have thought irony a new Holy Ghost, but for tens of millions of Americans, the Holy Ghost of an earlier era suited them just fine. Fundamentalism, meanwhile, functioned as a rejection of irony and a stern refusal to place quotation marks around eternal verities, a point made by the frequent Fundamentalist assertion about the Bible that "it says what it means and means what it says." Pentecostalism also rejected the rhetorical deconstruction of experience represented by the ironic mode. The language of Pentecostalism constantly asserted and reasserted the reality of the movement's religious experience, contrasting that deep reality against the doubt implied in the culture of irony.

Satan's brand proved durable for many, probably the majority of, Americans who felt threatened by the upheavals of the interwar period. Perhaps most telling of all, the strength of his image grew among individuals far removed from the American mainstream. Modern America borrowed old demonologies but also gave birth to new ones. In fact, powerful new reimaginings of Satan emerged from the world of the social sciences themselves. Egyptologist Margaret Murray, borrowing some of the techniques of both literary criticism and anthropology, fashioned a new mythic worldview that, at least for some, had the patina of academic respectability.

In the early twentieth century, the reigning scholarly interpretation of the witchcraft trials of early modern Europe viewed them as a series of delusional outbreaks connected to the religious intolerance of the inquisition. Margaret Murray, in her 1921 work *The Witch-Cult in Western Europe*, challenged this view by claiming that what the Christian churches had persecuted as witchcraft represented the survival of a religious vision that dated back to "pre-Christian times." In essence, this "old religion" was the worship and celebration of a Mother Goddess in the form of a fertility cult. Murray viewed the old religion as joyful, celebratory, and sensuous, in contrast to the censoriousness of Christianity. In later works, such as the 1933 *God of the Witches*, she argues that the "the horned one," defined by the Christian Church as the devil, was actually a joyful spirit connected to nature and fertility.[20]

Murray's views would later play a significant role in the emergence of "neo-paganism" as an organized movement in America. Some of her theories, in a much-revised form, would actually influence some genuine scholarship in the field of witchcraft studies. Unfortunately, some of the more fascinating assertions of her work are little more than elaborate historical fantasies. Her work, and her claims, became increasingly erratic. At the age of ninety she published a tome that made a number of absurd claims about the "ritual murder" of British kings, many of whom, she insisted, had been killed for practicing "the old religion."

Dark gods, reinvented and reimagined, also lived in the works of one of America's greatest pulp writers. H. P. Lovecraft, an extraordinarily inventive New England writer, began contributing his short stories to the pulp magazine *Weird Tales* on its founding in 1923 (by this time, he had already written his Reanimator tales, later made famous by what S. T. Joshi calls the "un-Lovecraftian" films of Stuart Gordon). Lovecraft was far from a typical writer of fantasy horror, embodying in his short stories and novellas a materialist conception of the universe that reimagined the conception of evil. In a view he called "cosmicism," Lovecraft evoked an existential dread in his readers by portraying the supernatural powers that truly ruled the universe as gigantic, alien beings that shared none of humanity's emotional or spiritual concerns. Human beings were alone in the universe—except for these powerful beings that might destroy them with indifference. Lovecraft, in stories like "The Call of Cthulhu" and "At the Mountains of Madness," rejected the category of the demonic just as he rejected the category of the divine. But in doing so he shaped the cosmos itself as a kind of devil, at least to human beings.[21]

Lovecraft's audience may have been small but he would have a wider influence in the history of Satan in the twentieth century. In the world of occultism, small groups of devotees, many of them ignoring Lovecraft's own philosophical materialism, became convinced that Lovecraft's tales intertwined together into a larger mythology they called the "Cthulhu mythos." Some even believed that demons had dictated his stories to him and that he had, unknowingly, fashioned them into a kind of unholy writ. Tracy Twyman, writing in the occult tabloid *The Arcadian Mystique*, claimed that Lovecraft had been dictated stories of a secret race of giant beings that had once been angels, referred to as the Nephilim. And a young carnival magician name Anton LaVey, future high priest of the Church of Satan, admired Lovecraft's writings and would incorporate some of his ideas into the rituals of his new religious movement in the 1960s.[22]

Those few who thrilled over Murray's and Lovecraft's creative reimaginings of the supernatural represent a small stream beside the flood tide of those who turned to popular entertainment to reaffirm the values of a racialized, Christian America. For most, Satan retained most of his traditional attributes as the enemy of God, of Christians, and of their society. Fundamentalism and Pentecostalism spoke to a profound unease in the culture over the dangers of modernity. Popular culture increasingly complemented traditional middle-class concerns, and the horror films of the 1930s provided them with the devil they desired.

Turn-of-the-century European (particularly Parisian) fascination with Satanism lay at the roots of the horror film in America. The decadent movement's interest in demonic and supernatural themes had slowly generated a popular audience for macabre entertainment, often presented as dark art for art's sake. By the 1920s, the Théâtre du Grand Guignol in Paris became infamous for its short tales of perversion, mutilation, murder, and Satanism, all presented as a bloodily realistic spectacle. During World War I, the theatre had its heyday, its horrors reflecting (and, in some cases, being inspired by) the horrors of the western front. In 1923, the Grand Guignol made a transatlantic trip to New York City that, according to historian of horror David J. Skal, proved a remarkable failure but still foreshadowed the later success of the genre in America. "The dark gods knew that the republic founded on principles of rational enlightenment," writes Skal, "would have more than an ample shadow side, where monsters might flourish and be free."[23]

Flourish they did. The popularity of Universal's horror films shows the continuing popularity of demonic themes. With one or two exceptions, all of the creatures that crawled, lumbered, and loped out of the faux foggy nights in these films embodied various aspects of satanic lore. Indeed, as Jeffrey Burton Russell suggests, creatures such as these became popular embodiments of the theological vision of satanic evil, just as trolls and giants had been in the Middle Ages. The vampire represents Satan as Mephistopheles, the suave seducer. Frankenstein's monster is the dark beast born out of satanic pride that exalts itself against the divine, mirroring the original Luciferian fall. The werewolf is a creature of secret demonic rites, a cursed and lonely figure in Lon Chaney Jr.'s 1941 incarnation of the beast but still one surrounded with the atmosphere of black, forbidden magic.[24]

Tod Browning's 1931 *Dracula* is perhaps the most significant of the Universal films in terms of tapping into traditional American fears of the devil as cultural enemy. Browning, a former carnival worker and magician, had a string of successes working with Lon Chaney Sr. in the 1920s. Browning had been hired because of his work with Chaney who, Universal executives assumed, would take the role of the Count. "The Man of a Thousand Faces," however, was diagnosed with terminal cancer in 1930, and after a number of other candidates were considered, Universal gave the nod to Hungarian actor Béla Lugosi (who had played the title character in hundreds of theatrical productions of *Dracula*).[25]

Lugosi's accent and operatic style, combined with Browning's easygoing approach to directing that allowed a gifted cinematographer to make crucial decisions, created a masterpiece of the horror genre and a popular success. Despite some early, poor reviews, the film sold 50,000 tickets in two days, a Hollywood landmark. The film would be Universal's highest-grossing entry for 1931. The unexpected success of the film pushed into production James Whale's *Frankenstein* as well as the entire genre of Universal horror films that kept the studio afloat through the Great Depression.[26]

Lugosi's Dracula became the early twentieth century's most powerful embodiment of the devil. Satanic imagery clustered around the character. The opening scene, a rocking carriage on a rugged Balkan road, features a group of frightened peasants and the Englishman Renfield making his way to Castle Dracula. The peasants warn him that he is setting out on Walpurgis Night, a night that, according to European folklore, marks a major gathering of witches with the devil. Goethe injected the idea of Walpurgis Night as a major witches sabbat into popular culture with his *Faust*. The frightened peasants give Renfield a crucifix for protection, a traditional weapon against diabolical power.

When we first see Count Dracula making his way down a spider-webbed stone Gothic stairway, the resonance with Faust grows even stronger. Lugosi appears as a dapper, Mephistophelean character, his aristocratic evening garb suggestive of hundreds of early twentieth-century magicians who used the figure of Mephistopheles in their publicity posters and donned his uniform for their shows. Lugosi's wooing of Renfield further suggests a satanic identity, as does the appearance of the "Brides of Dracula," redolent with a millennium of folklore about women/witches under the thrall of the devil.

The horrors perpetrated by Dracula replicated the American understanding of Satan. The growing American obsession with demonic possession, reflected by the popularity of the Earling, Iowa, account, fit nicely into the Dracula ethos. The self became displaced under the control of the evil count, much as millions of Americans believed the human soul could be lost in the grip of demonic possession. In fact, Pentecostals, as discussed in chapter 4, had a growing belief in the parasitic nature of demonic spirits, believing that they sometimes lived off of the blood of human beings (or even animals). The vampire count drew on all of the religious mythology about the devil.

Conservative anxieties about the "new woman" also play a central role in Dracula. Since the revivals of the eighteenth century, the devil had been seducer and tempter, the primary image conveyed by Lugosi's glaring eyes. Women in particular proved susceptible to his ghastly influence, especially those women who rejected traditional patriarchal controls. The character of Lucy, the opposite of the virginal and proper Mina, gives herself willingly to Dracula, a devil's bondswoman who literally vamps it up onscreen and must be destroyed by a gathering of deeply concerned males. Mina, the proper wife, spends the entire film under threat of seduction. The vampire represented a threat to bourgeois family values.

The conservative resurgence of the 1920s, especially in its distrust of the foreign, also makes itself felt in *Dracula*. The notion of a foreign menace coming to native shores, prowling the streets, seeking victims, and spreading a kind of pollution is at the heart of both Browning's film and

Stoker's earlier novel. This is exactly how the nativist movement of the nineteenth century, reborn in the decade before *Dracula*, imagined the immigrants to America. Notably, a kind of lynch mob or Klan forms around the patriarchal Abraham Van Helsing to destroy the creature and protect white womanhood from the foreign pollution, a climax that darkly resonates with Griffith's *Birth of a Nation*.[27]

Horror historian David Skal has suggested that the horror films of the 1930s became a kind of "popular surrealism, rearranging the human body and its processes, blurring the boundaries between *Homo sapiens* and other species." Horror films did interact with American anxieties about social upheaval and cultural chaos and, in the case of *Dracula* and the vampire tales of the twentieth century, would maintain a close connection with the satanic context of their origin.[28]

Why couldn't Satan himself, rather than his monstrous avatars, portray the ultimate supernatural villain for American audiences? The nature of the audience in the 1930s, as well as the powerful cultural forces that influenced the content of American movies, provide part of the answer. Early filmmakers dealt gingerly with religious themes. In fact, a number of Protestant leaders criticized Cecil B. DeMille's *King of Kings*, fearful that creating a cinematic image of Christ represented something akin to making a graven image and thus perilously close to idolatry and sacrilege. If the film industry had patrons nervous about inspirational portrayals of Jesus Christ, they certainly would not take the risk of creating a religious horror film.[29]

Roman Catholic leaders, meanwhile, exercised tremendous influence in Hollywood by the 1930s. The so-called Legion of Decency, organized by the Archbishop of Cincinnati in 1933, created a rating system for the faithful and encouraged them to take a pledge not to see any film rated "morally objectionable." A devout Catholic layman, Joseph I. Breen, took over the enforcement of the film industries own Production Code in 1934, giving it teeth (the first production code had been written in 1930 by a Jesuit priest, but had not been truly enforced). Such moves showed that the Catholic Church in America, because of its numbers and influence in urban areas, had major cultural capital to spend. It also meant that filmmakers would walk warily around demonic themes, and in fact around religious themes of all kinds, even if they previously had been used to enforce a profound cultural conservatism.[30]

Despite these restrictions, the devil did have a cameo in the monster films of Universal in the 1930s and 1940s. Indeed, soon after the adoption of the production code, he appeared in what has been called "one of the darkest films of the 1930s," *The Black Cat* (1934). The film, with a title borrowed from Edgar Allan Poe but based on nothing in particular in Poe's corpus, starred Béla Lugosi and Boris Karloff in the first, and most successful, of their onscreen partnerships. Karloff plays the head of a coven of Satan worshippers, with Lugosi portraying his enigmatic rival. The *New York Times* review of the film called it "more foolish than horrible," although the reviewer only saw the film after heavy editing by the studio eliminated much of what made it interesting. The original cut of the film, never released in Britain or America, included references to an orgiastic Black Mass, incest, a scene in which Karloff's character is flayed alive, and at least the suggestion of necrophilia. Censors swarmed around the film before its release, cutting and trimming with abandon. Universal executives even demanded specific cuts that replaced mention of "black magic" with an allusion to "sun worship" while also removing a number of references to World War I and the current political situation in Germany.[31]

Despite bad reviews and edits that made parts of the film incomprehensible, *The Black Cat* became Universal's top-grossing film for 1934. American audiences came in droves to see what David Skal calls "a moody mélange of Art Deco demonism and twisted eroticism." They came perhaps because the disturbing spectacle spoke to the anxieties of the era. This was a society with an official patina of traditional values that encircled a very violent nation, an America that generally expressed its support for the production code but also countenanced the continued growth of the Ku Klux Klan and the ongoing carnival of blood in the lynch-prone South. The violence of American life, as well as the moody despair felt by many in the midst of the poverty and hopelessness of the Great Depression, found some catharsis in a film that enacted, even in a shadowy way, the extremes of human behavior and framed it with a satanic plot.[32]

Undoubtedly, the reception of the film was helped by the fact that these evil acts were shown as the pastime of decidedly foreign characters. Karloff's character, chief Satanist Hjalmar Poelzig, lives in what Skal calls a "BauHaus fortress," built on the very site of a major battlefield of the Great War. Lugosi, with his unmistakable accent that had already constructed the satanic foreigner in *Dracula*, played his equally diabolical and equally foreign opponent, Vitus Werdegast. The expressionist lighting and modernist architectural aesthetic clearly rendered the story in a non-American, indeed un-American, milieu that reeked of continental European decadence. "Foreign devils" became a frequent theme even outside the horror genre. The American hatred and horror of the foreign continued in 1944 when Charles Boyer's Mephistophelean character with an Eastern European accent would seduce, menace, and almost drive to madness a nice English girl (Ingrid Bergman!) in *Gaslight*.

Popular culture provided an education in American diabology to the young during this era. Republic Pictures serials represented similar themes to young audiences in *The Mysterious Doctor Satan*. Republic serials created the paradigmatic "cliffhanger," in which young audiences watched short films ending with the hero in a desperate spot. In order to see his escape, the audience would have to return the following Saturday. In *Mysterious Doctor Satan*, the villain is a mad scientist trying to create an army of robots in the American West. Played by Eduardo Cianelli, film historian Grant Tracey describes Doctor Satan as a figure straight off New York's Lower East Side, "played with *Little Caesar* Bravado." The message to young audiences would be clear: the American West, an image redolent with traditional, American nationalism, was endangered by a demonic foreigner.[33]

Doctor Satan appeared before America's entrance into World War II, although also at a time when fears of foreign domination had reached a fever pitch. The end of the decade of the 1930s brought news of a growing threat in Europe combined with a surprisingly optimistic view of the future. By 1939, it seemed as if America had begun to pull itself out of the Great Depression and Rooseveltian optimism defined the official, public culture. The 1939 World's Fair in New York celebrated, even in the architecture of the structures built for it, a shiny, streamlined technological future that would raise standards of living and liberate the human spirit through scientific progress. The world the planners of the fair conjured seemed one swept free of evil spirits, a mentality that seemingly made Satan a relic of the past.[34]

But dark shadows gathered. The threat of fascism overseas coagulated with America's newfound optimism to create a desire for conflict within American culture. Henry Booth Luce, the editor of *Time* magazine, declared in 1941 that the twentieth century would be "the American Century" in world history. While a contrary myth suggests that many Americans felt a profound isolationism in the 1930s, a newer historiography has suggested that a large segment of the American public shared Luce's notion of expansive American power and favored war with the Axis powers. Cultural historians have described a frequently unexpressed longing for a war with evil in late 1930s American culture. The popularity of superhero comics in this period speaks to this longing. In the words of Gerard Jones, the superhero was "an expression of a rising American thrill," the desire to move beyond the doldrums of the Great Depression and flex American muscle. The caped and cowled super beings imagined in comics frequently had religious overtones, while early comic writers and artists imagined their enemies in demonic terms. The entrance of the United States into World War II became a kind of catharsis, a war effort that would provide America with significant degree of cultural unity against an evil foe.[35]

The American encounter with fascism created, at least for some, a willingness to deal with the problem of evil in a sophisticated fashion. Cultural critic Lewis Mumford castigated his fellow liberals in the spring of 1940 for being "unaware of the dark forces of the unconscious" that had found expression in Nazism. He further suggested that they had closed their eyes to the power of evil in the human personality. Franklin Roosevelt, according to one story, read the Danish religious philosopher Søren Kierkegaard during the war at the encouragement of his minister. While it is hard to see the sunny Roosevelt finding pleasure in the dour Dane, he did later tell his secretary of labor that Kierkegaard's scalding examination of human evil had helped him grasp the evils of fascism.[36]

Most Americans did not pursue the philosophical questions raised by the war with such intensity. Young American males, including and especially those who had been (or might be) mobilized in World War II, transmuted the horrors of the real world into the safe graphic terrors of the comic book. Comic books had become a substantial part of America's printed culture by the end of the war, with millions of copies sold each year to an audience made up of all age groups. The comic book sensibility had grown out of the pulp magazines and the radio serials of the 1920s and 1930s, borrowing heavily from these new realms of popular entertainment for narrative material and characters. The science fiction of *Amazing Stories*, the dark heroic deeds of the *Spider* and the *Shadow*, the superhuman prowess of *Doc Savage*, all came together by the late 1930s to produce Superman and Batman. Detective Comics (later known as DC) and Timely Comics (eventually taking the name Marvel) went on to create such iconic characters as Wonder Woman, Green Lantern, the Human Torch, and Captain America.

Comic books would seem to have provided a venue for writers and artists to explore a number of forbidden subjects in the 1930s and 1940s. Having no regulatory board or production code, comic books were theoretically free to explore any number of taboo subjects. Nevertheless, most comic book creators hewed a highly conservative line in the early years of the medium, largely because of fear of censorship. An early issue of Superman, for example, had the Man of Steel fighting against a secret band of "fifth columnists" threatening America. Superhero comics for children and teenagers never ventured very far to the edges of American sensibilities, and a whole genre of comics (known as "funny animal stories") catered specifically to young children.

Nevertheless, both comic books and pulp magazines (the latter largely directed at young males) still found ways to employ the satanic themes that would soon become the obsession of a whole underground cultural mood. Seeking to appeal to post-Victorian sexual mores, many of the pulps blended satanic imagery with erotic appeal. The January 1935 issue of *All Detective Magazine* featured a demonic cobra on its cover, raising its head over a buxom blonde. Imprinted on the vicious snake was an image of a Mephistophelian Satan, ready to pounce on the helpless, and sultry, woman. A novelette that appeared in the May 1936 issue of *Ace Mystery Magazine* told the story of "A Priestess of Pain." The cover depicts what appears to be a Black Mass, with a woman being flung into a sacrificial fire by red-hooded figures. A survey of the pulps from this era also yields stories like "Madame Satan's Yellow Legion" (*Strange Detective Mysteries*, May 1940), "Satan's Roadhouse" (*Terror Tales*, October 1935), and "The Devil's University" (*Mystery Tales*, February 1938).

In at least one case, Satan even appeared as a costumed hero. The 1938 pulp hero *Captain Satan* terrified the criminal underworld with his technological prowess and theatrical use of demonic imagery. Notably, he had only a short cultural life, disappearing after one or two novelettes. Americans, even those who consumed marginal cultural materials, were not ready (as they would be later in the century) for a hero connected to what their churches understood as the enemy of faith.

One comic title managed to create edgy material while constructing a set of tales well within the parameters of conservative cultural acceptability. Taking its name from an unrelated 1930 film, *Madam Satan* featured a supernatural version of the silent-era vamp in a comic that began its run in November 1941. Sensual and sultry, she walked the earth in search of male souls to devour. Ron Goulart's *Comic Book Encyclopedia* quotes the following caption from one of the now-rare books: "The Devil searched far and long for an ally to wreak havoc amongst mortals. . . . Then the black, corrupt soul of a beautiful woman, a victim of her own fiendish plan on earth, left its bodily habitation to stand before the king of purgatory . . . and his search was at an end . . . the Devil had found himself a fitting mate."[37]

Madam Satan blended together American misogyny and satanic lore into a tutorial in gender bias for the teenage boys attracted to her plunging necklines and Gene Tierney good looks. Life, especially male life, was viewed in the comic as lived in the midst of a web of devilish conspiracy. The beautiful vamp failed in most of her efforts to condemn souls to hell, although she did cut a swath of destruction through the lives she grasped at. Unlike some of her silver-screen predecessors, her association with the devil was no metaphor. She had supernatural powers (including the ability to turn into a giant bat) that presented her as the devil's literal partner. While parents could not have been pleased with the sensual packaging of the message, *Madam Satan* actually delivered a profoundly conservative cultural message about the dangers of sexuality and women's autonomy (and anatomy).

Satan also provided easy political satire in the 1940s, a register more of the seriousness of most Americans' belief in him than his usefulness as comic relief. The 1942 *The Devil with Hitler* recycled the plot of *To Hell with the Kaiser*, showing Satan dismissed by hell's board of directors for falling behind the German fuehrer in acts of evil. Satan incarnates himself as one of Hitler's advisors and uses trickery to convince the dictator to perform one good deed. This allows Satan to reclaim his throne. The comedy short ends with Hitler being poked and prodded into hell with pitchforks by some fairly unconvincing demons. While it would be easy to place too much cultural weight on a short film meant to complement a double bill on a long Saturday afternoon, it is notable that an America that generally believed in the reality of the devil could celebrate his triumph over its foreign enemies.[38]

In Fundamentalist circles, belief in the reality of Satan found expression during World War II in a growing fascination with the figure of the Antichrist. Robert C. Fuller notes that conservative Protestantism in America has, at one time or another, identified "Jews, labor unions, blacks, socialists, Catholics and liberal government leaders" as pawns in a much larger satanic conspiracy. Indeed, Fuller notes that historian Richard Hofstadter wrote that apocalyptic beliefs about the Antichrist in the twentieth century strengthened the nativist tendencies already present in American politics to the point that many American religious leaders came to believe that "History is a conspiracy, set in motion by demonic forces of almost transcendental power."[39]

A global conflict left plenty of room for speculation about which of America's enemies represented the Antichrist. Adolph Hitler had frequently been the center of speculation but, for the most part, American Fundamentalists concluded that Benito Mussolini, fascist dictator of Italy, fit the bill. In 1933, Gerard Winrod's *Mussolini's Place in Prophecy* suggested that the Italian leader had created a revived Roman Empire that would be a threat to true Christians (and to the United States). Fundamentalist leaders pointed to the dictator's 1929 concordat with the Vatican as proof of his satanic identity. The Antichrist, they believed, would have an alliance with a figure from the Book of Revelation known as the False Prophet. In the eyes of many conservative Protestants, what could this be but a symbol of the Roman pontiff? Apocalyptic speculation could be fueled both by anti-Catholicism and fervid nationalism.[40]

American nationalism proved to be at such a fever pitch during the course of the war that even small dissident groups who would seem to care little for the success of Christian America threw themselves into the effort. Ironically, some believed fervently that the devil was on the side of the United States and considered this a positive thing. Former pulp novelist and famed horror film director Val Lewton was renowned for wanting to learn as much about the phenomena he filmed as possible. In 1943, as he prepared to film the *Seventh Victim*, Lewton asked screenwriter Dewitt Bodeen to see if he could attend a meeting "of one of those devil-worshiping groups." Bodeen was able to find a small group of neo-pagans, inspired by Margaret Murray's work, meeting on New York's Upper West Side. Bodeen was surprised to discover a hardy patriotism among his hosts, who spent much of the meeting he attended casting hexes on Adolph Hitler. Bodeen described them as "tea drinking old ladies and gentlemen sitting there muttering imprecations against Hitler."[41]

Despite discovering that "Satanism" in American appeared to be fairly harmless, Bodeen and Lewton couldn't resist the opportunity to use the Prince of Darkness in one of the most important satanic films made in the twentieth century, one that set the tone for numerous cinematic portrayals to come. *The Seventh Victim* not only provided the plot structure for many of the films in what would become a late twentieth-century "satanic renaissance," but also drew on the growing belief among conservatives that modernity was being driven by a satanic conspiracy.

Lewton made use of his screenwriter's research in creating *The Seventh Victim* and in doing so marked a significant departure from previous fictional works concerned with the devil. Satan does not work through monstrous beings, nor does he bother with the temptation of individual souls. His concerns are broader. *The Seventh Victim* is not in the European wasteland of *The Black Cat* but rather a modern, if hellish, New York City. The story revolves around a group of well-heeled Satanists, all appearing at first to be little more than Upper East Side sophisticates, hunting down a former member played by Jean Brooks. Using many of the camera techniques of film noir, modern New York becomes a moving nightmare where the unfortunate characters discover secret Satanists almost everywhere they turn for help. Brooks, the traitorous former member of the group, finally commits suicide, the seventh victim to meet her death in an effort to escape what is apparently a very large, well-organized satanic conspiracy.[42]

Lewton's film marked the beginning of a new and influential image of Satan in American popular culture that easily entwined with new themes in American religion. Rather than a demon that must be combated by individuals, the devil in *Seventh Victim* seemed to have created a large network of followers at every level of modern American society. While nineteenth- and early twentieth-century Protestantism believed that spiritual warfare should be extended to the realm of social reform, the picture painted by Lewton suggested that the devil hid not only at the bottom of a bottle or in the immigrant sections of urban areas but also amid the ranks of the respectable. He is guiding a conspiracy with tendrils in every aspect of life, similar to the Rev. Timothy Dwight's belief about the Illuminati.

This image of Satan's work in America was less a departure than it seemed. Fundamentalism had already found its voice by challenging the American mainstream as corrupted by the devil. Pentecostals, many of whom remained outside of the sphere of social and cultural power, had little trouble believing that those on the inside had made a bargain with the Prince of Darkness. World War II, as we have seen, increased speculation about the identity of the Antichrist, a figure believed by most prophecy adepts to be hidden and secret, spinning out a conspiratorial web that would only be revealed when it was too late. *Seventh Victim* provided those anxieties with a reflection in popular culture. It became part of a new definition of spiritual warfare in which the devil was conceived to be, almost literally, everywhere.

The idea that the devil led a vast, conspiratorial network of followers found expression in a number of trends in American politics and popular culture. Both the HUAC hearings and Joe McCarthy's bitter anticommunist crusade show the influence of the idea that evil could be detected and driven out in a fashion not unlike many American Christians believed that evil spirits could be discovered and exorcised. American innocence might be (indeed would be) threatened by evil, but it could also be defended by Christian knights if only the conspiracy of evil could be exposed.

The mid-century popularity of detective stories and film noir underscores the significance of these ideas in popular culture. The 1920s pulp magazine *The Black Mask* (started by H. L. Mencken as a money-making scheme) told stories of hard-boiled private eyes and published the works of Dashiel Hammett, Lester Dent, Raymond Chandler, and other greats of the genre. The style of these writers catered to only a niche market in America until the 1940s, but they found expression in the larger culture through film. They created a moral universe—or perhaps an amoral universe—beyond good and evil, heroes who sometimes seemed to share in the corruption of their villains.

Hard-boiled fiction entered the American dreamscape when it came to Hollywood. The genre of film noir that exploded into popularity in the 1940s managed to embody some of the central themes of America's fascination with Satan, reflecting in popular secularized forms some of the nation's most naive assumptions about the nature of evil. A universe swept clean of moral absolutes, the popular perception of the meaning of film noir would be a universe in which Satan could find little purchase. In fact, film noir provided yet another arena in which America could reproduce its fear and hatred of the Other.

Women provided structure and form for the genre's demonology. American popular culture's tendency to identify satanic evil with women continued in both pulp crime fiction and film noir. John Leland describes "a river of misogyny" that flowed out of this genre. Writing on Dashiell Hammett, the author of the *Maltese Falcon*, Leland comments that he "restored the evil of Poe's horror stories, planting it in a plush office or a tight skirt." In classic films such as *Double Indemnity*, *Criss Cross*, *The Killers*, and *The Woman in the Window*, women offer erotic seduction that leads to destruction. In almost all of these films, they take on a Mephistophelean role of offering the male character a world of both erotic and economic bounty in exchange for his willingness to commit murder. Thus, Satan continued to appear in the shape of a woman, most explicitly in the first filmed version of *The Maltese Falcon* entitled *The Devil Was a Lady*.[43]

Film noir tapped not only America's misogynistic vein, but also its increasing fascination with the idea of the conspiracy of evil. The heroes are sometimes nihilistic detectives, but at other times the central characters are innocents entwined in a web of evil. Two of Bogart's classic films, *The Big Sleep* and *To Have and to Have Not* are grounded in a premise similar to Lewton's *Seventh Victim*: everyone is in on it, the conspiracy runs deeper than you imagine, the devil has infested every corner of the world, and you are left to stand alone against him. Many Americans worried, especially after World War II, that this was precisely the dilemma of America in the modern world. The threat of Communism, both internal and external, seemed to turn America into a lone hero in a noir drama facing a corrupt world and willing to do whatever was necessary in order to defeat that corruption.

Such anxieties fit well the America of the late 1940s and early 1950s. The postwar mood in America exhibited far more nervousness than is sometimes recognized. Although today the period is often remembered as a time of triumphal conservatism (especially by contemporary conservatives), America in the shadow of the bomb registered significant anxiety about the direction of the nation and the fate of the world. In fact, the assertions of traditionalism in domesticity and the escape into the materialistic comforts of the suburbs can be explained in part by the anxieties of a world in the midst of change.

Despite, and largely because of, these anxieties, American public culture in the postwar period embraced conformity and consensus. Mary Caputi has written that everything from advertising to film and television in the 1950s "contributed to . . . an image of wholeness" in American life. Caputi argues that, although the postwar era constituted a period of "collective angst concerning impending doom," the images in American popular culture shaped the belief that the world was a safe and beneficent place, that the secure domestic bliss of Ozzie and Harriet and the paintings of Norman Rockwell constituted the center of American identity. One striking example of this longing for consensus is the end of American film noir and the death of the gangster film. Dark tales, even ones that seemed to reaffirm the American fascination with evil, fell from popular favor. One of the final efforts, the 1955 *A Bullet for Joey*, starring old gangster pros Edward G. Robinson and George Raft, featured the FBI and organized crime teaming up to defeat a Communist threat. The age of consensus had truly come.[44]

The Cold War provided the context for most of the speculation about the devil's activities in the 1950s. Whittaker Chambers, a former Communist whose testimony before HUAC led to the prosecution of Alger Hiss, wrote that "Communism . . . is, in fact, man's second oldest faith. Its promise was whispered in the first days of creation under the Tree of Knowledge of Good and Evil." Some of America's most important religious leaders joined Chambers in the belief that Communism came from the lies of the serpent. The devil, according to Billy Graham, was the secret partner to America's Cold War nemesis. Graham in the early 1950s fully endorsed the Korean War as a crusade against evil and increasingly used the language of demonology to describe the enemies of America. Francis Cardinal Spellman of New York, the most powerful Catholic prelate in America in the 1950s, also defined Communism as a threat from hell itself.[45]

Joseph McCarthy's crusade against Communism had all the attributes of a witch hunt and fed off of the conspiratorial "paranoid style" of American politics. McCarthy's infamous February 1950 speech described his efforts as "the final, all-out struggle between communistic atheism and Christianity." His model of a Communist conspiracy at every level of government and society replicated the conspiratorial imaginings of Christian Fundamentalism and the pop-culture versions of the same ideas in *Seventh Victim* and *Madam Satan*. The unity of conservative Christians, Protestants, and Catholics behind his efforts also presaged the coalition building that would create the Christian Right of the 1970s.

The devil by the 1950s played a central role in the rhetoric of politicians and religious crusaders and made headlines in the *Washington Post* and the *New York Times*. At the same time, he briefly absented himself from popular film. Nicholas Schreck, in his study of the role of the devil in American film, notes that the monsters of science fiction seemed to take the place of the devil as the cinematic Other in the beginning of the atomic age. Efforts to censor comic books, given impetus by psychiatrist Fredric Wertham's *Seduction of the Innocent* and public hearings by a congressional committee, successfully exorcised the devil and the supernatural from sequential art. Countercultural voices, ironically, made an effort to bring him back. Increasingly, American writers and artists, instead of using the devil as a tool to inscribe marginality and otherness, used his marginality and otherness to subvert the dominant paradigms of American society.[46]

Ray Bradbury, the first fantasy/science fiction author in America to achieve success beyond the world of the pulps, used the devil to expose the dark underbelly of American life. Sometimes characterized as "an outspoken liberal," Bradbury is better understood as an outspoken political radical whose mountain of novels and short stories in the 1940s and 1950s (a mountain that continued to grow over subsequent decades) challenged American consumerism, misogyny, racism, and even establishment liberalism for its unwillingness to move from reform to a democratic social revolution. The devils of Melville, Poe, and Twain live in the satanic figures that Bradbury created.[47]

In his famous fictionalized memoir, *Dandelion Wine*, Bradbury evokes the small-town America of Norman Rockwell. But this same small-town innocence is haunted by a dark stalker who murders his victims in the abyss of a nearby ravine. If the films of Val Lewton had taken monstrosities out of Universal's faux European fairylands and placed them squarely in modern New York, Bradbury found evil living in small-town America. The devil prowls the margins of this supposedly safe American world and calls into question its basic assertions and understanding of itself. Similar themes emerged in *Something Wicked This Way Comes* (1962) in which "Mr. Dark" strikes a Faustian pact with the inhabitants of a supposedly innocent small town, granting their secret cravings for a price. Most of these Midwesterners long for lost youth, a metaphor for America's craving for innocence and freedom from moral guilt. As with so many dissident writers, Bradbury's vision imagines an America that has traded its soul to the devil. Both books would exercise enormous influence over novelist Stephen King's works *It* and *Needful Things*.

Less well-known than Bradbury, Charles Beaumont made even more frequent use of satanic imagery to critique postwar America's indulgence in racism, sexual repression, moralistic censorship, gender inequality, and unbridled consumerism. Satan represents the chaotic realties that upend the American applecart. The devil in this context could take the form of Twain's spirit of daring, offering liberation and freedom for the natural instincts. In his short story "The Dark Music," Beaumont has a Midwestern high school teacher, lost like Dante in a dark wood, seduced by a beautiful, somewhat androgynous, creature that is equal parts Satan and Pan.

In his essay "The Devil and Charles Beaumont," David Cochran writes that "Beaumont suffused his universe with religious underpinnings, though his theology placed greater emphasis on the Devil than on God." Beaumont's fiction challenged the economic rationalism of 1950s America by suggesting that the supernatural, often in its darkest form, lay beneath the stylized conformity of Levittown and the economic rationalism of the man in the gray flannel suit. An example of this appears in Beaumont's first published short story, "The Devil, You Say?" In this tale, Beaumont has a Luciferian newspaper editor take over the press of an American small town. Soon the outrageous stories he prints (such as "Farmer Burl Illing Complains of Mysterious Appearance of Dragons in His Backyard") begin to come true. He offers the owner of the paper the opportunity to enjoy continued success in exchange for his soul.[48]

In 1963, Beaumont's story of the small-town newspaper that went to hell was revised to become a *Twilight Zone* episode called "The Printer's

Devil." Significantly different from the published story, the televised version of the story tapped into themes of the two Americas that had emerged in the late twentieth century. "As a sophisticated, intelligent, educated twentieth-century man," Satan asks his prey, "You know the devil does not exist. True?" The devil has a laugh at the newspaperman's expense, a laugh that comes with layer of irony. "Imagine that," he says, "a grown man who believes in the devil." The irony of placing doubts about the devil's existence in the devil's own mouth clearly sought to shatter the self-satisfaction of America in the early 1960s. Beaumont here suggests, in the words of David Cochran, that Americans at the beginning of the 1960s were "unprepared to comprehend the extent and nature of modern evil."[49]

Satan had reached a turning point in his long life in America. A culture of irony continued to raise questions about the reality of the devil, while a significantly larger group of Americans believed that Satan was alive and active in the world, that he had followers who had created a world-wide conspiracy, that he was the secret force behind everything from Communism to urban riots. By the end of the turbulent decade, the rosy worldview and optimistic metaphysics of mainline Protestant liberalism seemed much further away than the early twentieth century. The powerful images of American popular culture, the dynamism of American religious enthusiasm, and the dark realities of American history were coming together in a perfect demonic storm. Robert Johnson met the devil at the crossroads of Henry Booth Luce's American century. In the decades ahead, Satan expanded his American realm even as America attempted to expand its own. The clock struck midnight, and Lucifer's time had come.

NOTES

1. Pete Daniel, *Standing at the Crossroads: Southern Life in the Twentieth Century* (Baltimore: Johns Hopkins University Press, 1996), 22.

2. Peter Guralnick, *Searching for Robert Johnson* (New York: Plume/Penguin Group, 1998), 1, 2. See also Elijah Wald, *Escaping the Delta: Robert Johnson and the Invention of the Blues* (New York: HarperCollins, 2004).

3. Francis Davis, *The History of the Blues* (New York: Da Capo Press, 1995), 129.

4. Edward J. Blum, *Reforging the White Republic: Race, Religion, and American Nationalism, 1865–1898* (Baton Rouge: Louisiana State University Press, 2005), 244–47.

5. Important studies of the economics of the 1920s include Irving Bernstein, *The Lean Years: A History of the American Worker, 1920–1933* (Baltimore: Johns Hopkins University Press, 1966), and Daniel, *Standing at the Crossroads*. On the growth of the Ku Klux Klan and its goals, see Kenneth T. Jackson, *The Ku Klux Klan in the*

City, 1915–1930 (New York: Oxford University Press, 1967). On racial violence, the so-called riots are covered by Herbert Shapiro, *White Violence and the Black Response: From Reconstruction to Montgomery* (Amherst: University of Massachusetts Press, 1988).

6. Peter Berger introduced the notion of "plausibility structures" in two important works, *The Sacred Canopy* (New York: Doubleday, 1967) and *The Homeless Mind: Modernization and Consciousness* (New York: Doubleday, 1974).

7. Lawrence Levine, *Black Culture and Black Consciousness* (Oxford: Oxford University Press, 1977), 160.

8. Levine, *Black Culture*, 233–34.

9. Rudi Blesh, *Shining Trumpets: A History of Jazz* (London: Cassell & Company, 1958).

10. Ellis Hanson, *Decadence and Catholicism* (Cambridge, MA: Harvard University Press, 1997), 3.

11. LeRoy Ashby, *With Amusement for All* (Lexington: University Press of Kentucky, 2006), viii. See also chapter 6 of Ashby's work that describes the American film industry's "search for respectability" that attempted to meld traditional values with a chic modern style, all in an effort to please America's "respectable classes."

12. Wyn Craif Wade, *The Fiery Cross: The Ku Klux Klan in America* (New York: Oxford University Press, 1998), 144.

13. Nikolas Schreck, *The Satanic Screen: An Illustrated Guide to the Devil in Cinema* (London: Creation Books, 2001), 28.

14. Schreck, *The Satanic Screen*, 29.

15. Janet Staiger, *Bad Women: Regulating Sexuality in Early American Cinema* (Minneapolis: University of Minnesota Press, 1995), xiii, 17.

16. Ronald Genini, *Theda Bara: A Biography of the Silent Screen Vamp, with a Filmography* (Jefferson, NC: McFarland & Co., 1996) 53; Schreck, *The Satanic Screen*, 29.

17. Andrew Delbanco, *The Death of Satan: How Americans Have Lost the Sense of Evil* (New York: Farrar, Straus and Giroux, 1995), 187.

18. Delbanco, *The Death of Satan*, chapter 5, especially 185–88.

19. Edward J. Larsen, *Summer for the Gods: The Scopes Trial and America's Continuing Debate over Science and Religion* (New York: Basic Books, 2006).

20. Margot Adler, *Drawing Down the Moon: Witches, Druids, Goddess-Worshippers, and Other Pagans in America Today* (Boston: Beacon Press, 1986), 46–49.

21. S. T. Joshi, introduction to *The Annotated H. P. Lovecraft*, ed. S. T. Joshi (New York: Dell Publishing, 1997), 11–13.

22. Christopher Knowles, *Our Gods Wear Spandex: The Secret History of Comic Book Heroes* (San Francisco: Weiser Books, 2007), 93; Gavin Baddeley, *Lucifer Rising: Sin, Devil Worship, and Rock and Roll.* (London: Plexus Publishing, 2006), 70.

23. David J. Skal, *The Monster Show: A Cultural History of Horror* (New York: Faber and Faber Inc., 2001), 55, 60–61.

24. Russell suggests that modern horror collects the attributes of Satan (and vice versa) in much the same way that medieval peasant folktales influenced, and were influenced by, theological beliefs about the devil. See Jeffrey Burton Russell, *Prince of Darkness: Radical Evil and the Power of Good in History* (Ithaca, NY: Cornell University Press, 1988), 111.

25. David J. Skal, *Hollywood Gothic: The Tangled Web of Dracula from Stage to Screen* (New York: Faber and Faber, 2004), 172–74.

26. Kendall R. Phillips, *Projected Fears: Horror Films and American Culture* (Westport, CT: Praeger Publishers, 2005), 13.

27. Phillips, *Projected Fears*, 22–25.

28. Skal, *The Monster Show*, 114.

29. W. Barnum Tatum, *Jesus at the Movies: A Guide to the First Hundred Years* (New York: Polebridge Press, 2004).

30. See Tatum, *Jesus at the Movies*, 48, 57, 62.

31. "The Black Cat: Not Related to Poe," *New York Times*, May 19, 1934; Schreck, *The Satanic Screen*, 55.

32. Skal, *The Monster Show*, 177–80.

33. Grant Tracey, "The Mysterious Doctor Satan," *Images*, issue no. 4.

34. David Gelernter, *1939: The Lost World of the Fair* (New York: Harper Perennial, 1996).

35. Gerard Jones, *Men of Tomorrow: Geeks, Gangsters, and the Birth of the Comic Book* (New York: Basic Books, 2004), 233.

36. Delbanco, *The Death of Satan*, 190–91.

37. Ron Goulart, *Comic Book Encyclopedia: The Ultimate Guide to Characters, Graphic Novels, Writers, and Artists in the Comic Book Universe* (New York: HarperEntertainment, 2004), 244.

38. Schreck, *The Satanic Screen*, 65–66.

39. Robert C. Fuller, *Naming the Antichrist: The History of an American Obsession* (New York: Oxford University Press, 1995), 137.

40. Fuller, *Naming the Antichrist*, 161.

41. Schreck, *The Satanic Screen*, 70

42. Schreck, *The Satanic Screen*, 70–73.

43. John Leland, *Hip: The History* (New York: HarperCollins, 2004), 96.

44. Mary Caputi, *A Kinder, Gentler America: Melancholia and the Mythical Fifties* (Minneapolis: University of Minnesota Press, 2005), 114, 115.

45. A full discussion of this issue appears in Thomas Aiello, "Constructing 'Godless Communism': Religion, Politics, and Popular Culture, 1954–1960," *Americana: The Journal of American Popular Culture* 4, no. 1 (Spring 2005).

46. Schreck, *The Satanic Screen*, 79.

47. David Cochran, *American Noir: Underground Writers and Filmmakers of the Postwar Era* (Washington, DC: Smithsonian Books, 2000), 69.

48. Cochran, *American Noir*, 74.

49. Cochran, *American Noir*, 88.

6

Lucifer Rising: Satanic Panics and Culture Wars

In December 1973, Satan's celebrity status reached its apotheosis in *The Exorcist*, perhaps the most significant horror film in cinematic history. In major cities, long lines snaked around entire city blocks as moviegoers waited for an opportunity to see a film that had become a cultural sensation. Enormous crowds forced the management of Cinema One in midtown Manhattan to turn away fans that had waited four hours to get in to an opening show, starting a small riot. In the Chicago suburbs, complaints of noise and property damage heralded the film's opening. In Beverly Hills, one theatre began showing the film at 8:00 AM to meet the enormous demand and still had to turn away thousands of people.[1]

The Exorcist is based on a novel by William Peter Blatty. Blatty's interest in demon possession was influenced by his own complicated relationship to Catholicism and inspired by a 1949 exorcism that had taken place in Mt. Rainer, Maryland, during Blatty's student days at Georgetown University. The novel and the film tell the story of an adolescent girl named Regan (echoing the rebellious daughter of Lear in Shakespeare's tragedy) possessed by the ancient demonic spirit called Pazuzu. Her mother is forced to turn to two priests, Father Karras and Father Merrin, as her daughter's upstairs bedroom becomes a carnival of horrors. The bed floats, sacrileges abound, and blood and green vomit splatter as the camera pulls audiences into the small, claustrophobic room with the demonic child and the embattled priests. The nuanced ending leaves many feeling that evil has triumphed.

Audience reactions at the time represented a phenomenon in and of themselves. Only days after the film's nationwide release, reports began to filter in of a bizarre physical and psychological reaction that American audiences were having in response to the disturbing images on the screen. Although some of these reports, especially those hyped by theatre managers, can be attributed to efforts at free publicity, hundreds of people did have reactions that ranged from vomiting, to weeks of nightmares to, in a slim number of cases, psychological breakdowns.[2]

The Exorcist, both in the story it told and the cultural impact it made, had implications that stretched far beyond its power to overwhelm audiences. The film drew on images of demonic evil that went back to the American founding and stretched back through the Middle Ages. It inaugurated a moment in American cultural life when the devil occupied a place in public discourse not held at any time or place in America since the New England settlements of the seventeenth century. While Satan had always been a primary site for the construction of American notions of innocence and of evil, by the 1980s the demonic had become a central cultural discourse, a social mechanism that worked on multiple levels of American religion and popular entertainment. The devil's stories and legends became more important than God's in defining cultural heroes and villains for millions of Americans. At the same time, other cultural voices reimagined the image of Satan, rejecting elements of the traditional imagery associated with the devil and turning him into a pop star or a metaphorical representation of rebellion against middle-class norms. Lucifer had ascended to a new height in the American cultural mentality, one from which the proud rebel could not be easily cast down.

Changes in the American Satan can be tracked along the trajectory of profound changes in American history. Violence, whether in the form of the Vietnam conflict or the assassinations of Robert F. Kennedy and Martin Luther King Jr., seemed endemic to American society. Watergate, meanwhile, suggested that a dark corruption worked at the highest levels of government. Conservative journalist William Safire later described the actions of the Nixon administration as a series of "evil offenses" that resulted in a profound constitutional crisis. The crisis, taking place in a context of post-Vietnam uncertainty, led to a ruthless questioning of not only the direction taken by the United States, but even the ideals of the nation.[3]

The change in the American experience from the inauguration of John F. Kennedy to the cold December morning in 1973 when crowds waited to view *The Exorcist* can be understood in part as an American confrontation with evil. The reality of history deconstructed the deeply held belief in American innocence, a cultural pattern solidly hardwired into the American system by the late 1950s. The struggle to preserve American innocence had never been more intense, as the reality of America's deep entanglement with real historical evil became undeniable.

More than anything else, the war in Vietnam and unease about its conduct brought Americans face-to-face with the reality of evil. In past wars and foreign adventures, the home front had always been able to legitimize both violence done to the enemy and violence endured by veterans. Popular culture had tended to shape public opinion, but before the late 1960s, limited media outlets had prevented Americans from hearing most of what their support for a particular war actually meant. The 1960s forever transformed these realities. American actions against Cuba in the Bay of Pigs debacle of 1962 had humiliated patriotic Americans while raising new questions about the national government's behavior around the world. Intervention in the Dominican Republic in 1965 seemed to identify the United States as little more than another global empire, eager to protect its spheres of influence. Vietnam represented not only the decline of American power but also the death of American innocence. The use of fragmentation bombing and napalm that scarred, wounded, and killed civilians, combined with Lyndon Johnson's boast that the air force "can't even bomb an outhouse without my approval," made all but the most traditionally patriotic anxious.

Vietnam prevented the American people from seeing themselves as "innocents abroad" and its soldiers as heroes and liberators. Incidents such as the My Lai massacre raised questions about individual American combatants as well as the institutions they represented. Films such as *The Deer Hunter* raised the possibility that, rather than being noble warriors in the struggle against evil, GIs were both perpetrators and victims of evil. Audie Murphy, once the symbol of the happy warrior abroad, was replaced by Christopher Walken's and Robert De Niro's portrayals of horrifically wounded, despairing, and suicidal former soldiers. Like some of America's most idealistic leaders of the past decade, they too were being destroyed by the violence living at the very heart of the American experience.[4]

Americans could not even pretend to be innocents at home in the 1960s. The civil rights struggle in the South, and similar initiatives in the urban North, lifted the dark veil off of a century-long story of violence and terror. National African American leaders such as Martin Luther King and Stokeley Carmichael joined with local activists like Fanny Lou Hamer and Fred Shuttlesworth to challenge Jim Crow, both as a legal structure and a cultural discourse. Their nonviolent campaigns of boycotts, marches, sit-ins, and other forms of public demonstration brought the realities of white violence into the national media. Torture, rape, and murder had always been the warp and woof of the Southern experience. The civil rights struggle took the serpent by the head with the intention of drawing out all of its poison. The serpent itself entered the national consciousness as American families watched images of dogs being unleashed on children in Bull Connor's Birmingham in 1963, the same year that a group of white Mississippians murdered three civil rights workers (two of them Northern whites) as retribution for their efforts to register voters during the Mississippi "Freedom Summer."

The civil rights struggle represented one of the most significant efforts in a broader wave of dissent that challenged the American consensus. At no other time in American history has the critique of American society become so trenchant, played such a role in popular culture, or influenced in some way every segment of society. Progressives in the women's and civil rights movements called on America to remember its promises of democracy while also damning America for its failure to live up to those ideals. The 1960s gave birth to a culture of protest.

Seemingly shell-shocked by the sudden, powerful emergence of voices long silenced by custom and by law, the mainstream struck back in the late 1960s. The candidacy of Richard Nixon, with his promise to bring "law and order" for the "silent majority," provided the first glimpse of the coming conservative ascendancy.

This construction of the world, in which America still represented a pristine innocence under attack by the darkest of foes, deeply influenced the course of American political and cultural history. The strength of political conservatism that would continue to grow during the 1970s was matched by the strength of newly powerful religious dynamism in some of America's most conservative religious denominations. While mainline Protestantism posted enormous membership declines, highly conservative denominations such as the Southern Baptists and the Churches of Christ grew in strength. Moreover, as has been noted in an earlier chapter, the Pentecostal movement exploded in strength during the 1960s, acquiring wealth and respectability.

The most striking aspect of Pentecostal, or what was increasingly called "Charismatic," churches is that after they acquired their new status in American society they returned happily and forcefully to some of their earlier themes about the power of the Holy Spirit to cast out devils. Exorcism, along with the phenomenon of "speaking in tongues" and healing, became the most clearly identifiable characteristics of the Charismatic movement. The 1960s would see the emergence of a number of Charismatic leaders, many of them coming from a mainline Protestant background, who founded so-called deliverance ministries. These organizations eschewed more conventional definitions of Christian ministries and perceived their efforts as, in essence, a struggle with the devil through exorcising souls beset by demonic forces. At a time when the downtown Presbyterian and Methodist churches became increasingly empty, this movement picked up many of the mainline denominations' lost sheep. Like the religious entrepreneurs of the eighteenth and nineteenth century Edwards, Finney, Moody, and many more, the new Charismatic leadership found a ready market for their dynamic brand of Christianity. Increasingly, they focused their attention on the power of Satan that, they claimed, had been unleashed in the social upheavals of American society.

Don Basham became one of the more influential of these leaders. Basham, a former Disciples of Christ minister, had been trained in a mainline Protestant seminary and was not even sure he believed in a literal devil until he experienced a series of encounters with demonic evil, which he recounts in *Deliver Us from Evil*. By the mid-1960s, Basham was performing regular exorcisms and had acquired Derek Prince, a well-known and highly influential Charismatic teacher, as his mentor. By the end of the 1960s, he and Prince were traveling the country performing "group deliverances," exorcisms of all the evil spirits in an enclosed room full of the possessed.[5]

If Basham's *Deliver Us from Evil* offered for Charismatic Christians an overarching narrative for their battle against the devil, Frank and Isa Mae Hammond's *Pigs in the Parlor* provided them with a handbook. This unlikely bestseller (over 1 million copies in print) actually bills itself as "a practical guide to deliverance" and cites Derek Prince as a primary influence. In Frank and Ida Mae's view, one did not have to be a leader like Prince in the Charismatic renewal movement to combat the devil. In fact, they insisted that "it is the responsibility of every Christian to deal with [demons] directly in spiritual warfare."[6]

The Hammonds held Satan responsible for almost all of the darker aspects of human life. An elaborate taxonomy of demons appears in their work, a chart that stretches over three pages of small print but that the Hammonds themselves insist "is by no means intended to be exhaustive." The chart assumes that demons inhabit an individual soul in "groupings," centered around a diabolical captain they call "a ruling spirit" or a "strong man." So, for example, a demon of the occult might enter the soul but likely bring with it lesser demons of "witchcraft," "charms," and "astrology." A demon of sexual impurity might possess but will likely bring with it a demon of "fornication," "adultery," or "frigidity" (although why the first two might want to inhabit a soul with the last is not explained).

In the Hammonds' view, a single soul might be possessed by literally hundreds of demonic spirits. In their cosmology, in fact, most human beings probably are possessed by such legions. The demon-hunting couple insisted that most of the sorrows to which the flesh is heir had their roots in demonic activity. So, for example, the soul might be taken over by a demon of indecision that would bring with it a whole household of evil spirits such as procrastination, compromise, and forgetfulness. Someone suffering from depression might be possessed by a demon of grief that would bring along its flunkies "sorrow" and "crying."

The Hammonds seem to have had little doubt about the validity of their elaborate map of the demonic world, even if it seems they had no epistemological basis for their certitudes. Notably, their taxonomy of the spirit world bears some relationship to similar charts of demonic spirits and "generals of hell" made by early modern witch hunters. The idea of the omnipresence of satanic evil, shared by most of the major leaders in the Charismatic deliverance movement, meant that almost everyone could benefit from an exorcism. In fact, they insisted, infants *and even fetuses* can be possessed by the devil. Children who are "rebellious and unmanageable" are likely possessed by a demon of self-will. Their often-bizarre treatise showed a willingness to give the devil credit for manifestations of childhood angst perfectly explainable from the very evidence they provide. In one instance, they describe a couple bringing to them a child they describe as "traumatized" by watching their parents have a "violent argument." The Hammonds concluded that the infant must have a "tormenting demon" and performed an exorcism on her.

Numerous efforts have been made to explain the rise in popularity of these naive explanations for personal and social ills at a time in American history when naïveté had seemingly gone out of vogue. One interpretation suggests that the rise of "Charismatic deliverance" constituted a religious version of the ideology of self-improvement and success shared by most of its white, middle class, suburban participants. The rise of these ministries occurred close to the time of the emergence of motivational speakers, who produced books, tapes, and seminars that promised white suburbanites success at work, at home, and in their inner life through reciting optimistic phrases and maintaining positive attitudes. Charismatic deliverance promised something similar (and perhaps no less magical) with the casting out of demons replacing self-help as the path to happiness and success.[7]

While the search for personal fulfillment that marked the baby boomer generation played some role in this phenomenon, the source for this cultural movement is more closely related to the political rather than the psychological. Charismatic deliverance practitioners passed along a far darker worldview than the one favored by the motivational speakers. They believed in a world where cruel and vicious spirits hunted humans for prey. They also believed that these same demonic forces had a political agenda. The preachers of Charismatic renewal were casting out the demons of the 1960s, seeking law and order in the spiritual realm even as they voted for it on Election Day. A profoundly conservative social and cultural message can be decoded within the discourse about demon spirits. "Hope for our nation and communities does not lie in government and social programs," *Pigs in the Parlor* assures us. After a decade of efforts directed at fulfilling the American promise through civil rights legislation, such rhetoric could have only one meaning. Moreover, the Hammonds' ministry seems largely directed at restoring traditional roles within the American domestic sphere. A series of "teaching tapes" offered at the end of *Pigs in the Parlor* promises a full explication of "The Husband's Headship" and "the Wife's Submission." Demonic discourse easily blended into efforts to replicate traditional social roles in a changing America.

Michael Cuneo, after a close examination of Charismatic deliverance ministries, has suggested that their struggle with the devil often reflected their hierarchal and patriarchal political and cultural assumptions. Cuneo notes that for many deliverance ministries, "deliverance seems to have been used . . . during the seventies and eighties as a mechanism of social control." Charismatic leaders did, in fact, believe that Satan had been the inspiration for everything from the struggle for gay and lesbian rights to the increasing numbers of women seeking options beyond marriage and child rearing. Cuneo describes the experience of a California woman, the wife of an Episcopal minister, who joined a Charismatic prayer group after struggling with depression over her highly regimented life as full-time wife and mother. The group diagnosed her condition as possession by "spirits of insubordination" and encouraged her to both accept her biblical role as helpmate to her husband and engage in spiritual warfare with the spirits bringing a "hellish atmosphere" into her home.[8]

The belief that Satan inspired almost every effort toward the expansion of rights in the American experience meant that "spiritual warfare" would enter the emerging culture wars. In post-1960s America, conservative evangelicals, traditionalist Catholics, and many Pentecostals believed they were in a literal struggle for the soul of America. Popular culture, frequently seen by conservatives as Satan's playground, ironically became a site where the conservative ideology of the new exorcists found resonance and even thematic highlights for their ideas. This is particularly true in a triptych of films that appeared between 1968 and 1974. In *Rosemary's Baby*, *The Exorcist*, and *The Omen*, the devil took over the American box office. A similar set of cultural anxieties, and even pathologies, found expression in all three of these films. All were films made in an America increasingly uncertain of its place in the world and its relationship to its alleged innocence.

These three films were not the first to tap into, as well as help structure and inspire, this new fascination with Satan. The early 1960s has seen numerous films with satanic themes make their way to the States from Italy and, particularly, from Britain where the birth of a new satanic chic reminiscent of fin de siècle Paris seems to have been in full swing. As early as 1960, a limited release of Italian director Mario Bava's *La Maschera Del Demonio* (*The Mask of the Demon* but released in America as *Black Sunday*) introduced audiences to Barbara Steele, who replicated her role as a sensual "black magic woman" repeatedly in both Italian and British horror films. Kenneth Anger, a devotee of the work of occultist Aleister Crowley and a close associate of the Rolling Stones, created *Scorpio Rising* in 1963, a film renowned for its desecration of Christian symbols and representation of a Black Mass as a homosexual orgy. The Rolling Stones themselves expressed a dilettante interest in the occult, titling their release *Their Satanic Majesties Request*. Their controversial single "Sympathy for the Devil," released in 1968, presents a cynical and world-wise devil who has witnessed millennia of humanity's catastrophes, cruelties, and absurdities. Mick Jagger claimed that Baudelaire served as his inspiration, although the song employs a number of thematic elements from Russian author Mikhail Bulgakov's masterpiece *The Master and Margarita*, a satire that describes a visit by the devil to a twentieth-century Soviet Union that does not believe in him.[9]

The stage had been prepared when 1968, a year marked by two assassinations, urban unrest, and the psychological jolt of the Tet offensive, brought to American audience's Roman Polanski's *Rosemary's Baby*. Polanski's film managed to place in a single, disturbing package many of America's cultural and religious anxieties. Drawing heavily on earlier notions of satanic conspiracy, the film borrowed elements of the *Seventh Victim* and made it into a broad reflection on the state of American family and gender mores in the wake of the sexual revolution.

Rosemary's Baby shocked American audiences for its style and setting as much as for its content. Val Lewton had taken horror and placed it in modern-day New York. Polanski placed his audience in what seemed to be the happy promise of a Doris Day picture. A young couple, Rosemary and Guy (played by Mia Farrow and John Cassavetes), find an apartment in the Bramford, a Gilded Age building with a shady past. They are befriended by their strange, but seemingly harmless, elderly neighbors who become especially close to Guy. Uneasy, Rosemary begins having strange nightmares of witches' sabbats and of sexual intercourse with a devil. Guy, a struggling actor, unexpectedly finds success when a rival goes blind. Rosemary becomes pregnant and feels increasingly isolated, while the grand old Bramford slowly becomes the crumbling mansion or castle-keep of nineteenth-century Gothic fiction, full of secrets and secret passages. At the end of the film she discovers that almost everyone she has come in contact with is part of a large satanic conspiracy to bring Satan's child to Earth. In the final harrowing scene, defeated Rosemary accepts her role as mother to the Antichrist, who has, in the words of one of the Satanists, "his Fathers eyes"—red and smoldering.

Rosemary's Baby proved an enormous commercial success perhaps because if its ability to render cultural anxieties in the context of a demon-haunted modern America. The idea that the child within represented a terror and even an enemy comported with increasing fears about overpopulation and the horrors of the thalidomide tragedy of the early 1960s. In the latter, stories from Western Europe about thousands of horribly deformed babies awakened ancient, deep-rooted fears of monstrous births. David J. Skal has noted that *Rosemary's Baby* became the first of many major Hollywood films that, for over a decade, dealt with what he calls "fetal and gynecological obsessions." Ridley Scott's *Alien* and David Cronenberg's *The Brood* represented the most visually shocking and powerfully told versions of this genre.[10]

Warner Brothers released *Rosemary's Baby* in a year that forced Americans to recognize the growing chaos and violence within their own society and also in which a great debate was taking place regarding sexuality, reproduction, and childbirth. In 1960, the FDA had granted its approval for the sale of Enovid as a contraceptive. By 1968, "the Pill" revolutionized America and laid the groundwork for a growing debate over abortion rights that led up to the January 1973 *Roe v. Wade* decision. The availability of birth control fundamentally transformed the dynamic of gender relations, altered attitudes about sexual intercourse, and gave renewed impetus to the long-silenced debate over reproductive rights. Conservative voices warned of the dangers the "sexual revolution" presented to traditional values. In response to the worldwide debate about birth control, Pope Paul VI, ignoring the recommendation of his own appointed commission of theologians, doctors, and laypeople, restated the Roman Catholic Church's opposition to artificial birth control in his July 1968 encyclical *Humane Vitae* ("On Human Life"). Widespread dissent greeted his decision. Theologians challenged it and some parish priests counseled couples to ignore it. Most did.

These cultural and religious convulsions found their way into Polanski's film. The character of Rosemary is, notably, a lapsed Catholic with strong yearnings to return to a faith she can no longer accept (we learn from the novel that she is estranged from her "fertile family" for having married outside of the Church). Much of her torment comes from being entrapped by female roles that, ironically, the Satanists seem to borrow from hierarchal and patriarchal Christianity. She conceives the devil's child by being held down and raped by her husband. Her panic increases through the course of the film as she feels herself surrounded and hemmed in by neighbors, doctors, and her spouse, all of whom carefully monitor the condition of the monstrous life growing within her, with little concern expressed for her own well-being and very little recognition of her autonomy. Her once-beloved apartment becomes a prison. At the end, she consents to accept a predestined role as mother to the Antichrist. Biology, and diabology, becomes Rosemary's destiny.

Darryl Jones has argued, very straightforwardly, that *"Rosemary's Baby* is a film about men controlling women's bodies."* Polanski's genius was to hide this critique of middle-class domesticity under the trappings of demonic worship and invest satanism with essentially the same values that conservative voices called for a return to in 1968. The film, not surprisingly, faced a powerful conservative backlash. Some of these critics focused solely on the use of the theme of devil worship, with little awareness of the movie's incisive critique. An exception was the National Catholic Office for Motion Pictures, formerly the Legion of Decency, which condemned the film for the "perverted use which the film makes of fundamental Christian beliefs, especially the events surrounding the birth of Christ."

The use of diabolical imagery in *Rosemary's Baby* suggests that something more than a straightforward screening of natal anxieties is at work. Polanski's vision of the meaning of Satan worship in modern America ironically borrowed much of the imagery from the American right, especially its fears of conspiracy, and used them to subvert conservative values. The film asserts the reality of a broad cultural conspiracy but portrays it as a conspiracy by traditional elites seeking to control sexuality and the female body. This is not a foreign threat but rather a corruption found in the heart of modern America and among the very people you would least suspect of perpetrating evil. Polanski's vision created a subversive document about the nature of evil, a truly idiosyncratic vision in a genre that would primarily buttress the most conservative elements in American society.

If *Rosemary's Baby* presented American culture with a new satanic nativity, the Dark Lord came of age with *The Exorcist*. We have already seen the powerful reaction that American audiences had to this film, reactions triggered in part by director William Friedkin's documentarian approach to the tale of possession and horror. As with *Rosemary's Baby*, female sexuality occupies a central place in the narrative. Images of both menarche and masturbation are used to illustrate the blasphemies of the demonic adolescent. The film's subtext suggests that the onset of adolescence, Regan's passage into womanhood, played some role in the demon Pazuza's control of her body.

The cultural politics of *The Exorcist* have been much debated. On one level, the film clearly traded in a conservative politics of the womb, presenting Ellen Burstyn's character as a single mother powerless to aid her daughter and forced to call upon the Catholic Church and its male representatives to save her. Horror historian Tony Williams views the film as a generalized comment on the changing state of the American family in the early 1960s in which a runaway divorce rate and the subsequent emergence of the single-parent household created a sense of the family in chaos. The missing patriarchal structure invites demons to enter the young girl's body, and the patriarchal structure must be invited in to save and redeem that body.[11]

Conservatives found that the film resonated with their sense of the nature of evil, even if they found themselves uncomfortable with much of its imagery. Two Jesuit priests acted as advisors to the film, and even the highly conservative *National Catholic Register* placed it on its list of "pro-Catholic films," right along with *The Song of Bernadette* and *The Bells of St. Mary's*. Evangelicals and Pentecostals had a less positive image of the film, if not of its overall message. Billy Graham even suggested that something evil resided in the original print of the film's very celluloid. Nonetheless, as Michael Cuneo points out, the Charismatic deliverance movement and the evangelical belief in the growing strength of the devil in modern society sometimes borrowed imagery and ideas from *The Exorcist* and related films. The success of *The Exorcist* drew on the growing fascination with Satan in American culture and religion but also helped to strengthen that fascination as well.[12]

An illustration of this unlikely partnership appears in a sermon given by Billy Graham in the summer of 1974 at, ironically, Sun Devil Stadium in Tempe, Arizona. Graham simultaneously attacked *The Exorcist* while highlighting and underscoring many of its major themes. His sermon proclaimed the continuing baleful influence of the devil in modern society, as illustrated by an increased fascination with the occult and the growing popularity of films that traded in satanic themes. Graham received applause from the 30,000-plus crowd when he insisted he had not seen *The Exorcist*, declaring, "I do not intend to expose myself to that sort of thing." Notably, however, Graham asked the crowd to accept the very premises found in the film. "The Devil knows his time is short" Graham insisted, and explained to his audience that this accounted for the growing number of cases of demon possession. He also suggested that, not unlike Regan's fascination with the Ouija board, a growing interest in America with matters related to the occult had opened the door to the devil.[13]

If *Rosemary's Baby* and *The Exorcist* reflected, and even helped to shape, a new evangelical fascination with the devil's influence, *The Omen* drew directly on this fascination for its plot and source material. Darryl Jones has called the Omen "The Exorcist for Protestants." The premillennial interpretation of the end times, popular among Protestant Fundamentalists since the beginning of the century, provided the basic story arc. In the final film, released in 1981, the Antichrist's rise to power is halted by the Second Coming of Christ.

In the more than thirty years since the release of *The Omen*, these ideas would become common currency in evangelical circles through the popularity of the Left Behind novels of Tim LaHaye and Jerry B. Jenkins. In 1974, they had only just broken out of the evangelical subculture, where they were born, through the works of Hal Lindsey. The popularity of the works of Lindsey by the mid-1970s signaled the beginning of this new phase of fascination with the devil. Lindsey's runaway best seller *The Late Great Planet Earth* gave to readers, in almost novelistic form, the premillennial dispensationalist view of human history that had been born in American Fundamentalism and remained popular in the Pentecostal and evangelical world. By the time *The Omen* premiered, Lindsey's book had outsold every nonfiction book in the United States except for the Bible. Lindsey's work claimed that world events provided clues for the nearness of the "End Times" and the fulfillment of biblical prophecy. Lindsey gave special currency to the idea that the history of the modern state of Israel, natural disasters, and the rise of the European Common Market provided a kind of prophetic clock for the rapture, that moment when premillennialists believe true Christian believers will be snatched physically from the earth and taken to heaven before the coming of a "period of tribulation" that would wreathe the world in chaos.

Evil, in this worldview, has a diabolical source, and only spiritual warfare, conducted in the heart and at the ballot box, prevents America from falling into a maelstrom of evil. Lindsey continued these themes in his best-selling *Satan Is Alive and Well on Planet Earth*. In it, Lindsey claimed that much of Western civilization, its philosophy, art, music, political movements, and films had become engineered by the devil to prepare the way for the Antichrist. Television represented the "demon eye" in every American living room. Music, particularly rock and roll, represented, literally, the devil's music, a soundtrack for the rise of the Antichrist. Moreover, Lindsey quoted unnamed "researchers," "authorities," and "experts" to suggest to the reader that the practice of Satanism, the actual worship of the devil, had become a widespread phenomenon in American society. While some readers certainly found Lindsey's claims ludicrous, he proved himself gifted in using popular idioms, his knowledge of current events, and a rather lurid writing style to convince millions of Americans of his claims.

Lindsey was helped in his effort by the appearance of a public face for Satanism in American popular culture. Although only attracting a tiny (to the point of being statistically uncountable) number of adherents, Satanism had a public relations agent in the late 1960s and early 1970s in the person of Anton Szandor LaVey, the high priest of the Church of Satan. Known in the media as "The Black Pope," LaVey was born in 1930 and spent much of his early life in what Gavin Baddely calls the "twilight underbelly of America." Working as an organ grinder for burlesque shows, a carnival barker, and a police photographer, LaVey later claimed that these experiences provided him with an encounter with the true nature of the human person, a nature defined by carnal animality rather than heavenly spirituality. Living in San Francisco in the 1950s and 1960s, he acquired a reputation as a renegade occultist, a kind of dark hippie who promised self-transcendence through fulfilling personal desires rather than universal love and peace. A group of his followers, known as "the magic circle," became the basis for his founding of the Church of Satan in 1966. The sensationalist nature of the new sect, and LaVey's talent for public theatrics, attracted enormous media attention as well as big-name Hollywood converts, including Sammy Davis Jr. and Jayne Mansfield.[14]

Ironically, LaVey completely, and very publicly, rejected the supernatural reality of the devil himself. LaVey taught his followers, in an echo of occult writer Madame Blavatsky, that the devil was "the best friend the Church had ever had, as he kept it in business all of these years." Satan, in his view, could not be worshipped as a "real" entity but rather understood as a symbolic representation of "indulgence" and "vital existence." His rituals, including the infamous Black Mass held at his San Francisco home, became psychodramas in which participants were encouraged to slough off the guilt and anxiety produced by their Christian upbringing. Friedrich Nietzsche, rather than Lucifer, was the real deity being worshipped.

Evangelical and Charismatic Christians, becoming ever more deeply convinced of the ongoing work of the devil in America, failed to recognize the schmaltz that LaVey submerged his Satanism in or the somewhat complex cultural point his campy theatricality attempted to make. LaVey and his imitators became for many conservative Christians the visible sign of a much larger, invisible conspiracy of "satanic cults" that sought to prepare the world for the end of days. A web of interrelated beliefs formed in the evangelical and Charismatic world in which the devil was believed to be active in everything from feminist ideology to active satanic groups who allegedly sacrificed children by the thousands. Rock music and role-playing games became the entry-point of Satan into their homes, even as Satan was seen as active in the efforts of liberal politicians and the American Civil Liberties Union. America found itself in the grip of a kind of mass psychosis that has variously been called the "Satanist scare" and "the satanic panic."

The 1980s, a decade that began with Ronald Reagan's proclamation that it was "morning in America," seem an unlikely time for such a gothic set of beliefs to take hold of the American imagination. Reagan's public persona and rhetoric celebrated a language of frontier optimism, a forward-looking conservatism that marked a departure from the popular image of the conservative before his appearance on the national scene. He, as Sean Wilentz has written, "conjured images of a brave new national destiny."[15]

This "brave new national destiny" would be built by rhetorically creating an America that never was, refashioning an image of wholesome innocence in the aftermath of the 1960s and 1970s. Wilentz concludes that

"Reaganism was nostalgic in the literal and original sense of the term, a longing to return to the homeland." Popular television shows of the era, such as *Little House on the Prairie*, romanticized a lost America. But why had this pristine world been lost? Reagan's mythological world was full of good guys and, in his words, "neighbors helping neighbors." But it was also a world full of evil, of "ghetto rioters" and "flag burners" who had stalked and killed the American dream over the previous two decades. The rejuvenation of America meant the destruction of the enemies that had threatened and corrupted her.

Some of the Reagan Revolution's most ardent foot soldiers shared this Manichean worldview. The Christian Right represented a major part of the coalition that elected him in both 1980 and in 1984. Bringing together Charismatics, evangelicals, some traditionalist Roman Catholics, and a small number of neoconservative Jews, this new movement put aside older theological differences in an effort to turn back the pace of change in post-1960s America, especially in regard to issues of gender and sexuality. Mobilizing voters through conservative Christian churches, the Christian Right used the hoary and powerful language of spiritual warfare to describe their efforts to reclaim American culture for "Christian values."

The origins of this movement are complex. Conservative Christian voices have, as we have seen, critiqued the culture through much of the American experience. But in the 1970s, a significant degree of coordination among conservative religious leaders helped to mobilize the growing number of evangelical and Charismatic Christians on controversial culture issues such as abortion and homosexuality. These various efforts came together after a meeting of evangelical leaders with Jimmy Carter in 1979. Believing that the Southern Baptist president had been unresponsive to their concerns on social issues, Jerry Falwell came away from the meeting convinced, as he later wrote, that "Satan had mobilized his forces to destroy America. . . . God needed voices to save the nation from inward moral decay." Falwell founded the Moral Majority as the primary organizational voice for the movements, but there were many others. Tim LaHaye, later to become the co-author of the runaway best-selling Left Behind series, was a long-time Falwell ally who joined him in this effort.

The Christian Right functioned as a movement for social rejuvenation that drew on the themes of American innocence and a simplistic conception of evil. The leaders of the movement found in the notion of satanic influence a ready image to explain what they perceived as America's decline as a moral innocent and as a global power. The foot soldiers of the movement, many of them the aging "silent majority" of the Nixon era, found in the rhetoric of the movement an explanation for social and cultural changes that made them anxious. Most significantly, they deployed the imagery of spiritual warfare in an arguably even more effective way than had nineteenth-century Christian reformers. The new Christian Right believed that they fought a supernatural battle in heavenly realms even as they struck at the minions of Satan on Earth (feminists, abortionists, liberals, and progressives of all stripes).

The influence of the Christian Right over the Reagan Revolution is hard to exaggerate. Leaders in the movement raised close to $20 million for Reagan's election and then found themselves with extraordinary access to the administration. James Watt, a leader within the Christian Right, received a cabinet position as Secretary of the Interior. Robert Billings, formerly executive director for the Moral Majority, served as Reagan's liaison to the Christian Right and held a position within the Department of Education.

This close relationship between Reagan's White House and the Christian Right provided the context for Reagan's own use of satanic and apocalyptic rhetoric. In 1983, Reagan used the annual meeting of the National Association of Evangelicals to proclaim the arms race as a "struggle between right and wrong, good and evil." Borrowing from Billy Graham and Whitaker Chambers, Reagan referred to Communism as "the faith first proclaimed in the Garden of Eden with the words of temptation." The Soviet Union represented more than America's ideological and geopolitical rival. It was the instrument of the devil on Earth.[16]

Americans who accepted the idea of satanic activity in Soviet Communism had little trouble believing he targeted them in their homes and churches. Soon they would believe he was coming for them in their children's day care centers. Spiritual warfare of the type preached by the Christian Right suggested not only a mighty struggle, but also powerful and well-organized enemies. Informed by images of Satanism that included *Rosemary's Baby* and older American conspiracy theories, the "satanic panic" was born.

The "satanic panic" had three interrelated and mutually reinforcing expressions. First, the widespread belief, mostly based on urban legend and rumor, that a network of satanic covens existed throughout the country and that these groups were responsible for everything from animal mutilation to the kidnapping of children. Second, it grew from the belief by many adults that, as children, they had suffered "ritual abuse" at the hands of parents, teachers, and even clergy. Finally, the belief that Satan and his minions had infiltrated the popular media, using its influence over the young in very specific ways, mobilized the Christian Right to expose these forces. Heavy metal music, fantasy role-playing games, comic books, and films all displayed the signs of the devil's influence. Moral crusades against these media became a new kind of American reform movement, often led by parents groups, ministers, and even sometimes by members of the law enforcement community.

Sociologists, folklorists, and cultural historians have examined the diverse roots of the satanic panic. Its origins can be located in the late 1960s and early 1970s when rumors of "cult" activity among disaffected young people terrified parents. The horrific Manson murders intensified the connection between "cults" (soon to become a catch-all term for new religious movements) and antisocial behavior. A series of urban legends mushroomed in the late 1970s concerned with alleged "cattle mutilations" in a number of Midwestern states. Some claimed that this phenomenon, which later turned out to have a simpler explanation, was the work of organized groups of Satanists (although, notably, some claimed it was the result of extraterrestrial activity rather than devil worship).[17]

By the early 1980s, increased concerns over missing children and moral panics over child abuse found expression in rumors about the work of devil worshippers. In 1983, accusations against workers at the McMartin Preschool in Los Angeles took on a satanic theme. Several parents made allegations that their children had been subjected to everything from secret sexual rites to cannibalism, all in the context of the worship of Satan. Years of investigations and a twenty-eight-month trial followed. One of the accused spent five years in prison until he was able to post a $1.5 million bond. The group of parents, joined by "satanic investigators" who flocked to Los Angeles, became increasingly reckless in their accusations. One of the parents, clearly mentally unbalanced, eventually claimed that goats had been sacrificed at the center, a baby had been murdered and its brains set on fire, and even that a lion had been introduced into the recurrent episodes of satanic torture. Many of the children shared similar stories after being interrogated for days by therapists, police, and parents, who rewarded the increasingly bizarre stories with praise. Not surprisingly, many of these children began to show signs of severe emotional disturbance.[18]

Popular evangelical and Pentecostal leaders seized on incidents such as the McMartin case to claim that millions of American children suffered bizarre abuse at the hands of Satanists. Radio evangelist Bob Larson claimed in his 1989 book *Satanism: The Seduction of America's Youth*, that 95 percent of all missing children in the United State had become victims of satanic groups. Such bizarre claims were calculated to elicit response, and donations, leading to the rise of a number of "anti-occult" ministries that focused on the alleged influence of Satanism in America. They also resulted in local "rumor panics" at schools and day care centers.[19]

Traditionalist Catholics, especially those who opposed the reforms of the 1960s, often joined their evangelical and Charismatic brethren in ramping up the diabolical rhetoric. Malachi Martin became one of the more popular of the Catholic demon hunters. Martin, a former Jesuit scholar who had once been a theological advisor at the Second Vatican

Council and a former professor at the Vatican's Pontifical Institute, had been released from his vows in 1965 under uncertain circumstances and thereafter become a best-selling author and, in his own mind, a kind of rogue demon hunter. His book *Hostage to the Devil* purported to tell the story of five exorcisms in modern America, though his refusal to divulge names and sources makes his claims unlikely.

Martin represents the link between the phenomenon of "deliverance" and the panics revolving around alleged satanic conspiracies. Martin's writings became famous in Protestant "deliverance circles," and his outlandish claims about satanic conspiracy contributed to the growing sense among many evangelicals that the devil had become especially active in late twentieth-century America. In the 1992 edition of *Hostage to the Devil*, Martin claimed that over 8,000 satanic covens operated in the United States and that these covens celebrated the Black Mass regularly in every major American city. He further claimed that "politicians, clergy and the religious" held membership in these covens, where human sacrifice and other unnamable rites took place. Conservative evangelicals relied on his statistics, possibly also attracted to his contribution to the literature of anti-Catholicism with books like *The Jesuits* and *The Keys to This Blood*, which he filled with the plotting Jesuits and Vatican conspiracies of nativist legend.[20]

Martin was far from the only influential voice making baseless and unsubstantiated claims during this era. One of the most successful of the new religious entrepreneurs of the 1980s was Mike Warnke, an evangelist who specialized in an odd mix of Christian-themed comedy, traditional Charismatic preaching, and tales of his preconversion experiences as a Satanic high priest in a large and well-organized network of California covens. Warnke's book *The Satan Seller* related his experiences in a satanic mafia, heading up over 1,500 followers in three major cities and given wealth and power by the Illuminati (that same shadowy organization that had been popular with American conspiracy theorists since the Jefferson era). Warnke proved enormously appealing to his white, suburban, Charismatic, and evangelical audiences. His comedy albums became top sellers in the burgeoning world of Christian contemporary recordings by 1991 with 1 million-plus sales. *The Satan Seller* topped 3 million in sales over a ten-year period. Such an important figure had he become in the conservative subculture of evangelical America that in 1988 the mayor of Nashville honored him with "Mike Warnke Day," a tribute to his efforts on behalf of the Nashville-based Christian publishing house Word.[21]

Warnke's voice became one of the most influential in the evangelical war on Satan. While only one of a chorus of voices that called for a moral crusade against Satan in popular culture, his alleged past as a satanic high priest seemingly gave him unbounded authority on the topic. Audiences in churches and civic auditoriums from coast to coast accepted his bizarre claims without question. In one such gathering, Warnke claimed that he knew of a coven of Satanists who "took a little girl and they killed her by cutting out her sexual organs while she was still alive. After she was dead, they cut her chest open, took out her heart and cut it into little pieces and had communion on it." Warnke became an expert in theatrical representation of the role he portrayed. By the early 1990s, he ended his shows by being processed out by a phalanx of husky bodyguards, since, he claimed, the international satanic conspiracy made constant threats against his life.[22]

The very nature of Warnke's tall tales makes it clear that anyone who bothered to investigate his surreal claims would quickly discover their falsity. Two reporters for the evangelical magazine *Cornerstone* undertook just such an investigation, finding a pattern of lies, tax fraud, and manipulative fictions. Warnke had never had any association with satanic cults, never had an all-expenses paid trip to a gathering of the Illuminati in Salem, Massachusetts, never uncovered proof of human sacrifice. And yet, as reporters Mike Hertenstein and Jon Trott admitted after their detailed investigation, "a generation of Christians learned what they knew of Satanism and the occult from *The Satan Seller.*"[23]

Warnke was not alone in providing grist for the satanic rumor mills. The coerced testimony of children was joined by a chorus of adult voices who claimed that they had suffered the most bizarre abuse imaginable at the hands of parents, teachers, and clergymen. These stories became highly stylized and followed the template provided by a 1980 book entitled *Michelle Remembers*.

Michelle Smith entered therapy with Lawrence Pazder in the summer of 1976 to work through a severe depression following a miscarriage. In Pazder, she found a therapist with traditionalist Roman Catholic beliefs combined with ideas borrowed from the Charismatic movement. Moreover, Pazder held a strongly literal belief in the power of Satan and black magic, informed by his previous medical practice in West Africa. In Africa, Pazder interpreted traditional African religion through the Western missionary lens in which sacred ceremonies of native peoples are viewed as diabolical ceremonies. He brought these ideological and religious positions to his treatment of this troubled woman.

Pazder interpreted Michelle Smith's dreams through his conception of demonic activity and notions of satanic conspiracy, finally leading her to interpret her nightmares as evidence of fourteen months' worth of repressed memories. In *Michelle Remembers*, patient and psychiatrist (soon to leave their respective spouses and become lovers) recounted a horrific tale of ritual sexual abuse at the hands of a satanic coven. These tales became the template for numerous claims of "recovered memories" and resulted in what Bill Ellis calls "a conduit of information" in the form of "conferences, workshops and training sessions" for therapists, child welfare advocates, and law enforcement officials. Therapists and social workers who accepted this worldview even classified a host of symptoms in adults as SRS, or "Satanic Ritual Abuse Syndrome." Pazder himself journeyed to Los Angeles to serve as a consultant with local therapists on the McMartin case. There he would claim that the satanic conspiracy that had abused Michelle was the same one behind the McMartin case. Indeed, he told local media that "anyone could be involved in this plot including teachers, doctors, movie stars, merchants, even . . . members of the Anaheim Angels baseball team."[24]

The involvement of health care professionals and the police ensured that the satanic panic would be far more than an underground urban legend among conservative Christians. Robert Hicks has examined the emergence of "occult crime experts" in police departments across the country, "experts" who beginning in 1984 held seminars for their fellow police that Hicks calls "a pastiche of claims, suppositions and speculation." White, male, and Protestant with strongly conservative religious and political beliefs, one study found, is the typical profile of an occult investigator. This cultural and ideological background led the "occult cops" to define a wide variety of beliefs as "satanic," even to the point of classifying traditional Latin American and Afro-Caribbean belief systems as "devil worship" or "evidence of occult criminal activity." Lieutenant Larry Jones of the Boise Police Department even got much of his information from the religious tracts of Chick Publications, an extremist Fundamentalist sect known for its tendency to define Catholicism itself as part of a larger satanic plot to usher in the reign of Antichrist.[25]

Although a number of authors have examined the role of local and state police forces in the satanic panic, the larger framework of this phenomenon, the changing ethos of police work since the 1960s, has not been examined. The emergence of "occult cops," alleged experts in dealing with satanic crime, are actually part of a larger transformation of police work in which fighting social deviance and keeping a check on marginal groups constitutes a major part of both urban and rural police responsibility. The rise of police forces under centralized control, a phenomenon of the early modern era, has long been associated with the control of social deviance in the interest of class and nation. Seldom in the nation's history has the work of police departments simply been limited to the prevention of crimes against life and property. American police history has entwined with the history of strikebreaking and efforts to ferret out "foreign radicals" in the country's immigrant population. This role expanded as the 1960s saw the rise of a special set of concerns related to student protestors, civil rights protests, and the urban uprisings at mid-decade. Richard Nixon's promises of "law and order" on behalf of the "silent majority" moved the American middle class, who had come to see public protest and "rioting" as monsters that had to be slain rather than widespread dissent rooted in complex social problems. The FBI, by the mid-1960s, offered state and municipal leaders conferences and seminars that encouraged the use of overwhelming force to quell the very threat of social uprising. South Carolina governor Robert McNair attended one such conference in 1967, a factor in his fateful decision to send heavily armed highway patrol and state police to a small student protest against a segregated bowling alley in Orangeburg. The result was three college students dead and twenty-eight wounded.

In such a climate, the violent control of college campuses and the urban landscape became the primary response to unrest. Such attitudes persisted after the 1960s among Nixon's "silent majority." In the 1970s, 1980s, and 1990s, many middle-class Americans viewed the phrase "tough on crime" as a panacea for a whole range of social problems. Police work, in their eyes, should essentially function as social control, fighting a war on drugs and on gangs of "urban youth." Conservatives constructed this urban enemy using the vocabulary of evil. A *Time* magazine article from 1977 informed its readers that "behind the ghettos' crumbling walls live a large group of people who are more intractable, socially alien and more hostile than almost anyone had imagined. They are the unreachables: the American underclass." The 1980s would see a dark flowering of political rhetoric, some of it from President Reagan himself, about the "crack heads" and "welfare queens" who constituted the urban proletariat.[26]

Not surprisingly, middle-class America and its spokespeople turned to the language of evil to describe the plight of the poor, the drug addicted, and the marginalized. William Bennett, later touted by conservatives as "virtue czar," described "moral poverty" as the real problem with the inner city. Conservative social critic James Q. Wilson described African American men in the inner city as "feral, pre-social human beings." Municipal authorities, building their philosophy around this set of beliefs, mobilized heavy firepower to deal with these demonic predators. By the 1970s, large urban areas had outfitted paramilitary squads known as SWAT teams. By the late 1980s, 30,000 communities in the United States had these heavily armed military units, some of whom patrolled African American neighborhoods daily. The Reagan administration fully supported these efforts. Throughout the 1980s, the Department of Defense dispensed battlefield military hardware to these often slightly trained units, including grenade launchers, armored personnel carriers, and even helicopters.[27]

Given this enormous expansion of police power, it is less surprising that urban legends related to occult crime received some attention from police on high alert to squelch social deviance. White suburbanites, somewhat secure knowing that paramilitary assault squads in armored vehicles patrolled the inner city streets, still feared that evil could make a sudden, subtle entrance into their well-ordered neighborhoods.

The connection between the changing role of the police in American society and efforts to control culturally subversive groups is illustrated in the backgrounds of some of the most well-known of the "occult cops." Debbie Nathan and Michael Snedecker's examination of these usually low-ranking detectives found that many of them "had spied on groups opposing racism or the Vietnam War in the late 1960s." Before morphing into "occult experts" they traveled the "small town lecture circuit" warning mainly white, middle-class audiences about the danger of "Moonies" and other alternative religious movements. The role of the police in the satanic panic of the 1980s appears to be symptomatic of a much larger problem. Rather than asking its police to prevent and prosecute crimes against person and property, white America asked it to crusade against evil, to slay monsters and demons. In an urban America prostrated by the growing economic inequality of the 1980s and the consequent deadly mix of entrepreneurialism and despair that constituted the crack epidemic, politicians gravitated to the "tough on crime" rhetoric that became such an important part of the successful campaigns of Reagan, Bush, and Clinton. Meanwhile, the leadership of the evangelical and Charismatic worlds adopted a very similar rhetoric in which their followers were asked to engage in an unrelenting war on the forces of darkness threatening their homes, children, churches, and communities.[28]

Fear of these subterranean forces ignited a series of moral crusades among conservative Christians. Many of these efforts did not focus on bringing about actual social change, but rather took the form of exposés of immoral and demonic messages allegedly hidden in popular culture. Like the moralist crusades in the late nineteenth century, they sought to restrict and contain behaviors and cultural images they considered dangerous. Heavy metal music, and rock music in general, received special attention from evangelical and Charismatic traveling clergy, who detailed the more lurid aspects of the rock world for teenagers and their parents. Clergy and parent groups also found the devil lurking in the newly popular role-playing games and in the changes that had come to the style and content of the American comic book.

Jacob Aranza, a young Louisiana evangelist and popular speaker deeply involved in the independent Christian School movement of the 1970s, became the primary propagandist of the antirock message by 1980. Aranza focused his attacks heavily on Ozzy Osbourne and other heavy metal musicians who made use of satanic imagery in their concerts and on their album covers. Aranza also attacked more mainstream pop, making the claim that the Eagles' 1976 single "Hotel California" celebrated

Anton LaVey and the beginnings of the Church of Satan (in fact, it was an allegory of the decadent attractions of the California music and film scene). Aranza is also largely responsible for introducing the idea that "backwards masking," hidden messages imbedded in rock music that affect the subconscious, constituted the major threat to America's youth in the public discourse. Such messages, he and others claimed, appeared not only in heavy metal but in radio pop as well. Aranza asserted, for example, that rock-pop group Styxx embedded the phrase "Satan move in our voices" in their song "Snowblind." Aranza's book, *Backward Masking Unmasked* (1983) went through several printings and became the textbook for antirock crusaders in the Christian Right as well as a popular tool for evangelical youth ministries.[29]

The genre of heavy metal earned most of the ire of these antirock crusaders. The cultural politics of the musical form made the confrontation inevitable. Heavy metal as a musical genre had its birth among alienated working-class youth in the England of the 1970s. From its beginnings, dark, occultic imagery played some role in the lyrics and in what could be described as the performance art of the concerts. *AC/DC* employed satanic symbolism in songs such as "Hell's Bells" and "Highway to Hell" although they personally had little interest in the occult beyond its shock value. Black Sabbath from Birmingham, England, came out of the same angry, hard-drinking proletarian world where references to Satan offered a way for the culturally alienated to punch traditional mores directly in the face. Sabbath front man Ozzy Osbourne happily employed much of the successful satanic imagery throughout his career. Ironically, most of Osbourne's music carried notably unsatanic messages about the dangers of the military-industrial complex ("War Pigs"), the stupidity and exploitation of pornography ("No Bone Movies"), and the frightening effects of alcoholism, one of Ozzy's own personal demons ("Suicide Solution"). Osbourne was never especially dark at all if his musical themes, rather than his persona, are used as a guide.[30]

An examination of the struggle against this angry, if largely apolitical, music illuminates a style of cultural politics that was born out of the Satanism scare and grew into a major force in American politics with the rise of the Christian Right. The Christian warriors of the Right had a much broader political and cultural agenda than the devil in rock music. Aranza's popular exposé of the satanic roots of heavy metal, which featured a preface by conservative Louisiana state senator Bill Keith (legislative sponsor of a bill that would have made the teaching of "creation science" law in Louisiana public schools), includes Aranza's "personal testimony" of his teenage attraction to drugs and alcohol and the negative effects of his parents' divorce. "As if all this wasn't bad enough," Aranza exclaims, "they had just started integration in the schools. . . . Our school already had problems with drugs, sex, and violence. All integration did for our school was put the match to the fuse of a bomb that was already there."[31]

Aranza's and other conservative Christian attacks on popular culture drew on the growing fascination with demonic themes that had been inspired by *The Exorcist* and related films. Ironically, their attacks only helped to make Satan, sorcery, dark fantasy, witchcraft, and related topics a growth industry. Evangelical religion and popular culture together spawned the urban legends about the influence of Satan in America, as the country became a kind of demonic echo chamber of rumor, panic, conspiracy theories, and deep cultural unease.

Since the 1960s, magic and occult themes had thrived in a vibrant subculture among American youth. In 1965, the first paperback edition of J. R. R. Tolkien's *Lord of the Rings* trilogy appeared and quickly became a pop culture sensation. "Frodo Lives!" buttons and "Go, Go Gandalf" bumper stickers appeared on college campuses. Even rock gods Led Zeppelin expressed their love for Middle-Earth (especially in "Ramble On" and "Misty Mountain Hop"). The popularity of the Tolkien trilogy and its fantastic themes created a flood of paperback fantasy novels, role-playing games, comics, films, and eventually online games. The "sword and sorcery" genre became for American teens of the 1970s and 1980s what "cowboys and Indians" had been for the 1940s and 1950s.

Mobilized activists on the Christian Right read this cultural interest in sorcery as the growth of satanic evil. Dungeon and Dragons (D&D), by 1984, had become a special target of conservative Christian animus. Dungeons and Dragons, created in 1974 by Gary Gygax and Dave Anderson, is a role-playing game (RPG) in which players take on the role of various figures of fantasy largely, though not entirely, drawn from the medieval folklore of northern Europe. Scenarios are created by game leaders (known as "Dungeon Masters") and usually revolve around the exploration of caves and dungeons filled with treasure but guarded by various powerful creatures (trolls, goblins, and, of course, dragons). For the most part, the simulation revolves around the rolling of dice to determine the outcome of physical and magical "combat." The general popularity of fantasy literature since Tolkien, as well as the social aspects of the game, enthralled young participants in high school and college in the 1970s and 1980s.[32]

The structure of a game centered on magic and sometimes including references to "gods" and even "demons" became a target for local groups affiliated with the larger Christian conservative movement. The fantasy universe in which D&D took place was not a universe that posited the existence of Christianity, and thus Satan was not a force to be faced or a character to be played within the context of the game. Nevertheless, groups such as BADD (Bothered about Dungeons and Dragons) as well as larger evangelical organizations warned that the occult nature of the themes made the game a recruitment tool for Satanist organizations. One BADD brochure described the game as "addictive and evil. . . . It is a device of Satan to lure us away from God. It is occult."[33]

Warnings from such groups about the dangers of D&D meshed with the larger discourse in the 1980s about the influence of satanic covens. Patricia Pulling, the founder of BADD, has claimed that there are 30,000 Satanists active at all levels of American society. Such claims had local consequences. In Putnam, Connecticut, conservative parents petitioned their board of education to ban the playing of D&D at Putnam High School. An angry parent described the game as "another of Satan's ploys to pollute and destroy our children's minds." A participant in a similar controversy in Minnesota described D&D as opening the "realm of the occult" up to its players. They are, he claimed, "games that Satan has connived to bring about war on God's kingdom."[34]

The discourse about widespread satanic conspiracy clearly influenced the way millions of Americans interpreted leisure and recreation. But the influence of these ideas can also be seen in the new urban legends of the 1980s, legends that depended on the subculture of the Christian Right for their origin and spread. In 1981, a flyer circulated, frequently in evangelical congregations, claiming that Proctor and Gamble (P&G) donated a significant part of its corporate profits to Anton LaVey's Church of Satan. According to one version of the tale, an unnamed "president" or "executive" of the company had appeared on national television and bragged about his commitment to Satan. The flyer also noted the company trademark, a man in a moon encircled by thirteen stars, and claimed it represented a satanic symbol.

While such tales might be expected to be met with skepticism, the Proctor and Gamble Company acknowledged a considerable loss of profit and of image over the last twenty years because of the rumor. P&G has aggressively pursued litigation against anyone caught spreading the rumor and even changed their trademark. In 1995, P&G sued Amway products, a competitor known for the evangelical nature of its corporate culture, when an Amway distributor in Utah spread the rumor on the phone message system of the company.[35]

The "satanic panic" of the 1980s crested between 1985 and 1988. National media outlets picked up the story of local panics such as the McMartin case (as well as similar imitations across the country) and sensationalized them. In 1985, the television news magazine *20/20* presented a special report called "The Devil Worshippers" that suggested that Satan worship and ritual sacrifice were widespread phenomena. Geraldo Rivera, known for his flamboyant showmanship and sloppy reporting, claimed that over 1 million Satanists operated in the United States. His 1988 special *Devil Worship* relied on a variety of unidentified sources, footage from horror films, and an effort to connect Charles Manson, Anton LaVey, heavy metal music, and the allegedly widespread incidence of ritual murder to convince millions of Americans that the devil had hundreds of thousands of agents active in their communities. "Occult cops" and special workshops held in local churches made use of *Devil Worship*, often setting off or strengthening local rumor panics.[36]

By the early 1990s, the worst of the rumor panics had passed. This may be because much of the animus of the Christian Right toward its cultural opponents would be absorbed by the Clinton administration after 1992. Around this same time, Mike Warnke's ministry, a major conduit for false and misleading information on the subject of Satanism, all but collapsed. A number of articles began to appear in the professional journals of psychiatry that effectively debunked the claims of "SRA" advocates. Many of those same advocates ceased using the "satanic coven" paradigm to interpret cases and passed on to other, sometimes equally mythological, conspiracy theories. Other advocates' claims became so bizarre that even the most credulous found difficulty accepting them. In June 1992, Dr. Corey Hammond, long-time advocate of SRA, made the claim that the origins of America's satanic covens dated back to "a Hasidic Jew" who had collaborated with the Nazis during World War II, teaching them "mind control techniques he learned from the Kabala." Hammond claimed that after the war, this Nazi cabal had helped Allen Dulles and the CIA perfect mind-control techniques and "was given free reign [*sic*] to practice on children in U.S. military hospitals."[37]

Elements of the satanic panic remained, finding expression in other forms. Meanwhile, other cultural voices reshaped and reimagined the role of the devil in their imaginative lives. Unlike earlier moments in American history, when a dominant discourse about Satan prevented the spread of alternative visions, the diffuse and decentralized nature of late twentieth-century popular culture allowed for the discourse about Satan to become much more than an echo chamber. Countless subcultures, especially among the young, borrowed centuries-old imagery of Satan in order to create new fantasy worlds free of America's dominant Christian paradigm.

Some of the uses of satanic imagery in this period was derivative of the "satanic panic" discourse itself. The direction taken by heavy metal music in America by the mid-1980s provides a perfect example of this approach. Bands such as Mötley Crüe and Twisted Sister engaged in self-parody while attempting to create a "satanic conspiracy" for promotional purposes. Mötley Crüe's 1984 album *Shout at the Devil*, with its infamous cover featuring a pentagram, is the crudest example of these efforts. The band not only deployed satanic imagery in their songs about drugs, sex, and alienation, but also attempted to "underdub" the phrase "Jesus is Satan" in order to satire allegations of "backward masking." Attempting to mirror (and make a commercial appeal to) the current climate, the original album even came with a fake "Warning" stamp that noted that the recording "may contain backwards masking." Iron Maiden, much more creatively, created a "satanic legend" to surround themselves in with albums such as *The Number of the Beast,* the title song of which shows similarities, conscious or not, to Hawthorne's "Young Goodman Brown."

Comic books in the late 1980s borrowed heavily from satanic imagery and often became the medium in which notions about the devil were reshaped most creatively. The use of the devil as a character, often a villain but almost as frequently a hero, grew from the transformation of the comic's medium after 1985. Two graphic novels in this period, Alan Moore's *The Watchmen* and Frank Miller's *The Dark Knight Returns,* became watershed events in their deconstruction of the nature of comic book heroism. Artists and writers turned to a grittier and grimier ethos. Dark antiheroes in morally ambiguous situations became the stock-in-trade as the artists focused their efforts on an adult readership rather than children and teenagers.[38]

The dark supernatural often figured into these new narratives. Heroes such as Marvel Comics' *Ghost Rider* became fan favorites, portraying a character, Johnny Blaze, who sold his soul to the devil in order to save the life of his beloved. As part of the deal, Blaze is possessed by a demon who, with his skeletal body burning with "hellfire," rides a demonic motorcycle through the night. DC Comics had *The Demon,* another superhero who was actually a demonic being. In the early 1990s, artist entrepreneur Todd McFarlane broke with the large comic conglomerates to create Image Comics and its flagship character, *Spawn.* A deadly assassin working for a secretive government agency, Spawn is betrayed and murdered by his employers and finds himself in hell. Much as in the traditional Christian ethos, he suffers for his sins but does so by being transformed into a powerful and terrifying being, "a hellspawn," that will one day lead Satan's armies in a war against heaven. As the story progressed, readers learned that if Satan and his demons are the bad guys, Heaven and its cronies are arguably even more villainous. Spawn must battle both to hold on to a remnant of his humanity and protect the human race. The tone of the series had a deep, if very adolescent, streak of cynicism that viewed all authority figures as corrupt and corrupting, mocked traditional pieties about religion and patriotism, and took a profoundly pessimistic view of human nature.[39]

The popularity of these themes led DC Comics, long the home of traditional heroes such as Superman, Batman, and Wonder Woman, to create an adult comic line called Vertigo. The flagship series for this new imprint became best selling fantasy author Neil Gaiman's series *Sandman*, in which a sympathetic Lucifer became one of the most popular characters. Gaiman created a world in which seven gods ("The Endless") ruled over their own bailiwicks. The title character, Sandman, rules "the Dreaming" and his brother, Lucifer, has, of course, charge of hell. Early in the series, Lucifer (who looks a great deal like a young David Bowie) gives up his rule of the infernal regions and retires to Earth. While not exactly turning the devil into a superhero, Gaiman radically reinterpreted Christian categories in ways that show the influence of William Blake and elements of John Milton. Lucifer becomes the spirit of creative rebellion against predestined fate and all the powers of boundary and limitation (including the role he was predestined to play in the great cosmic drama).[40]

In the 1980s and early 1990s, an entire subculture of dark fantasy had emerged that reimagined Satan and God, heaven and hell. Attractive especially to the alienated young, this subculture allowed them to navigate the fantasy world of comics, provided them with a heavy metal soundtrack, and shaped attitudes that their parents and clergy found blasphemous and socially dangerous. This outpouring of often angry, while also deeply apolitical, pop culture fascinations perfectly suited the first post-boomer generation, a cohort labeled "Generation X" by commentators in the media and in academe who worried about this generation's tendency toward ennui and addiction to irony that had little sympathy for the verities of their parents.[41]

Few in this generation dabbled in anything resembling the "Satanism" of the Christian Right's understanding, and most understood the satirical irony of some of their interests. In fact, such concerns represented another adult attitude worthy of satire. In the 1986 cult hit *Trick or Treat*, a heavy metal musician sells his soul to the devil. Ozzy Osbourne played a right-wing Christian evangelist, obsessed with discovering "backwards masking" in music and censoring heavy metal.

Not everyone had gotten the joke as America entered the last decade of the twentieth century. During the 1980s, belief in Satan as a supernatural force corrupting America's youth and heading an army of human and demonic minions represented the dominant American conception of evil. Rumor and panic became the nation's epistemology of evil. Evangelical preachers used rhetoric that seemed to ignore the complexities of the Vietnam era and hearken back, by their own admission, to the patriotic pieties of the immediate post–World War II era. Politicians joined them, and the "Reagan Revolution" itself would become an effort to escape from history into a mythic time of innocence when the struggle with the devil could be painted in stark terms.

"Spiritual warfare" continued to represent a powerful aspect of the American Christian experience in the 1980s. In fact, by the last decade of the twentieth century the idea had more resonance with American Christians than ever before due to a number of social and cultural forces that had come together at once. Belief in demonic possession and the activity of the devil in the world strengthened the idea among conservative Christians that they engaged in daily combat with evil forces. The ramping up of the culture wars took on the lineaments of a spiritual struggle for those who believed Satan had plotted to expand reproductive rights, remove prayer from schools, and bring homosexuality out into the public square as an acceptable lifestyle. Moreover, as the twenty-first century approached, highly influential Christian leaders and their millions of followers came to believe that the increasing strength of the devil they perceived in their society was building to a crisis point. Premillennialist theology assured them that they would be the victors but that the struggle would be cataclysmic. Satan, many believed, was getting ready to make his final assault on God and his servants. The End of Days had come.

NOTES

1. Mikitta Brockman, *Hollywood Hex: Death and Destiny in the Dream Factory* (London: Creation Books, 1999), 92–95.

2. *The Fear of God: The Making of the Exorcist*, DVD, produced by the BBC (New York: Time Warner, 1998).

3. Safire quoted in Sean Wilentz, *The Age of Reagan: A History, 1974–2008* (New York: Harper, 2008), 16.

4. Vincent Canby, "Screen: *The Deer Hunter*," *New York Times*, December 15, 1978; Andreas Killen, *1973: Nervous Breakdown: Watergate, Warhol, and the Birth of Post-Sixties America* (New York: Bloomsbury, 2007), 105-107, 109-110.

5. Michael W. Cuneo, *American Exorcism: Expelling Demons in the Land of Plenty* (New York: Doubleday, 2001), 89–95.

6. Frank and Ida Mae Hammond, *Pigs in the Parlor: The Practical Guide to Deliverance* (Kirkwood, MO: Impact Books, 1973, 2007), 5.

7. Cuneo, *American Exorcism*, 126.

8. Cuneo, *American Exorcism*, 119–21.

9. Gavin Baddeley, *Lucifer Rising: A Book of Sin, Devil Worship, and Rock 'n' Roll*, 2nd ed. (Medford, NJ: Plexus Publishing, 2006), 45.

10. David J. Skal, *The Monster Show: A Cultural History of Horror* (London: Faber & Faber, 2001), 298.

11. Tony Williams, *Hearths of Darkness: The Family in the American Horror Film* (Madison, NJ: Fairleigh Dickinson University Press, 1996), 112–15.

12. *National Catholic Register*, "100 Pro-Catholic Movies," at www.ncregister.com/info/top_100_pro_catholic_movies/ (accessed December 31, 2008).

13. "Graham on Demons," *Christianity Today*, June 7, 1974.

14. Peter H. Gilmore, "LaVey, Anton Szandor," in *Satanism Today: An Encyclopedia of Religion, Folklore, and Popular Culture*, ed. James R. Lewis (Santa Barbara,

CA: ABC-Clio Press, 2001), 144–47; Mike Hertenstein and Jon Trott, *Selling Satan: The Evangelical Media and the Mike Warnke Scandal* (Chicago: Cornerstone Press, 1993), 424, 425.

15. Sean Wilentz, *The Age of Reagan: A History, 1974–2000* (New York: Harper, 2008), 129–30.

16. George Johnson, *Architects of Fear: Conspiracy Theories and Paranoia in American Politics* (Los Angeles: J. P. Tarcher, 1983), 167.

17. Bill Ellis, *Raising the Devil: Satanism, New Religions, and the Media* (Lexington: University Press of Kentucky, 2000), 240–78.

18. Debbie Nathan and Michael Snedeker, *Satan's Silence: Ritual Abuse and the Making of a Modern American Witch Hunt* (New York: Basic Books, 2001), 84–87.

19. Jeffrey S. Victor, *Satanic Panic: The Creation of a Contemporary Legend* (Chicago: Open Court, 1983).

20. Malachi Martin, *Hostage to the Devil* (San Francisco: HarperOne, 1992), xii.

21. Hertenstein and Trott, *Selling Satan*, 1–5.

22. Hertenstein and Trott, *Selling Satan*, 16.

23. Hertenstein and Trott, *Selling Satan*, 3.

24. Ellis, *Raising the Devil*, 116, 117.

25. Robert D. Hicks, "The Police Model of Satanism Crime," in *The Satanism Scare*, ed. James T. Richardson, et al. (New York: Aldine de Gruyter, 1991), 175, 182; Ben M. Crouch and Kelly Damphousse, "A Survey of Cult Cops," in *The Satanism Scare*, 195. See also Robert Hicks, *In Pursuit of Satan: The Police and the Occult* (Buffalo, NY: Prometheus Books, 1990).

26. "The American Underclass," *Time*, August 29, 1977, 14–15; "Welfare Queens Become Issue in Reagan Campaign," *New York Times*, February 15, 1976.

27. William Bennett, John DiIulio, and John Walters, *Body Count: Moral Poverty and How to Win America's War against Crime and Drugs* (New York: Simon & Schuster, 1994); James Q. Wilson, "What to Do about Crime," *Commentary* 98 (September 1994): 25–34.

28. Nathan and Snedeker, *Satan's Silence*, 113.

29. Joe Selvin, "Q&A with Don Henley," *San Francisco Chronicle*, November 26, 1995, 41, Sunday Datebook; Jacob Aranza, *Backward Masking Unmasked* (Shreveport, LA: Huntington House, Inc, 1983), 7, 15, 18–20.

30. The best academic study of heavy metal, with a focus both on its origins and cultural content, is Robert Walser, *Runnng with the Devil: Power, Gender, and Madness in Heavy Metal Music* (Hanover, NH: University Press of New England, 1993). See especially x, xi, 154.

31. Aranza, *Backwards Masking*, 112.

32. Victor, *Satanic Panic*, 172–75.

33. Daniel Martin and Gary Alan Fine, "Satanic Cults, Satanic Play: Is Dungeons and Dragons a Breeding Ground for the Devil?" in *The Satanism Scare*, ed. James T. Richardson, et al. (New York: Aldine de Gruyter, 1991), 109, 110.

34. Martin and Fine, "Satanic Cults, Satanic Play," 110, 111; more on the role played by Dungeons and Dragons in the satanic panic can be found in Hicks, *The Pursuit of Satan*, 286–301. Hicks notes that Patricia Pulling, founder of BADD, has had "an extraordinary influence on the police," as well as on media portrayals of the game's influence.

35. Dana Camedy, "Advertising: After Two Decades and Counting, Proctor and Gamble Is Still Trying to Exorcise Satanism Tales," *New York Times*, July 19, 1997.

36. Victor, *Satanic Panic*, 46, 69, 216–17; Nathan and Snedeker, *Satan's Silence*, 113.

37. Victor, *Satanic Panic*, 294–95.

38. Matthew Pustz, *Comic Book Culture: Fanboys and True Believers* (Jackson: University Press of Mississippi, 1999), 137, 138.

39. Christopher Knowles, *Our Gods Wear Spandex: The Secret History of Comic Book Heroes* (San Francisco: Weiser Books, 2007), 155; Todd McFarlane, "Spawn," *Spawn* no. 1 (May 1992). Christian conservatives noted, and decried, these themes and characters. In *Seduction of the Innocent Revisited* (Lafayette, LA: Huntington House Publishers, 1990), evangelical author John Fulci describes comics as being "deep into occultism." This did not result in a moral crusade of the sort directed against music and RPGs, perhaps because of the socially marginal nature of comic book fandom.

40. Christopher Knowles, *Our Gods Wear Spandex*, 202–3.

41. An examination of the concept of "Generation X" (and the social and economic factors that shaped it) appears in Geoffrey T. Holtz, *Welcome to the Jungle: The Why behind Gen. X* (New York: St. Martin's Press, 1995). Holtz emphasizes how ennui and cynicism grew amid changing familial and economic structures.

7

The Beast: Satan and the Theology of American Empire

Frank Peretti's *This Present Darkness* became one of the best-selling evangelical books of the late 1980s. A combination of science fiction, sword and sorcery saga, evangelical/Charismatic beliefs about demon possession, and the Christian Right's political agenda, Peretti's work mirrored the "satanic panic" of the times. The novel told the story of the struggle for the soul of a small town fought between devout evangelicals and the servants of Satan (represented by a professor who teaches a course on goddess worship allied with a "secular" journalist and a "liberal" Christian pastor). Behind the devil's human servants are powerful forces of darkness directed by Satan to craft a "new world order" that will bring the Antichrist to Earth and begin the final struggle against God. In Peretti's imagination, only evangelicals and their prayers stand in the way.[1]

Tens of millions of evangelicals and Pentecostals in modern America believe that they are engaged in just such a struggle against Satan every day of their lives. The version of reality presented in *This Present Darkness*, spiritual combat being waged between true believers and demonically inspired liberals and secular humanists, found resonance in the politics of the Christian Right. In fact, this view informs the spirituality and voting practices of a significant number of American evangelicals and Pentecostals. The struggle with the devil has become part of the struggle for the outcome of the end-time; a struggle that many thought, and some hoped, would coincide with the coming of the new millennium.

The link between the work of Satan and the coming apocalypse is certainly not a new idea. But in the last two decades of the twentieth century, a perfect cultural storm developed that created a frightening image of the eschatological devil. The strength of the Christian Right at the end of the Reagan Revolution, anxieties over national safety and security that had been part of the American experience since World War II, and cultural conflicts in the increasingly complex moral life of the nation all helped to produce the most powerful and frightening images of Satan in American history. At the same time, some cultural voices continued to raise questions about America's simplistic concept of the devil and its failure to truly confront the reality of historical evil. Moreover, the events of September 2001 brought to the American psyche a new confrontation with the realities of history, a confrontation that would focus and concentrate the American conception of evil with disastrous effects.

Apocalyptic thought in America has a long history. Philosopher and cultural critic John Gray has written that a strong strain of millennial thought has been present in American institutions from the founding as a set of ideas that intertwined with the Puritan belief in America's special destiny and the more secular notion of American exceptionalism. The conception of America as a "redeemer nation" has informed not only national identity, but foreign policy as well. Although there have been periods in American history when the redeemer nation idea has been muted (notably the period leading up to World War II), it returned in strength with the close of the Cold War. The world after 1989 became a world in which both secular and religious apocalypticists proliferated. While the sale of evangelical "prophecy" titles soared, neoconservative thinkers described a secular "end of history" in which market capitalism and liberal democracy replaced the traditional geopolitics of the nation-states.[2]

American evangelicalism, meanwhile, has always exhibited a strongly apocalyptic impulse given its belief that the supernatural can suddenly explode into the mundane. The "great awakenings" of the eighteenth and nineteenth centuries generally had as their subtext the possibility of the approaching end. In the twentieth century both Fundamentalism and Pentecostalism drew on nineteenth-century eschatological ideas that would have enormous influence not only over how Americans viewed the devil but also how they understood the very meaning of history.

The evangelical and Pentecostal conception of "the end of the world" has its roots in the nineteenth century. In the 1860s, British theological eccentric John Nelson Darby became enormously influential in evangelical circles with his teaching that the "rapture" (or "taking up") of all of the world's true Christians could occur at any moment. Darby theorized that God dealt with humanity through successive stages or "dispensations" and that the world had entered the "Church age" in the first century. As noted previously in this study, this belief included the idea that the present age would end with the rapture, to be followed by a new era called the "Age of Tribulation" in which Satan would be given almost complete control over the earth. The Antichrist would appear as Satan's agent to rule the world, and at the end of his reign, Christ would make his visible Second Coming in wrath, destroying the Antichrist and his new world order. These ideas filtered into America through the work of Cyrus Scofield, a Missourian who appended dispensationalist notes to the King James version of the Bible. Published in 1909 as the Scofield Reference Bible, this version of scripture seemed to give the sheen of divine authority to the dispensationalist viewpoint.

Premillennial dispensationalism would acquire strength and texture from a diverse number of cultural sources in the late twentieth century. American apocalypticism was not confined, after all, to evangelical Christians. Apocalyptic ideas appeared in traditionalist Catholicism in believers' obsessions with twentieth-century apparitions of the Virgin Mary that came bearing messages about the end of the world. In 1992, Hasidic Jews who gathered around Rabbi Menachem Mendel Schneerson in Brooklyn became convinced that he was the Messiah and that he had predicted a number of events that would bring about an end of the age. Schneerson had as many as a quarter of a million followers worldwide.[3]

During this same era, devotees of New Age movements propounded beliefs in such impending events as "harmonic convergence" and various UFO scenarios, convinced that otherworldly powers, or the forces of the universe itself, had begun the process of bringing global existence to completion. In many cases such views were more optimistic than apocalyptic, viewing the coming transformation as the next stage in cosmic evolution or as a friendly extraterrestrial helping hand. An exception to this was the secretive Los Angeles group known as "Heaven's Gate" that, in the late 1980s and early 1990s, began warning of a coming destruction of the planet heralded by a worldwide satanic conspiracy. Heaven's Gate drew on the anxieties of the satanic panic to assert that "Luciferians" controlled all aspects of world government and economy. In the spring of 1997, the group committed mass suicide, believing that this allowed them to leave their "earthly containers" and unite with a spaceship that had appeared with the Hale-Bopp comet. This conception of the apocalypse reveals how flexible premillennial discourse about the devil and the end-time could be in cohabitating with ideas far removed from the evangelical and Pentecostal worlds.[4]

In the world of end-time imaginings, Satan was part of a much larger complex of cultural ideas. Apocalyptic foreboding had arguably been growing in the United States since the 1950s and had not always had a clear connection to religion or religious symbols. The possibility of a secular apocalypse had long been the theme of Cold War America given the possibility of a nuclear conflict that would, in fact, mean the destruction of human life on Earth as we now know it. The 1959 novel *On the Beach* and the 1963 Stanley Kubrick masterpiece *Dr. Strangelove* captured the very real, and very appropriate, anxiety about the outcome of the nuclear arms race. During the 1980s, the made-for-television series *The Day After* portrayed the struggles of survivors of a nuclear holocaust, while films from *Mad Max* to *Waterworld* proposed the rise of brutal postapocalyptic societies in which environmental catastrophe invalidated the social contract and left survivors in a quasi-medieval state of conflict.

Coming as they did in the wake of massive cultural upheavals that began in the 1960s, these documents from popular culture are as much about anxiety over social chaos as about the possibility of mass apocalyptic destruction. Indeed, much of this fictional material dwelt less on traditional apocalyptic themes of the end-time and more on the dangers of social dissolution. These concerns are reflected in some elements of progressive and alternative rock in the 1990s, with bands such as Smashing Pumpkins and R.E.M. echoing apocalyptic themes. Industrial "grunge" rock actually sought to replicate the sounds and the feeling of urban decay at the end of the world. Meanwhile, images of technological doom based on anxieties over the so-called Y2K bug filled American society in the late 1990s. Early computer designers had represented the year with two digits, raising the possibility that January 1, 2000, would become an "event horizon" that would lead to serious computer failures. There was speculation that such failures would unleash chaos in government, corporate operations, and public services. Books such a *The Crash: The Coming Financial Collapse of America* raised the possibility that this would fundamentally undermine American society.

Secular images have proven far less durable than images of theological doom. A definitive boundary exists between the idea of secular and religious apocalypse. The intervention of supernatural forces, as opposed to ecological catastrophe or technological hubris, plays the decisive role in the latter. And yet, in the context of American history, the concepts of spiritual warfare have so frequently blended with what might normally be thought of as largely secular questions that they have become hard to separate in the popular American mind. In the early 1950s, Billy Graham pointed to the possibility of an atomic exchange with Russia as a sign of the coming judgment of God on a sinful world. In the 1990s, some evangelical doomsayers pointed to the mounting ecological crisis as one more sign of the End of Days, while Jerry Falwell suggested that "Y2K is God's instrument for shaking this nation, for humbling this nation." Falwell ally and prophecy guru Tim LaHaye suggested that Y2K would bring about a financial collapse that would pave the way for the coming of the Antichrist. Premillennial dispensationalism could thus live parasitically off of secular fears that would seem to have little relationship to religious and theological anxiety.[5]

In fact, the evangelical and Pentecostal movements in America read almost all political and cultural events in the 1990s as part of the ongoing struggle with Satan and his minions. Premillennial dispensationalism viewed the end of time, in its most basic form, as a final showdown between God and Satan. The Antichrist (also known as "the Beast") has been the most prominent symbol of this worldview. Evangelical and Pentecostal Christians see the Antichrist as the devil's final gambit. Robert C. Fuller, who sees the identification of the Antichrist as a peculiarly dark American obsession, writes that the Antichrist is "understood to be Satan's chief disciple or agent for deceiving humanity in the final days. . . . [T]he Antichrist assists Satan by working through various persons and social movements to spread chaos and thwart the redemption of souls."[6]

In the waning days of the twentieth century, the effort to identify the Antichrist conjoined with the struggle of the Christian Right to identify the assault of the devil on American values. This struggle is a continuation of earlier efforts to fashion a sense of American identity that allows for no shadow, that asserts the reality of American innocence in the face of history. Although apocalyptic scenarios frequently make use of the language of evil, they do not deal directly with the problem of personal guilt or collective social guilt. Instead, they represent attempts to create a mythic conception of evil that will cast all cultural and political conflicts as an eschatological struggle.

Daniel Wojcik, in his comprehensive study of apocalyptic thought in American culture, has suggested that these ideas become "imbued with the culturally relevant behavior of particular historical epochs." The Antichrist appears as the cultural enemy of the moment. Just as some ministers saw the breakup of the American union in 1860 as a sign of the end, so did writers in the mid-1980s declare Soviet leader Mikhail Gorbachev to be the Antichrist. In the nineteenth century, Louis Napoleon of France was considered a candidate, while in the early 1990s, at least one major evangelical "prophecy" writer suggested that Saddam Hussein was "rebuilding Babylon" to make it his base of end-time operations.[7]

In almost all of these cases, political figures who represented ideas, values, and constituencies that mainstream America finds exotic or objectionable have become the primary candidates for the Antichrist. John F. Kennedy was rumored by some right-wing, nativist elements to be Satan's chief disciple, due to his Roman Catholicism and because, it was claimed, he had cast 666 votes during his term as senator. Barack Obama, too, has been suggested as a possible candidate for the apocalyptic role by Fundamentalist Christian authors, evangelists, and pastors. These speculations work from the fringe of society to affect, in subtle ways, the cultural understanding of the center. In a time of apocalyptic musing, such suggestions of satanic evil have easily found credulous audiences.

Premillennial dispensationalism had largely been the preserve of the most marginalized of American religious movements through most of the twentieth century. Since the 1920s, American Fundamentalists had grasped at the idea of the "rapture" as a salve for their marginal status. The world was not their home and they might, at any moment, abandon it to be taken up with Christ in the air. This "blessed hope" as many called it, appeared especially attractive given the changing social terrain of that era, combined with the black-eye Fundamentalism received from the 1925 Scopes Trial.

These marginal ideas reemerged in the American mainstream of the early 1970s with the writings of Hal Lindsey. Lindsey's materials, published and distributed almost entirely though evangelical Christian channels, nevertheless achieved best-selling status and affected the views of tens of millions outside of the evangelical fold. Shaping premillennialism into an exciting adventure/disaster novel appealed to many who never attended religious services of any kind. A profound biblical illiteracy made Lindsey's use of scripture in tandem with current events seem all the more compelling. Folk beliefs about the devil, nourished at all levels of popular culture, furthered the acceptance of Lindsey's conception of Armageddon.

Lindsey's best sellers set the stage for an even more spectacular entrance of premillennialism into the American mainstream. Tim LaHaye and Jerry B. Jenkins's Left Behind series made these ideas not only mainstream but also shaped them into a pop culture phenomenon. Published in 1995, *Left Behind* became the first of a twelve-book series (accompanied by several spin-off series) that told the story of the Rapture; the rise of Satan's servant, the Antichrist; the resistance of those who converted to evangelical Christianity after the Rapture; and the final coming of Christ and the new divine order. Aided by a multimillion-dollar promotional campaign in partnership with Wal-Mart, Costco, and Barnes and Noble, Tyndale House grew from a $40 million specialty publisher to a $160 million dollar behemoth.[8]

The cultural phenomenon of Left Behind perfectly embodied America's apocalyptic mood and invested it with the satanic imagery of premillennialism. Tim LaHaye, one of the founders of and a long-time activist in the Christian Right, created Left Behind's fictional narrative from a combination of premillennialist theology, the conspiracy theories of twentieth-century right-wing movements, and contemporary conservative politics. By the late 1990s, the Left Behind series had sold about 60 million copies, with 20 million more sales of the related book series (including a series specifically designed for children).[9]

Left Behind found its greatest resonance among practicing evangelicals, though its themes proved attractive to a much larger audience, who looked with some trepidation on cultural change and the coming twenty-first century. Its themes had a demonstrable effect on speculation about the meaning of the approaching millennium. A *Time*/CNN poll taken in 1993 suggested that many Christians looked to the coming of Christianity's third millennium as the likely date for the Second Coming. Twenty percent of the poll's respondents asserted that the Second Coming would occur before the millennium while 31 percent were willing to say that it might occur before the year 2000.[10]

The narrative context of Left Behind, a world in which satanic conspiracies have come to full fruition and "true Christians" must fight for their very lives, allows all manner of simplistic scapegoating on the part of the authors. The anti-Catholic, nativist tradition grows freely in the Left Behind books, as the pope himself is portrayed as a tool for the Antichrist. Muslims appear only as terrorists, and LaHaye does his best to provide premillennialist justification for American Middle Eastern policies regarding Iran, Israel, and Iraq. Jews are represented as little more than souls to be converted or destroyed, depending on whether or not they refuse their final opportunity to accept Christ as their Messiah.[11]

Left Behind also sought to make an evangelical case for some of the contemporary cultural and political struggles of the 1990s. Its emergence as a publishing phenomenon coincided with a public movement for gay, lesbian, bisexual, and transgender (LGBT) rights. Emerging first in the 1960s, the public LGBT community forged a powerful social movement during the 1980s to respond to the catastrophe of the AIDS epidemic. The 1993 controversy over "gays in the military" and the "Don't Ask Don't Tell" policy adopted by the Clinton administration became a flashpoint point both for Christian conservatives and human rights activists. Over the course of the decade, LGBT activists fought to secure same-sex partnership rights and began to seek legal remedies against sodomy laws and antigay violence. Conservatives, many of them affiliated with the Christian Right, warned darkly of the "homosexual agenda" and began the so-called pro-marriage movement that would eventually result in calls for constitutional amendments at the state and federal level that sought to "preserve traditional understandings of marriage."[12]

LaHaye had long been an opponent of civil rights for gay and lesbian Americans and as associated with some of the most extreme elements in the antigay movement. His 1980 book *What Everyone Should Know about Homosexuality* combined scriptural references to homosexuality with the writings of Paul Cameron, a researcher expelled from the American Psychological Association for a variety of absurd claims, including that homosexuals were responsible for half of all sex-related murders and that Thomas Jefferson had favored castration for gay men and facial mutilation for lesbian women.[13]

LaHaye definitely links homosexuality with the devil in Left Behind. In the series homosexuality becomes the literal conduit through which Satan enters the world of the last days. In a prequel novel entitled *The Rising*, the birth of the Antichrist is described as being brought about by a conspiracy of "international bankers" who accept sperm donations from two gay men. The Antichrist has two daddys, claims LaHaye, a point the author seems to use to represent a kind of satanic inversion of the Christian doctrine of the virgin birth. Much as the horror films of the 1960s, 1970s, and 1980s had reflected anxieties about abortion, contraception, and women's control over their own bodies, the Christian horror genre created by LaHaye drew on fears about changing cultural mores and the slow but steady gains for human rights in American politics. Satan, once again, was constructed as the ultimate origin of any effort toward progressive political change.[14]

Commentators on the apocalyptic genre have traditionally pointed to its representation of what Robert Fuller calls "a curtailment of agency," the tendency to adopt a fatalistic attitude about earthly matters. What does social policy, and even the moral temperature of modern society, really matter if Armageddon approaches? Frequently, apocalyptic schemas have seen moral degeneration as a sign that true believers will soon leave this world rather than a call to arms to try to transform it. Left Behind, on the other hand, seeks to inspire readers to become fully engaged in contemporary struggles, indeed to become soldiers in the culture war. Given this charge, violence becomes redemptive rather than an aspect of evil. The books feature a symmetrical amorality in which both the forces of the Antichrist and the "Trib Force" (evangelical believers who are "saved" after the Rapture) make use of deadly violence in their struggle against one another. In fact, "Trib Force" resembles nothing so much as a Christian Fundamentalist al Qaeda, a secret, underground network willing to make use of cyber-terrorism, assassination, and targeted bombing to challenge a satanic modernity. As one member of the groups says, "Woe to those who believe God is only love. We are engaged in a worldwide battle with Satan himself for the souls of men and women." Jesus Christ himself gives his blessing to these ideas when he returns in *Glorious Appearing*, book number twelve in the series. His "Second Coming" marks the death of tens of thousands, "their blood pooling and rising in the unforgiving brightness of the glory of Christ."[15]

The Left Behind series allowed the image of Satan in American culture to grow freely, and often exotically, from the soil of the American culture wars of the 1980s, which only gained strength in the last decade of the century. Often initiated by the Christian Right, the culture clashes brought a vigorous response from critics on both the secular and religious left, and for many evangelicals, they represented the struggles against the forces of darkness at the twilight of the world depicted in the fictional narratives of Tim LaHaye and Frank Peretti.

The anger generated by the American culture wars owed much to the idea that disagreement over social and cultural issues had, at back of them, a struggle with evil. Tim LaHaye has said that a "religious war" is being waged in America. "We," he explained to one evangelical audience, "need to aggressively oppose secular humanism; these people are as religiously motivated as we are and they are filled with the Devil." In LaHaye's understanding, there are only two stark options in America's ideological divide. The secular left, inspired by Satan himself, and the Christian Right, which seeks to overturn *Roe v. Wade*, stop the expansion of gay and lesbian rights, introduce prayer into public schools, and remove the teaching of evolutionary science. Just as in previous moments in American history, the ability to identify one's opponents with the devil creates a dark assurance of one's own religious certitudes, turning every cultural conflict into a holy war.[16]

The culture wars even made popular holidays such as Halloween into sites of contest. Satan had always had a powerful presence in the world of dime museums, carnivals, and so-called dark rides. In the 1930s, fun house mazes and "Laff in the Dark" attractions functioned as tours of an American inferno where devils and witches attacked delighted and frightened children and teenagers. The American invention of the "Haunted House" grew out of these rides in the 1950s and 1960s, soon becoming, especially for adolescents, a rite of passage connected to Halloween. In these updated dark rides, the devil at times took a back seat to chainsaw killers, mad scientists bringing shambling horrors to life, and even the occasional lettuce-headed alien seeking to probe laughing customers. The same generation that helped make Forrest Ackermann's *Famous Monsters of Filmland* magazine a pop culture phenomenon found these attractions the perfect mix of irony and macabre fun.[17]

Evangelicals in the 1990s created a new kind of horror ride, one haunted by the ghosts of the culture wars and presided over by Satan himself. In October 1991, the *Boston Globe* wrote of what appears to have been the first "Hell House" or "Judgment House," an evangelical Christian version of the dark ride in which vampires, ghosts, and slashers are replaced by covens of Satanists, unrepentant homosexuals dying of AIDS, and women dying in agony during botched abortion procedures. Almost everyone ends up in convincingly designed hells where the devil and his servants torment them in the most sadistic ways imaginable. These efforts proved enormously successful. George Ratliff's 2001 documentary *Hell House* told the story of one large Texas youth ministry that, over a ten-year period, attracted 75,000 people to its evangelical haunted house.[18]

By 1995, these "Christian Haunted Houses" had become common throughout the country and were seen by many evangelicals as useful conversion tools. Abundant Life Christian Center in Colorado planned one of the largest and most controversial of these annual events. Their "Hell House" made use of some of the central themes of the satanic panic, with one scene purporting to show a human sacrifice by a coven of Satanists. While Hell Houses frequently relied on sensationalist images of abortions that drew on late nineteenth-century imagery, Abundant Life Christian Center sought to make their point even more crudely by using animal entrails to represent an aborted fetus. While controversial, this effort was also successful in leading Abundant Life to market a 280-page book explaining how other evangelical congregations could create their own Hell House.[19]

The Hell House phenomenon expressed evangelical anxieties about the nature of Halloween itself. The holiday had come under attack during America's satanic panic, with many evangelical and Fundamentalist leaders claiming that the celebration had "satanic roots." Some Christian leaders even claimed that the large satanic conspiracy that threatened American society became especially active on October 31. David J. Skal has written that for evangelicals and others who believe in satanic conspiracy, Halloween seemed "an open invitation to an orgy of human and animal sacrifice—a kind of Superbowl for the 666 set." Skal notes that the Fundamentalist publishing house Chick Publications not only produces cartoon religious tracts that rail against Darwinism, Catholicism, homosexuality, abortion, and feminism but also reads Halloween as the satanic high unholy day when devilish conspirators tamper with candy, cast spells on believing Christians, and even invade high schools in Salem, Massachusetts.[20]

By the 1990s, claims about Satan's role in Halloween gelled perfectly with a strong folkloric discourse in American society. Unsettled by the larger social and political anxieties of the era, persistent stories of candy tampering (razor blades in apples, cocaine masquerading as powdered sugar) convinced many parents and church groups of the dangers of the holiday. Moreover, while these stories seemed to percolate out of the popular mind, they did receive some cultural imprimatur from a poorly done 1974 piece in the *New York Times*. The article speculated on the possible horrors that could accompany a round of "trick or treating" without any evidence that such things had, in fact, occurred:

Take, for example, that plump red apple that Junior gets from the kindly old woman down the block. It may have a razor blade hidden inside. The chocolate "candy bar" may be a laxative, the bubble gum may be sprinkled with lye, the popcorn balls may be coated with camphor, the candy may turn out to be packets containing sleeping pills.[21]

These baseless assertions ultimately relied on folkloric associations that had long been the foundation of hysteria. "The kindly old woman down the street" who may have implanted a razor blade in your child's apple clearly draws on the crone imagery of early modern Europe that made older, single, unattached, and unprotected women the target of witch hunts. David J. Skal points out that the closest thing to an "authority" quoted in this seminal article was Reginald Steen, a culturally conservative psychiatrist who claimed that the leftover social dissent from the 1960s was the cause of the alleged danger. Skal quotes Steen as saying that "People who give harmful treats to children see criminals and students in campus riots getting away with things. . . . [T]hey think they can get away with it, too."[22]

Anxious parents responded immediately to the possibility of Halloween terrorism. "Trick or Treating" became relatively uncommon by the 1980s, with most parents taking their children to visit friends and family. American films in the 1970s reflected the anxieties over what had once been a childhood rite of passage. John Carpenter's *Halloween* became the top-grossing independent film of all time with its tale of an unstoppable and mysterious killer (Michael Meyers in the film but referred to simply as "the Shape" in the script). Carpenter's original vision, somewhat lost as the *Halloween* franchise proliferated with often absurd sequels, was to imagine an inhuman and unstoppable evil in the suburbs, an invasion of meaningless violence into middle-class Americans' well-ordered world. Americans believed in this vision and pulled their children close.[23]

Some evangelical leaders made use of Halloween in their campaigns against their cultural opponents. One of the most striking of these was the effort by evangelicals to challenge the use of the holiday by gay and lesbian revelers as a major celebration of identity and of joy in alternative sexualities. The famous Greenwich Village Halloween Parade draws in part on the cultural energy unleashed by the Stonewall uprising of 1969 in which gay men, many of them drag queens, struck back against draconian police harassment. San Francisco's Castro Street celebrations have been even more unrestrained, although they have frequently been overshadowed by the efforts of antigay activists to inject violence and harassment into the event in the late 1970s and early 1980s.[24]

In 1990, Texas evangelist Larry Lea introduced spiritual warfare into these street battles. Lea and his colleague Richard Bernal told the *Wall Street Journal* that some of Satan's top lieutenants, "high ranking evil spirits," were operating out of Castro Street. The duo managed to attract over six thousand "Prayer Warriors" who would gather to pray against "territorial spirits" who controlled and directed the "homosexual agenda." The spiritual warfare on Halloween 1990 became something like a real street battle, with protestors pelting the prayer warriors with eggs and police moving in with riot gear.[25]

Much of popular culture reinforced, rather than critiqued, the notion that the final struggle against the devil had come. In one case, the apocalypse was turned into an action film, with Satan given a starring role. Released in 1999, *End of Days* presented action hero (and future Republican governor of California) Arnold Schwarzenegger as the last best hope for the human race in the struggle against the Antichrist. A big-budget shoot 'em up, *End of Days* pitted brawn and gunplay against the devil's efforts to impregnate a young woman with his child, the Antichrist. Based on some of the same cultural premises that inspired the religious right, *End of Days* is largely the story of massive violence employed to prevent coitus. Schwarzenegger's cynical cop must accept religious faith in order to prevent the sexual act that will bring about the world's damnation.

End of Days represented only one entry into what can be described as the "religious horror" genre that grew increasingly popular at the end of the decade. Drawing on themes of eschatology and demon possession, these films asserted the power of religious faith to confront and defeat the power of satanic evil, averting the end of the world. *Prince of Darkness, Bless the Child, Stigmata, The Devil's Advocate,* and *The Exorcism of Emily Rose* all employed theological themes within the traditional horror-film format. Apocalyptic anxiety tended to blend with themes from gothic horror; another newly popular genre after the runaway hit *Scream* (1996) deconstructed the slasher genre through postmodern irony. The success of the Left Behind novels gave filmmakers plenty of material, reshaping premillennial dispensationalism into frightening forms. Even renowned actor Al Pacino portrayed an effective Mephistophelean Satan in the otherwise colorless *The Devil's Advocate.* Pacino plays Satan as the head of a multinational legal and corporate conglomerate, a lover of the sensual delights of the human world who comes across as equal parts Miltonic Rebel and Michael Corleone. In one of the film's few successful moments, Satan delivers a soliloquy on his long struggle with God and his triumph at the end of days.

> I'm here on the ground with my nose in it since the whole thing began. I've nurtured every sensation man has been inspired to have. I cared about what he wanted and never judged him. Why? Because I never rejected him, in spite of his imperfections. . . . I'm a humanist, maybe the last humanist.[26]

The most striking aspect of the genre of religious horror was its ability to trawl through the cultural unconscious of America and re-present the fearful images of urban legends and more generalized horrors of the Other. The deployment of the archetype of the "serial killer" as a figure in the apocalyptic consciousness provides one example. The 1980s had seen the rise of the "serial killer" as a cultural archetype, a mysterious, predatory force lurking on the edges of American society. The slasher/ horror genres create countless theatrical images of these unstoppable killers, from Jason Voorhees to Freddie Kruger. But real-life monsters such as Ted Bundy and John Wayne Gacy haunted America in this era as well, suggesting to Americans that inhuman evil had a reality beyond the world of the teen scream fantasies. Novelist Thomas Harris perfectly captured this strange cultural fascination with the psychotic killer in his successful novels *Red Dragon, Manhunter*, and *Silence of the Lambs*. His murderous protagonist, Hannibal Lector, is equal parts serial killer, Machiavelli, and incarnation of Mephistopheles, almost a heroic figure. The 1991 film *Silence of the Lambs* became an enormously successful horror film that drew on traditional satanic imagery to shape the serial killer into a compelling cultural icon.[27]

In the 1990s, the satanic panic came together seamlessly with anxiety over the omnipotent serial killer to produce films such as *The First Power*, *Mr. Frost*, and *Fallen*, in which human incarnations of the devil spend their time on Earth massacring everyone who crosses their path. *The First Power* drew heavily on the racial and class codes of the Right, portraying drug addicts and Ronald Reagan's "Welfare Queens" as easily led astray by Satan. These films played on the fears stirred by the satanic panic, specifically the concern that the devil endangered middle America by bringing the terrors of marginal society into the safe, enclosed suburban worlds of the middle class. The murderous rampage of Richard Ramirez, the "Night Stalker," seemed to confirm these fears. Ramirez, ironically, seems to have borrowed much of the gothic imagery from the "satanic panic" in the perpetration of his crimes.[28]

American horror films in the 1990s tell us much about American anxieties in the same era. Cultural critic James Ursini describes the horror genre in popular culture as "based on recognizing the unfamiliar something familiar." Kendall R. Phillips views this familiarity lurking under terrifying forms as a kind of violation of audience expectation, a "jolt" to the familiar that awakens feelings of terror. Horror films in the 1990s drew on familiar themes within America's religious culture to achieve moments of horror. In doing so, filmmakers did much more than simply reflect ideas already found in America culture. They added background screams to the ongoing American conversation about evil, providing images that resonated with what millions of American Christians believed they had learned from their religious tradition. The devil was stalking humankind, incarnated in the grotesque forms of the Other. They themselves were in a struggle with this king of terrors, a struggle taking place at the twilight of the world. Spiritual warfare, always a powerful theme in American Christianity, drew renewed strength off of the "jolt" of the cinematic image.[29]

Mel Gibson's *The Passion of the Christ* (2004) provided the capstone for an era that had been fascinated with cinematic images of religion-themed horror. *The Passion*, certainly the most controversial religious film ever made, portrayed the final hours of the life of Jesus using blood and gore in proportions large enough to draw comparisons to the slasher genre. Numerous reviewers, theologians, Jewish leaders, and historians attacked the film's implicit anti-Semitism, drawing as it did on the long tradition of the medieval passion play in which Jews are portrayed as "deicides" and "Christ killers." Moreover, many noted that Gibson's strongly traditionalist Catholicism (which questioned the legitimacy of Vatican II and the authority of the papacy since Pius XII) itself had a strong tinge of anti-Semitism. Despite this criticism, Gibson's film proved hugely successful, grossing $370 million dollars in the United States alone and becoming the highest-earning R-rated film of all time. Evangelicals proved to be the film's most stalwart constituency, despite the film's heavily Catholic symbolism.[30]

Satan plays a central role in Gibson's bloody spectacle, a role far larger than that assigned to him by the traditional Gospel narratives of Christ's death. An androgynous, hooded, and cowled figure (Gibson used a female actor but dubbed a male voice in the single scene in which the devil speaks), Satan slithers through the film, tempting Jesus in a nightmarish scene at the beginning of the film and appearing at each crucial turning point. Demonic forces literally swirl through the movie. Mark Allen Powell notes that at one point in the film "a stereotypical Hollywood Ghoul" pops up to frighten Judas. Despite this, Powell suggests that Gibson's "visual representation [of the devil] is creative and profound."[31]

Mel Gibson not only made Satan a primary character in his film, he also believed Satan played a role in the audience response. In an interview with EWTN, a traditionalist Catholic broadcasting network, Gibson attributed negative critiques of the film to what he called "a big dark force that didn't want us to make this film." Part of the enormous cultural significance of *The Passion of the Christ* was its ability to become yet another symbol at the heart of the culture war. Embracing the film symbolized the embrace of the Christian Right's conception of America, an America in which a deeply conservative theology could find confirmation and validation in significant elements of popular culture.[32]

Writers and artists in popular culture did not, however, simply replicate these themes and provide aid and comfort for dispensationalist hopes. At times, American popular culture sometimes borrowed dispensationalist themes and used them to satire their source and reimagine the nature of evil. Perhaps nowhere was the 1990s obsession with apocalypse and the struggle against evil better parodied, nuanced, and complicated than in the pop culture phenomenon *Buffy the Vampire Slayer*. Based on an unsuccessful 1992 film, the television series told the story of a teen-age girl who is "The Chosen One," the "one girl in all the world" given the supernatural power to fight gothic evil. Her high school sat atop a "Hellmouth," a convergence point of dark mystical energy that, week after week, spewed forth some nameless evil for Buffy and her friends to combat. Rich with metaphor and layered with meaning, the show became a phenomenon that fascinated academics even as it created a deeply loyal, global fan base.[33]

Given the show's use of gothic themes, the devil is noticeably absent throughout the series. And yet, an apocalypse that sounds a lot like the one imagined in premillennialist thought is always a live possibil-ity. Throughout the 144-episode, seven-season run of *Buffy*, she and her cohort face what Wendy Love Anderson calls "a multiplication of Apocalypses." Indeed, this endless recurrence of the end became one of the running jokes of the series. At one point in season five, Buffy queries her friends about just how many apocalypses they have had to face. Clearly, series creator Joss Whedon has borrowed an idea from the 1990s apocalyptic imaginings and the broader Christian myth. And yet the very frequency of the imagery undercuts the explicit Judeo-Christian meaning of the idea: in Christian thought, there can be only one apocalypse, and it cannot be averted. But in the world of *Buffy*, it is averted again and again through human agency; acts of unconditional love; and, in the final epi-sode, by a dismantling of the patriarchal religious source material that the show had itself borrowed and redacted. Women throughout the world, in the climatic scene of the series, had Buffy's powers bestowed on them instead of those powers being limited to a single "Chosen One."[34]

Most arresting, given the hard-nosed culture wars being fought in the America of the late 1990s, the series repudiated the uncomplicated moral absolutism that generally accompanies the idea of the apocalypse. Evil is a force of violence and destruction not easily identified with any single character or being. "Good" vampires and demons make an appearance in the series and in its spin-off, *Angel* (the story of a vampire-with-a soul's crusade against evil), while some of the show's main characters can find themselves tempted to destructive evil. The closest the series ever comes to having Buffy combat Satan is in the final season when she faces "The First." Portrayed as the origin of evil, "The First" works primarily through seduction, deception, and temptation to accomplish its destruc-tive ends. Notably, one of its greatest powers is the ability to appear in any shape and under any guise, thus making the identification of evil a difficult exercise.

Buffy was not the only pop culture phenomenon that reimagined the apocalypse in the 1990s. Comic creator Mike Mignola used apocalyptic imagery to suggest that the very image of the demonic could, in fact, be the world's savior. The Other is our ally in Mignola's *Hellboy*, a demon child complete with vestigial horns, born in the midst of World War II. Raised by a kindly Catholic occult expert and fighting in the ranks of the U.S. government's super-secret BPRD (Bureau of Paranormal Research and Development), the adventures of Hellboy drew on religious themes, the dark folklore of numerous cultures, and the writings of H. P. Lovecraft to shape a mythical world where the devil actually fights on our behalf. In sharp contrast to the unstoppable apocalypse of premillennialism, Hellboy (who, we learn in the course of the series, is himself the Beast of the Apocalypse and still on our side anyway) has made the decision to prevent the end by refusing to play his role in the destruction of the world. This willingness to revolt against his own demonic nature in order to preserve the human race seemed to novelist and cultural critic Joyce Carol Oates a living critique of America's behavior in the world. "In the ruins of American empire," Oates asked, "what more appropriate figure of salvation/damnation than Mike Mignola's Hellboy?" Director Guillermo del Toro would create two successful *Hellboy* films in 2003 and 2008.

In 1999, independent filmmaker Kevin Smith, further subverted the apocalyptic narrative in his comedy hit *Dogma*. Playing with the complexities of Catholic moral thought, apocalyptic imagery, and the traditional concerns of demonology, Smith crafted a theological fairy tale in which the demon Azrael has kidnapped God (portrayed by Alanis Morissette as a compassionate, playful, and female deity) and a female messiah must save Her. As in *Buffy* and *Hellboy*, compassion and love prevent the apocalypse (and the fallen angels themselves are redeemed with a kiss). Vociferously attacked by the conservative Catholic League of America for its irreverence and satirical portrayal of the Church, most thoughtful critics have actually seen *Dogma* as a film deeply imbued with the Catholic imagination. Smith has responded to his critics by pointing out that he is a practicing Catholic and saw *Dogma* as an effort to present moviegoers with a more relevant, modern iteration of Catholicism.[35]

Buffy, *Hellboy*, and *Dogma* clearly show that a large segment of Americans remained fascinated with the apocalyptic images so predominant in fin-de siècle American culture. But they also show that the images of conservative evangelical theology would not simply be accepted and replicated. The influence of conservative evangelicalism in America also failed to limit the influence of religious experimentation in American life at the millennium. Many Americans showed a willingness to experiment with religious systems that departed in significant ways from traditional Jewish, Christian, and Islamic monotheisms. America has always been a nation of religious experimentation, as well as strict religious traditions, and the late 1990s saw a continuing proliferation of new movements. In terms of the American Satan, one of the most interesting of these movements was the continued growth of a loosely organized set of beliefs known as neo-paganism.

The 1960s had seen the growth of new and "alternative religious movements" that rejected traditional Christian theology in favor of an earth-centered spirituality that chose to describe itself as "pagan." Although many on the Christian Right viewed these movements as expressions of worship of the devil, neo-pagans themselves tended to see Satanism as a variety of Christian theology, regarding it almost as another Christian denomination. After all, neo-pagans pointed out, Satan played no role in their own worldview and only had any meaning within the context of the Christian tradition. Satanists, on the other hand, self-consciously responded to a set of Christian theological ideas, while neo-pagans refused to accept the premise that the devil of the Christian universe even existed.

A significant amount of diversity exists in the neo-pagan movement, much of it defined by attitudes related to traditional categories of witchcraft and alleged devil worship. Neo-pagan leaders have chided some Wiccans for trading too heavily on the traditional imagery of witches in shaping their tradition. Occultist P. I. Bonewits even described those who call themselves practicing witches as shaping a new tradition he calls "gothic witchcraft." Bonewits claimed that most "witches" are simply borrowing Christian delusions about witchcraft found in the trial reports of the early modern period. Practitioners of Wicca have, in turn, been strongly critical of the small number of self-styled "Satanists" in the United States. Margot Adler, a scholar of neo-paganism and a practicing Wiccan priestess, dismissed Satanism as "misplaced neo-pagans who have not been able to get beyond Christian terminology and symbolism."[36]

Some of the early "ecumenical" gatherings of neo-pagan practitioners sought to make clear their repudiation of the Christian mythology of witchcraft. In 1973, the Council of American Witches met in Minneapolis, Minnesota, for the express purpose of drawing clear parameters around the meaning of their ritual practices. Gathered under the auspices of Llewellyn Press, an occult publishing house, these late twentieth-century practitioners of the "craft" expressed the hope that the gathering would force the media to move beyond sensationalist readings of Wicca and the tendency to link it to the worship of Satan. The Council gathering declared that:

> We do not accept the concept of "absolute evil" nor do we worship any entity known as "Satan" or the "Devil" as defined by the Christian tradition. We do not seek power through the suffering of others, nor do we accept the concept that personal benefit can only be derived by denial to another.[37]

Wiccan efforts to affirm the validity of their religious identity have borne fruit in American courts. In 2001, Darla Wynne of Great Falls, South

Carolina, a town of 2,100 people, sued the town for opening its town council meetings only with invocations of Jesus Christ. Wynne faced significant harassment but, after a four-year battle, managed to prevail in the Fourth Circuit Court of Appeals. The town council was not only ordered to cease prayers in the name of Christ but to pay Wynne's legal expenses.[38]

The story of the "Great Falls Witch," as Wynne became known, points to a significant cultural shift in images of the occult in American culture. Neo-pagans at the turn of the millennium could look with pleasure on numerous positive images of witchcraft in American society. Salem, Massachusetts, has been a favored destination for neo-pagans since the 1960s and has a thriving community of alternative religious traditions eager to make an ironic comment on the town's dark past. Laurie Cabot, her name as New England as maple syrup, became the "official witch" of Salem and a media personality in the 1990s. Willing to wear black capes and dye her hair to please media stereotypes, Cabot has nevertheless become a goodwill ambassador for religious tolerance and alternative spirituality (as well as a boon for the Salem tourist industry).[39]

Popular culture, moreover, provided numerous positive representation of witchcraft. Most striking of all, J. K. Rowling's Harry Potter book series and the subsequent films became one of the most important popular culture events of the new millennium. The Harry Potter series, the story of a boy wizard who gradually comes to understand his integral role in an ongoing struggle against evil, revolved around magical objects, spell casting, and fantastic beings. The books alone have sold 400 million copies worldwide and, beginning in 2000, bookstores around the world held prerelease parties for books in the series that included games and live entertainment.

The centrality of magic and sorcery to the series predictably raised the ire of evangelical groups. In the 2006 documentary *Jesus Camp*, which goes behind the scenes of the "Kids on Fire" summer camp, we hear Pentecostal evangelist Becky Fischer tell the campers "Let me tell you something about Harry Potter. Warlocks are enemies of God. . . . Had it been the Old Testament, Harry Potter would have been put to death! You don't make heroes out of warlocks!" In 2000, when the online satirical news magazine *The Onion* ran a humorous piece entitled "Harry Potter Sparks Rise in Satanism Among Children," evangelical opponents of the series created an e-mail chain letter to circulate the story. Those unaware that *The Onion* satirizes odd and peculiar trends in popular culture used this article as proof of their claim that the series promoted satanic rites. Nevertheless, there is some evidence to suggest that even most evangelical parents found the books harmless and that a few even saw them as teaching important moral lessons. *Christianity Today* published a positive review of the series in January 2000.[40]

Harry Potter was not the only magical hero in America's millennial pop culture. The popular television series *Charmed* told the story of a coven of witches who use their powers to fight the forces of evil, often forces that are demonic in nature. *Buffy* featured Willow Rosenberg as a powerful witch who uses her powers in the struggle against evil (and also struggles with the dangers of their misuse). Gregory Maguire even rehabilitated the Wicked Witch of the West from L. Frank Baum's *Wizard of Oz* in a way that urged his readers to think about the nature of evil and the Other in a more nuanced way. His book *Wicked*, later a Tony Award–winning Broadway show, provided its readers with a complex metaphor for how society constructs the demonic out of its own cultural and religious anxieties. Maguire's own experience as a gay man, a parent, and a Roman Catholic gave him a powerful sense of the challenges faced by the marginalized and the dangers of the dominant culture's fascination with defining the Other as evil (as well as a timely political satire that warned of the dangers of absolutist politics).[41]

The millennium came to an America with the most sophisticated popular culture it had ever had and a reigning sense of optimism about the future. The United States, riding a wave of economic prosperity, had every reason to be optimistic at the beginning of the twenty-first century. The Y2K bug turned out to be a technological difficulty solvable by human ingenuity, rather than a digital Armageddon. Those who expected a rapture of true believers and the rise of the Antichrist by the year 2000 were disappointed. Fears of ecological crisis, though grounded in hard science and grim reality, helped to create the early beginnings of a global green revolution that may be productive of world-historical change in global culture and economy. The millennium came and went for America, with the most dangerous occurrence of the year being a contested presidential election, the outcome of which seemed to call into question the reality of America's democratic processes.

September 11, 2001 brought apocalyptic frenzy to the fore once again, injecting the language of satanic evil into political discourse in a way that transformed it into a clarion call for war mobilization. The deaths of more than three thousand Americans and the looming threat of further attacks created an entire cultural discourse focused on the security of the "homeland" threatened by a stalking, evil presence. In response to this threat, the United States had more political unity in the fall of 2001 than perhaps any other time since World War II. Along with this political unity came widespread reports of increased stress; sleepless nights; and, most seriously, attacks on the American Muslim community.

The uses to which the Bush administration put this new sense of unity and mission underscore how much Satan has entwined with the history of American self-identity. Increasingly, the president and his surrogates used the language of satanic evil to describe the nation's enemies in "the War on Terror." As the months passed, this rhetoric about evildoers expanded beyond the immediate threat of small terrorist networks to include all of America's real and perceived foreign policy obstacles. Bush, drawing on Reagan's description of the Soviets, described Iran, Iraq, and North Korea as an "axis of evil." Although careful not to describe Islam itself as satanic, Bush did describe the enemies of America in religious terms, calling "the terrorists" a "cult of evil" and the newly proclaimed War on Terror a "crusade." Bush made use of a quote from a survivor of 9/11 that described the fall of the Twin Towers as being "like the roar of the devil." Neoconservative David Frum wrote approvingly of Bush's choice of words, noting that "In a country where two-thirds of the population believes in the devil, Bush was identifying Osama bin Laden and his gang as literally satanic." The destruction of this satanic evil became the official, public mission of the Bush administration. In his September 14, 2001, address to the memorial service for 9/11 victims at the National Cathedral in Washington, D.C., Bush promised to "rid the world of evil." The military operations that would begin the "War on Terror" would be code-named "Operation Infinite Justice."[42]

George W. Bush's evangelical faith deeply informed his conception of evil, but it would be simplistic to simply see the president co-opting traditional Christian categories and applying them to American foreign policy. America's belief in its innocence, shored up by earlier notions of "spiritual warfare," allowed the Bush administration a strong ideological base for rejecting criticism, even criticism from some elements of the Christian church. While there has been much discussion of America's traditional allies challenging Bush's decision to go to war, little has been made of the Christian tradition's almost unanimous response to the conflict. John Paul II, spiritual leader to 1 billion Roman Catholics, warned the president in person that he had embarked on an immoral course. Rowan Williams, Archbishop of Canterbury, criticized the war, as did major leaders from the Orthodox tradition. In America, national leaders of the Lutheran and United Methodist traditions (of which Bush is a member) raised moral concerns about a preemptive attack by the United States. Despite this, America's Christian Right proved the strongest supporters of the invasion of Iraq and the larger goals of the War on Terror.[43]

The larger Christian tradition's response to the Bush administration is not surprising. Some of the most powerful strands of Christian thought, informed by the theological corpus of Augustine, would deride as human pride and vanity the idea that the world can be rid of evil or that the state could create the conditions of "infinite justice." This point only underscores how Bush's own faith, and the faith of millions of Americans, is active in the formulation of the peculiarities of American historical experience. The belief in American exceptionalism, and its corollary of American innocence, informs much of American religion. The nation-state has a special destiny, in this view, as a redeemer nation and only confronts evil as the enemy and in combat. There is no shadow-side to the American story, and thus the interests of America and of God run on parallel tracks. "War without end" can be conducted if the warrior-state is fighting for the redemption of the world rather than for limited military and political objectives.[44]

The conception of America as a nation of innocence wielding a sword of righteousness gelled with George Bush's own evangelical faith. A convert in middle age, Bush's religious attitudes served him well in shoring up his base of support in the Christian Right and among evangelicals more generally. He also became a creature of neoconservative thinkers who had long hoped to expand American imperial ambition and who saw the American concept of evil as an effective way to generate support for overseas adventurism. In fact, some of his closest foreign policy advisors had been working toward this new American empire since the late 1990s. A working group known as the Project for a New American Century that included Dick Cheney, Donald Rumsfeld, and Richard Perle had, for example, issued a paper in 2000 that called for military intervention in Iraq, Iran, Syria, and North Korea.[45]

The forces that guided the Bush administration's policies could rely on a concept of evil that would support almost any foreign adventure, and Bush's simplistic conception of the devil's work in the world helped to make him impervious to criticism for these policies. After he received severe criticism for his decision to invade Iraq from foreign policy experts from his father's administration, he told reporter Bob Woodward that he had "a higher Father" he had to be concerned with pleasing. In this worldview, the struggle against "the instruments of evil" is wholly identified with American foreign policy. Indeed, Bush constructed a rhetorical world in which refusal to support his policies represented collaboration with evil and a rejection of the will of God. In language redolent with the monotheistic "holy war" tradition, Bush told Palestinian leader Mahmoud Abbas in 2003 that "God told me to strike al-Qaeda and I struck them, and then he instructed me to strike Saddam, which I did."[46]

This is not an entirely new American language about the nature of evil and America's enemies. But the tendency to think of war as an instrument with which to bring the world a cleansing apocalypse, as opposed to a strategy that seeks to accomplish limited goals and prevent greater evil, is new. Contrast, for example, the grim determination with which the American public, led by FDR, undertook the war against fascism with the religio-utopian sentiments embodied in American policy since 9/11. Bush told journalists in September 2006, for example, that the War on Terror was

"A third great awakening," a religious revival that had forced the American people to understand that American foreign policy was shaped by "the confrontation between good and evil." Even with the end of the Bush presidency, these ideas show little evidence of abating on the Christian Right. Georgia governor Sonny Perdue, for example, referred to Sarah Palin, Republican vice presidential nominee in 2008, as presidential nominee John McCain's "soulmate in the struggle against all evil in this world."[47]

These ideas made their way through the ranks of the American military as it began the 2003 invasion of Iraq and conducted the subsequent occupation. In the spring of 2004, American forces launched an assault on the insurgents of Fallujah by destroying the city and hideously killing the inhabitants with "white phosphorus" (known colloquially as "Willie Pete"), an "improved napalm" that poisons the lungs. The Pentagon at first denied the use of this controversial weapon, in part because Saddam Hussein himself had once used it in one of his own campaigns of terror against dissidents.[48]

Lieutenant Colonel Gareth Brandl (USMC) had no qualms about the use of "Willie Pete" against the enemy (or against the noncombatants who died horribly from it). "The enemy has got a face," Brandl told the BBC during a second chemical assault on the city in November 2004, "He's called Satan. And we're going to destroy him." Brandl was simply reiterating the view of the Bush administration's undersecretary of defense, William Boykin. Boykin, a highly decorated soldier, told a church audience in June 2003 that the real enemy facing America was "a spiritual enemy; he's called the principality of darkness. The enemy is a guy called Satan." Boykin's beliefs had been strongly influenced by the "deliverance" movement in American Christianity that sees the world inhabited by a powerful hierarchy of demonic spirits. In 1993, he reportedly told another evangelical audience that he had taken a picture of a demonic spirit that hovered over the city of Mogadishu.[49]

Boykin provides a perfect example of how the Christian Right's concept of spiritual warfare buttressed the goals of the neoconservatives in the Bush administration. The propaganda war waged among millions of American Christians provided crucial support for the decision to go to war. Tim LaHaye made clear that he saw the Iraq conflict as part of the precursor of the end-time scenario portrayed in the Left Behind books. Texas evangelist Gary Frazier, speaking at a Detroit church near the beginning of the Iraq war, called Islam a "satanic religion" and warned of "sleeper cells" that hived the country. He coupled this with a warning about the influence of Satan among major political organizations such as the ACLU and the NAACP and at "Harvard, Yale and over 2,000 colleges." The struggle against Satan had to be carried out both here and abroad.[50]

In an apocalyptic struggle against enemies who are instruments of the devil, any methods are acceptable. Dick Cheney, whose influence within the Bush administration reached extraordinary heights never before attained by a vice president, described the need for America to "work with the dark side" in order to defeat the looming threat of evil ("dark side" apparently became Cheney's nickname within the administration). Within weeks of the attack on the Twin Towers, the Bush administration did go to "the dark side" in its quest to destroy the "cult of evil." Under the administration's first attorney general, John Ashcroft, the struggle against evil included the use of torture, domestic espionage, and the restriction of constitutional liberty.[51]

A war on the devil and a "satanic religion" legitimizes almost any action. One example of where these ideas could take American domestic policy is the so-called Ashcroft raids in the months following 9/11. The Justice Department created a nationwide dragnet that detained Muslim noncitizens, some of them for almost a year, with little or no cause beyond being designated as "persons of interest" by the Justice Department. Of the 766 persons detained during this period, none have had charges brought against them, although over 500 have been deported. Six thousand more automatic deportations have also never been explained.[52]

The U.S. Patriot Act, passed six weeks after September 11, became the basis for the attorney general's actions. In its original form, it gave the attorney general wide latitude to detain noncitizens without trial and to prevent immigrants from entering the nation on the basis of their political opinions. The "special registration" requirement has been termed a state act of racial profiling, requiring male citizens of twenty-five designated countries who were required to appear at an immigration office in February and March of 2003 to be photographed, fingerprinted, and interviewed. They are required to reregister annually. The willingness to use torture at Abu Ghraib and elsewhere, including torture techniques meant to insult and denigrate the cultural and religious traditions of detainees, further underscores the willingness to believe that the enemies of the United States represented ultimate evil.[53]

The argument of this book has been that America has always had a lush and exotic vocabulary of evil, energized both by popular religion and by popular culture. This vocabulary made the devil a shape-shifter in which a variety of ideas, social groups, and institutions were defined as "satanic." This, in turn, allowed for a suspension of moral scruples. These trends continued in the 1990s and into the twenty-first century. During this period, American culture and religion sensationalized evil, fashioning global politics and religious belief into a cartoonish struggle between clearly defined adversaries. Films in the "religious horror" genre strengthened such simplistic views. More often than not, sermons, printed materials, and media produced by the Christian Right itself encouraged Americans to adopt a view of Satan and of evil that ignored complexity and nuance (or that rejected it as yet another temptation of Satan).

By the twenty-first century, the language of satanic conspiracy had worked its way through the discourse of American culture for generations. Satan continues to be a powerful figure in religious rhetoric. In fact, his alleged work in America shaped the worldview of spiritual culture warriors such as Republican vice presidential candidate Sarah Palin. Her spiritual mentor, Thomas Muthee, had publicly prayed in 2005 that the emerging Alaska politician would be "delivered from witchcraft." In the summer of 2008, before she became John McCain's running mate, Palin attributed her gubernatorial victory to Muthee's prayer on her behalf. Muthee has a long acquaintance with spiritual warfare and the struggle against witchcraft. He won fame in Pentecostal circles for his claim that he had successfully driven a witch out of a town in his native Kenya. His defeat of "Mama Jane" in his hometown of Kiambu did lead to her being driven out of town, an incident of ostracism replicated over and over again in the larger phenomenon of witch hunting in postcolonial Africa. This phenomenon, often driven by Western missionaries or local pastors with Western links, has led to an outbreak of violence against women suspected of witchcraft. The American Right has, in this way, exported its conception of spiritual warfare. Reporter Max Blumenthal visited the Wasilla Assembly of God (Palin's former church) in September of 2008 and heard Muthee warning about the need for the congregation to wage "spiritual warfare" against "the enemy" in the media, what he called "the python spirit." "We come out against the python spirits!" Muthee proclaimed, "We come out against the spirit of witchcraft!"[54]

Millions of Americans still believe in the power of "The Beast," an image from the Book of Revelation of a powerful system of evil opposed to God's Kingdom on Earth. In the worlds of popular religion and popular culture (most especially *The Omen* that received an updated remake in 2003), the Beast has been combined with traditional images of the Antichrist. Such imagery surfaced in the 2008 presidential campaign as hundreds of right-wing blogspots, websites, and radio talk shows raised the question of whether or not the charisma, popularity, and progressive politics of President Obama qualified him as the devil's anointed. An ad released by the McCain campaign in August called "the One" seemed to allude to traditional fears of the Antichrist. Tim LaHaye even commented to the *Washington Post* that he saw similarities between the ad and the Left Behind series (though LaHaye also graciously acknowledged that there was no reason to believe Obama to be the Antichrist).[55]

Robert C. Fuller has called the fixation on "the Beast" an "obsession," one that has frequently served what he regards as our "tribal" impulses.

He goes on to argue that the image in the waning days of the twentieth century acquired new importance as evangelical Christianity found itself an increasingly marginal value system under attack from a variety of viewpoints. This view has much to recommend it given the tendency of the Christian Right in America to regard disagreement and challenge as "persecution" and to read themselves as a marginal community.[56]

At the same time, Fuller made these arguments in 1995, a full five years before evangelical Christian leaders saw one of their own in the White House and the Bush administration melding the language of foreign policy and apocalypse. Bush's invocation of a "third great awakening" surely cheered those who saw an innocent America endangered by godlessness, convincing them that the nation's immutable innocence had burned through the post-1960s malaise.

Since 2008, the Christian Right may feel marginalized yet again, given the election of Barack Obama and the repudiation of conservative misrule. And yet for many, Satan, so long an enemy in spiritual warfare, is still the enemy confronted on foreign battlefields. America fights, banners flying, against the armies of hell. America the innocent confronts the Beast.

Recent writing by biblical scholars has noted the profound irony that the New Testament language of "the Beast" first emerged as a symbol of the godless imperial society, the Roman Empire that persecuted the minority Christian faith. It was an image that offered a prophetic critique of the power of empire and its violent foundations. The politics of the devil were the politics of violence. Evil was not found lurking in the hearts of the marginalized whose struggles might upset the status quo but rather in the established order built on the massacre of the saints who had opposed it. Transposing contemporary evangelical assumptions about the apocalypse to the first century would have created a very different reading of politics and society. Indeed, if the politics of the Christian Right had been operative in 90 CE, John the Revelator would not have been challenging the presumptions of godless empire but instead writing symbolically about the need for Emperor Nero to extend his geopolitical influence, crush the heathen barbarians, and call all Roman citizens to a renewed commitment to imperial power in a war without mercy and a war without end.

NOTES

1. A full discussion of *This Present Darkness* and where it fits in the Pentecostal movement of the 1980s and 1990s can be found in Harvey Cox, *Fire from Heaven* (New York: Da Capo Press, 2001), 282–84.

2. John Gray, *Black Mass: Apocalyptic Religion and the Death of Utopia* (New York: Farrar, Straus and Giroux, 2007), 107–10, 123–25.

3. Daniel Wojcik, *The End of the World as We Know It: Faith, Fatalism, and Apocalypse in America* (New York: New York University Press, 1997), 9.

4. Mark Miller, "Secrets of the Cult," *Newsweek*, April 7, 1997.

5. Wojcik, *The End of the World*, 110–12; Michael Standaert, *Skipping Towards Armageddon: The Politics and Propaganda of the Left Behind Novels and the LaHaye Empire* (Brooklyn, NY: Soft Skull Press, 2006), 102–3.

6. Robert C. Fuller, *Naming the Antichrist: The History of an American Obsession* (New York: Oxford University Press, 1995), 5.

7. Wojcik, *The End of the World*, 148.

8. Amy Johnson Frykholm, *Rapture Culture: Left Behind in Evangelical America* (New York: Oxford University Press, 2004), 22.

9. Standaert, *Skipping Towards Armageddon*, 11–13.

10. Wojcik, *The End of the World*, 212.

11. Standaert, *Skipping Towards Armageddon*, 184.

12. The best examination of the struggle for gay and lesbian rights in relation to Christian conservatism in America is Chris Bull, *Perfect Enemies: The Battle Between the Religious Right and the Gay Movement* (Lanham, MD: Madison Books, 2001).

13. Standaert, *Skipping Towards Armageddon*, 132–33.

14. Tim LaHaye and Jerry B. Jenkins, *The Rising* (Wheaton, IL: Tyndale House Publishers, 2005), 74–76, 253–55.

15. Tim LaHaye and Jerry B. Jenkins, *Glorious Appearing* (Wheaton, IL: Tyndale House Publishers, 2004), 241.

16. Amy Johnson Frykholm, *Rapture Culture: Left Behind in Evangelical America* (New York: Oxford University Press, 2004), 175.

17. On *Famous Monsters*, see Gary Cross, *The Cute and the Cool: Wondrous Innocence and Modern American Children's Culture* (Oxford: Oxford University Press, 2004), 151.

18. Jeff McLaughlin, "Haunted House Abortion Scene Sparks Protest," *Boston Globe*, October 30, 1991.

19. "Hell House Ignites Debate," *Denver Post*, October 21, 1995; Gayle White, "'Trick or Treat?' No, 'Turn or Burn,'" *Atlanta Journal Constitution*, November 1, 1995. See also Lynn Scofield Clark's excellent discussion of the Hell Houses and the role of Satan in what she calls "the dark side of evangelicalism" in *From Angels to Aliens: Teenagers, the Media, and the Supernatural* (New York: Oxford University Press, 2003), 35–43.

20. David J. Skal, *Death Makes a Holiday: A Cultural History of Halloween* (New York: Bloomsbury, 2003), 78–80.

21. Judy Klemensrud, "Those Treats May Be Tricks," *New York Times*, October 28, 1970.

22. Skal, *Death Makes a Holiday*, 5, 6.

23. See Vera Diker, *Games of Terror: Halloween, Friday the 13th, and the Films of the Stalker Cycle* (Rutherford, NJ: Farleigh Dickinson University Press, 1990).

24. Susan Stryker and Jim Buskirk, *Gay by the Bay: A History of Queer Culture in the San Francisco Bay Area* (San Francisco: Chronicle Books, 1996).

25. Skal, *Death Makes a Holiday*, 134–35.

26. From *The Devil's Advocate*, quoted in Darryl Jones, *Horror: A Thematic History in Fiction and Film* (London: Arnold Press, 2002), 190–91.

27. A full discussion of the connections between horror films and "the dramatic rise in prominence of the real-life serial killer" in the 1980s appears in Kendall R. Phillips, *Projected Fears: Horror Films and American Culture* (Westport, CT: Praeger Press, 2005), 145–47. Phillips notes that the media context for *Silence of the Lambs* was coverage of serial killers "at times bordering on hysteria."

28. Nikolas Schreck, *The Satanic Screen: An Illustrated Guide to the Devil in Cinema* (London: Creation Books, 2001), 219–22.

29. James Ursini, introduction to *The Horror Reader*, ed. Alain Silver and James Ursini (New York: Limelight Editions, 2000), 5.

30. The introduction to Timothy K. Beal and Tod Linafelt (eds.), *Mel Gibson's Bible: Religion, Popular Culture, and the Passion of the Christ* (Chicago: University of Chicago Press, 2006) provides one of the best general introductions to the film's success and the controversy that surrounded it. See especially 2–3, 6–7.

31. Mark Allan Powell, "Satan and the Demons," in *Jesus and Mel Gibson's "The Passion of the Christ": The Film, the Gospels, and the Claims of History*, ed. Kathleen E. Corley and Robert L. Webb (London: Continuum, 2004), 71–78.

32. Gibson quoted in John Dominic Crossan, "Hymn to a Savage God," in Corley and Webb, *Jesus and Mel Gibson's "The Passion,"* 20.

33. A description of the show's global popularity appears in the introduction to Elana Levine and Lisa Parks (eds.), *Undead TV: Essays on "Buffy the Vampire Slayer"* (Durham, NC: Duke University Press, 2007), 2–6.

34. Wendy Love Anderson, "Prophecy Girl and the Powers That Be: The Philosophy of Religion in the Buffyverse," in *"Buffy the Vampire Slayer" and Philosophy: Fear and Trembling in Sunnydale*, ed. James B. South (Chicago: Open Court, 2003), 222.

35. Amy Frykholm, "Catholicism Wow!" in *Catholics in the Movies*, ed. Colleen McDannell (New York: Oxford University Press, 2008), 297–98.

36. Margot Adler, *Drawing Down the Moon: Witches, Druids, Goddess-Worshippers, and Other Pagans in America Today* (New York: Penguin/Arkana, 1997), 68–69.

37. Margot Adler, *Drawing Down the Moon*, 102–3.

38. Will Moredock, "Who You Calling a Witch?" Pagans Struggle to Come out of the Broom Closet," *Charleston City Paper*, December 12, 2007.

39. Dave Morrison and Nancy Lusignon Schultz, *Salem: Place, Myth, Memory* (Boston: Northeastern University Press, 2004), 55–61.

40. "Why We Like Harry Potter," *Christianity Today*, January 10, 2000.

41. Chuck Colbert, "Gay, Catholic, and Parents of Three," *National Catholic Reporter*, March 16, 2007.

42. Ira Chernus, *Monsters to Destroy: The Neoconservative War on Terror and Sin* (Boulder, CO: Paradigm Publishers, 2006), 125–26; Michael Northcott, *An Angel Directs the Storm: Apocalyptic Religion and American Empire* (London: I.B. Tauris, 2004), 7, 11, 140–41.

43. On the broader, Christian opposition to the war, see Kevin Phillips, *American Theocracy: The Peril and Politics of Radical Religion, Oil, and Borrowed Money in the 21st Century* (New York: Viking Press, 2006), 235–36.

44. Journalist Chris Hedges has thoroughly examined and critiqued this concept of American origins and destiny in *American Fascists: The Christian Right and the War on America* (New York: Free Press, 2006).

45. Project for a New American Century, *Rebuilding America's Defenses: Strategy, Forces, and Resources for a New Century* (Washington, DC: PNAC, 2000).

46. John Gray, *Black Mass: Apocalyptic Religion and the Death of Utopia* (New York: Farrar, Straus & Giroux, 2007), 115.

47. Ari Berman, "Defeating Evil and Defending Palin," *The Nation* online, www.thenation.com/blogs/state_of_change/353134 (accessed September 2, 2008).

48. BBC News, "U.S. General Defends Phosphorus Use," http://news.bbc.co.uk/2/hi/americas/4483690.stm (accessed November 15, 2008).

49. CBS News, "The Holy Warrior," www.cbsnews.com/stories/2004/09/15/60II/main643650.shtml (accessed November 15, 2008); BBC News, "U.S. Is 'Battling Satan' Says General," http://news.bbc.co.uk/2/hi/americas/3199212.stm (accessed November 15, 2008).

50. Hedges, *American Fascists: The Christian Right and the War on America* (New York: Free Press, 2008), 192–94.

51. See *Taxi to the Dark Side*, DVD, directed by Alex Gibney (New York: ThinkFilm, 2008).

52. John Bellamy Foster and Robert McChesney, *Pox Americana: Exposing the American Empire* (New York: Monthly Review Press, 2004), 153–54.

53. Foster and McChesney, *Pox Americana*, 153–54.

54. Max Blumenthal, "The Witch Hunter Anoints Sarah Palin," *Huffington Post*, September 24, 2008, www.huffingtonpost.com/max-blumenthal/the-witch-hunter-anoints_b_128805.html (accessed November 15, 2008).

55. Michelle Boorstein, "Left Behind Authors: Obama Not Antichrist," *Washington Post*, http://voices.washingtonpost.com/44/2008/08/14/left_behind_authors_obama_not.html (accessed August 14, 2008).

56. Fuller, *Naming the Antichrist*, 99.

Epilogue

Shame the Devil:
The Problem of Evil and
American Cultural History

The idea of satanic evil has been the progenitor of much mayhem in America's national history. Satan provided America a metaphor for what our culture hates and fears most at each moment in our history. Worse, the devil and our fascination with him, has served as a blind for our society's darker moments, those times when the United States has renounced its collective moral obligations and acted out of its anxiety or lust for power. Puritans found Satan lurking in the "howling wilderness" and in marginal members of their own community rather than their genocidal wars against the native peoples of New England. In fact, they defined those peoples as "children of the devil." In the 1970s, more concern seemed to be focused on discovering the "truth about exorcism" than facing the hard truths of the Pentagon Papers. In the 1980s, the absurd SRA upheaval unleashed anxieties over satanic conspiracy and ritual abuse that seem straight out of the peasant village politics of early modern Europe. During the same decade, millions of children in the United States actually did suffer, not from the actions of conspiratorial Satanists, but from poverty, poor schooling, the emerging crack epidemic that gutted inner cities, and inadequate health care. Those religious traditions and religious leaders most interested in speaking of the devil remained the most silent on those grinding social problems, even as they created intricate demonologies. Exclusion, persecution, and violence followed in the wake of these satanic speculations.

A look at the American experience shows that we love the notion of evil. Moralists and social conservatives may insist that Americans have lost the sense of evil and the sense of sin. This is not the case. As noted earlier, partisan identity mattered little in the days after 9/11, not only because of collective grief, but because President Bush deployed the ideas of evil and evil-doers, hard and clean ideas that swept all ambiguity from history and historical experience while focusing rage and sorrow to a sharpened spear tip. A chorus of voices joined him and soon we no longer faced a human tragedy or even human enemies. We were instead in a mythic battle with monsters. Like those who murdered our fellow citizens, we were fighting the Great Satan.

The story of Satan in America reveals central truths about American culture. The religious history of America has been informed by the concept of spiritual warfare, combat with evil. The images that have shaped American misogyny, racism, and imperial hubris are largely demonic images. We have seldom asked the more profound questions about evil and instead constructed the nature of evil using the mythical language of apocalypse. This language has fed a thirst for power and violence while also allowing us a language of innocence.

This book has been, in some respects, primarily a history of the American experience seen through the lens of one of its cultural fascinations. But while the American Satan tells us something about America, his story may also tell us something about the nature of evil. René Girard's scapegoat mechanism, operative in all eras of American history, has functioned as the devil in almost every human society. It is a mechanism that has blinded its participants as much as it has illuminated the way to their victims.

Authoring a book about the devil leads to interesting conversations. The traditionally gaudy nature of beliefs about Satan inspires great enthusiasm. Invariably, these conversations lead to a question: "Does the devil exist?" When I first began this project, a conversation with a politically and religiously conservative student proved revealing. The student knew me to be a practicing Roman Catholic and assumed this meant that I would write a book about what he called "the real devil." Too often, he believed, scholars "wrote the devil off as a metaphor or a symbol." I tried as best I could to help the student unpack his thoughts about this topic. What does it mean to say something is a metaphor? Is it the same as denying its existence? Why might one believe in a devil and why might one wish to? Most of all, I tried to explain that, as a scholar of American history, it really didn't matter what my own belief or unbelief about Satan might be, since a phenomenological approach had to be taken to any study of this nature. As a scholar, and not as a specifically Catholic scholar, I had to believe in the devil believed in by many different kinds of Americans in order to describe him. I was pursuing this research with the understanding that most of the people I would study believed in the devil and that, therefore, Satan did exist in the cultural context of the Western world and in American history. The basis of the historical study of religion, I told him, was the idea that one can study how an idea appears, changes, and functions without engaging in metaphysical speculation or creedal assertions about it and also without denying and debunking speculations and assertions. To paraphrase the old formulation, one must suspend both belief *and* disbelief in order to describe and analyze.

The student went away unedified, to say the least. This is perhaps because something very specific was being asked of me that I could not and would not provide—a reaffirmation rather than an explanation. I think behind this young person's comment was really a request: will you tell me, please, that there is a Satan? I think he would have been in every way relieved, on a very deep level, if I had said yes. But why, I wonder, might anyone be relieved to have his belief in Satan reinforced? In a world of violence, warfare, natural disaster, and incurable disease, all of those evils we see inflicted on others and ourselves, what could possibly be comforting about an invisible Prince of Darkness, seeking to destroy and damn us?

The heart of the answer is the heart of evil itself. We want to believe, strange as it might seem, that a malevolent force stalks us. If it is, we can learn and use techniques to fight him. We can name evil and deal with it. We can even go to a skilled practitioner of exorcism and have him name the evil and cast it out. We never have to ask hard questions of ourselves or of our culture. The refusal to ask hard questions about the nature of evil has been evident at every phase of the American experience. The assertion of the devil's power has been a convenient way to assert the reality of evil while avoiding the spiritual, cultural, and political implications of its existence.

Early in this work we met Cotton Mather. The Puritan theologian, famous for his abhorrence of the body, believed that everything from sexual gratification to the enjoyment of food and drink represented "the lusts of the flesh," a trick of the devil. His hatred of his own desires found twisted expression in his sensual descriptions of the burning flesh of native peoples, his hatred of women as a source of impurity. Unable to come to grips with his humanity, viewing his humanity as a source of evil, he became inhuman. Mather's psychosis may be the primary infection plaguing the American soul: a belief in purity that seeks to destroy every trace of corruption in the world.

The transformation of our social and economic life in the nineteenth century provides an even more sinister explanation for America's fascination with the devil. Our material comfort has unleashed a profound narcissism that denies the reality of evil even as it asks the national government to slaughter the enemies of our comfort. The devil remains a powerful part of our public consciousness and political rhetoric, although, for most of us, the theological and moral systems that created him have withered and died. Religion plays a powerful, usually too powerful, role in our public culture, and yet generally what are preserved are the darkest impulses of fanatical atavism.

Belief in a metaphysical Devil allows us to ignore the fact that America has been a fallen angel from the beginning. The rhetoric of religious declension, used by Puritan ministers and today by the religious right, is generally an ahistorical diversion for powerful cultural forces that imagine a golden age destroyed by the growth of sexual freedom and secularization. Their golden age was an age of segregation, disenfranchisement, the restriction of women's lives and bodies, and the birth of an imperialistic hubris that is still with us, that wishes to save a village by destroying it, that seeks to make the stars fall from the heavens in the pursuit of millennial dreams.

My response to my student, while not inaccurate, was too watery and insubstantial. There is a devil. He lives in our collective history at the intersection of violence and hubris. Charles Baudelaire was wrong. The devil's greatest trick is not to convince us that he does not exist. It is, instead, to convince us that he lives in our enemies, that he surrounds us, and that he must be destroyed, no matter the cost, no matter the collateral damage. What better tactic could be employed by a creature that lives off violence, that, in a fundamental way, is violence? The Devil is negation, and the negation of negation, but not in some purely abstract, philosophical sense. The devil is the negation and hatred of the Other, a sinister force working its will in our social order and then disappearing into the shadows

Ian McEwan's short novel *Black Dogs* is perhaps one of the more moving modern meditations on the problem of evil, especially in its relationship to history, culture, and violence. McEwan slowly unravels the tale of a failed marriage between June, an aging female author of mystical texts, and Bernard, a progressive British Labour politician with a socialist background. By the end of the compelling work, the reader learns that the life of the couple soured on a fateful day in France just after World War II when June came face-to-face with two enormous and vicious black dogs. Soon after, she hears a local folk legend that these dogs had been cruelly tortured by the Gestapo, perverted into becoming instruments of torture themselves. This encounter destroys the couple's marriage, largely because June had confronted an evil that "no social theory could account for." She could no longer share her husband's hopes for political and social change, and so she sought another path.

In the closing pages of the novel, June describes her understanding of the evil she had encountered decades before, in the heady days of her early marriage, when the threat of fascism, and of evil, had seemingly been defeated forever.

The evil I'm talking about lives in us all. It takes hold in an individual, in private lives, within a family and then it's children who suffer most. And then, when the conditions are right, in different countries, at different times, a terrible cruelty, viciousness against life erupts and everyone is surprised at the depth of hatred within himself. Then it sinks back and waits. It is something in our hearts.

McEwan's ability to connect the personal lives of his characters with the torments of history makes June's statement something other than solipsism, a confessional look into the human heart. Collective violence seems to come from every direction and not simply from our psyche. The study of history tells us that the devil is no metaphor for the human heart but a collective rage at the outsider, the weak, the marginal. It lives not in "our hearts" but in our histories.

Given the historical reality of the destructive power of evil in human experience, perhaps the impulse to hear the tale of "the real devil" should be honored. Secular rationalism has been rightly critiqued for its too easy dismissal of the invisible world, as if rational argument can easily prove that something does not exist. Denis de Rougemont, best known as the author of the highly regarded *Love in the Western World*, also wrote a deeply intriguing small book called *The Devil's Share*. In it, he dismisses the sophomoric rationalism that simply says "Satan is a myth, myths are not true, therefore there is no Satan." While not going to the opposite extreme and accepting the notion of a literal, demonic consciousness, de Rougemont does assert that evil exists as a "special dynamism" in human history. The devil may be, in the strictest sense of the term, a myth. But it is a myth that does exist and that structures the reality of the world.[1]

Critics of post-Enlightenment trends who castigate America for losing its sense of evil are, then, perhaps at least partially right. Americans do not confront evil or recognize how luxuriantly it grows within their social structures. But they have not abandoned belief in the devil. Belief in devils has become a substitute for the confrontation with evil. The devil is real, but in one of the sharp ironies that seems inextricable from thinking through moral and theological profundities, Americans' fascination with him has prevented them from recognizing this fact in any meaningful way.

In August 2008, presidential candidates John McCain and Barack Obama made a joint appearance at Saddleback Church in Orange County, California, for a public discussion of the role of faith in public life. Pastor Rick Warren, the foremost of a new generation of evangelical leaders, asked both candidates a series of question about contested social issues, their worldviews, and even their personal religious beliefs.

One of the more interesting moments occurred when Warren asked the candidates if they believed in evil and, if so, should America "defeat it or negotiate with it." Senator Obama asserted that he believed in evil and that any observer would find it at work in Darfur or even in the streets of America. Moreover, he cautioned against the dangers of doing evil in the pursuit of the good. While he did not quote Nietzsche, he could have to make his point: "Beware when fighting monsters that you do not become a monster. When you stare into the abyss, the abyss stares into you."

Senator Obama's answer was not especially compelling to the audience, as it simply did not have the kind of visceral response that the question really called for. It stood in striking contrast to McCain's, who adamantly asserted that evil was to be defeated, a simple and straightforward assertion that drew loud and long applause from the conservative Christian audience. Rather than raising the possibility that the nation must beware of doing evil in the pursuit of the good, McCain quickly pivoted to the War on Terror and even to an evocation of the devil by promising the assembled believers to chase Osama bin Laden "to the gates of hell." The cheering, at that point, would not stop.

The candidates' very different answers illustrate two very different understandings of evil and two very different understandings of America. If we are a redeemer nation, baptized in our own innocence, then any action we take on the world stage is a priori the right one. Moreover, those moments in our history when internal dissent has been squelched, when our own people have been brutalized and marginalized by those who controlled the culture, these have only been signposts on the way to progress, moments when we had to insure the cohesiveness and strength of our identity. Exclusion of the morally and culturally suspect becomes an act of strength, preparing the nation for its hard fight against the devil and his agents.

On the other hand, if we are as implicated in history as every other society, if our past contains a record of savagery against the marginalized, if the story of America is in part the story of her victims, then our desire to "fight evil" has a very different meaning. Our invocations of the devil, in this case, become the worst kind of hubris, a cynical legitimation of past error and the prologue for future mayhem. We are looking into the abyss and not realizing that it is looking into us. We have, as Vice President Cheney suggested, decided to "spend some time in the shadows." We have chosen to become evil.

The folk traditions of Central Europe might have some accidental wisdom here. A Czech folk saying, *Nemaluj certa na zed*, can be translated "don't paint the devil on a wall." In other words, to create his image is to summon him from the depths. According to Radu Florescu, Romanian folklore warns to be careful not to give a name to the devil and his legions, to instead speak of "he who may be killed with a cross." He may be less dangerous, teaches these sayings, if left alone. We have met plenty of exorcists in this study, and almost all of them have claimed that to use the name of Satan is to cast him out. The peasant traditions of Central Europe raise another possibility. Using the name of Satan calls the devil to your side.[2]

In our national experience it has generally been those who were certain that they were fighting evil and thus preserving the idea of American innocence who have been the perpetrators of evil. David Frankfurter is right when he says that evil is a discourse, horror brought into existence by our own imaginings. But the willingness to create such a discourse reveals that evil also has an objective side: acts of violence and terror that degrade and destroy human beings, that fundamentally violate the dignity of the human person. We have seen how Puritans, preachers, and presidents have evoked Satan again and again in our history, unleashing the Dark Prince to walk the earth. We have also seen the many victims of these invocations. Perhaps to be silent about him and instead deal with injustice as a human problem with human solutions will lay the prideful angel to rest forever.[3]

"Tell the truth and shame the devil" is another folk saying that suggests a proper path for dealing with the devil. The discourse of evil is comforting because it feeds our worst appetites, calling us to supine indifference or explosive violence. Individual and collective introspection is that more difficult choice. But with it comes the recognition that it is America whose name is legion. It is our dark history, not devils that must be cast out.

NOTES

1. Denis de Rougemont, *The Devil's Share* (New York: Meridian, 1957).

2. Erazim V. Kohak, "Speaking of the Devil: A Modest Methodological Approach," in *Disguises of the Demonic: Contemporary Perspectives on the Power of Evil*, ed. Alan M. Olson (New York: Association Press, 1975), 48; Radu Florescu, "The Devil in Romanian Literature," in *Disguises of the Demonic*.

3. David Frankfurter, *Evil Incarnate: Rumors of Demonic Conspiracy and Ritual Abuse in History* (Princeton, NJ: Princeton University Press, 2006), 9–12.

Hunting the Devil:
A Bibliographic Essay

The materials that have been most useful to this study are found in the endnotes for each chapter, and yet the published material on the devil, in English alone, is so voluminous that the reader interested in pursuing the topic further needs a guide. Moreover, this study has examined a number of ideas, movements, and cultural expressions in American history that are given fuller examination and much more precise nuance in other works. The following brief bibliographic essay offers the reader an interpretive path to some of the best of these materials.

Not surprisingly, the vast majority of the works concerned with the devil are religious in nature, seeking to help believers define their beliefs about Satan and prepare to do battle with him. Some have been used as primary sources in this book. Others are insightful in ways useful to the historian beyond their value as primary texts. Catholic apologist and cultural commentator F. J. Sheed (of Sheed & Ward) assembled an essay collection called *Soundings in Satanism* (New York: Sheed & Ward, 1972) that contains valuable historical interpretations of Cotton Mather, the role of Satan in Christian history, and aesthetic renderings of the devil. The late John Updike wrote a trenchant introduction that reflects on the theology of Karl Barth, the nature of belief, and, of course, the nature of evil.

Another large amount of literature exists that explores belief in the devil as part of Western folklore. A good place to begin in the American context is David Adams Leeming and Jake Page's *Myths, Legends, and Folktales of America: An Anthology* (New York: Oxford University Press, 1999). Amy M. McElroy in "The Devil Is Alive and Well: Devil Legends in American

Folklore" (PhD dissertation, DePaul University, 1997) examines the role played by Satan in various American folktales to the ubiquity of his importance in the American consciousness. Catalog of beliefs about Satan and related matters can be found in Nancy Campbell's *Folklore: Hoax Stories, Devil Stories, Beliefs, and Proverbs* (New York: Houghton Mifflin, 1971).

Historians of religion have created a much smaller body of literature dealing with the cultural, social, and political influence of belief in Satan. The definitive, and monumental, work of this genre remains Jeffrey Burton Russell's four-volume history of the devil. I have used Russell to help explain the "past lives" of Satan and found especially useful his *Mephistopheles: The Devil in the Modern World* (Ithaca, NY: Cornell University Press, 1986). Russell, a deeply learned scholar, also offers a number of interesting reflections on the nature of belief in Satan, continually confronting the reader with the idea's relationship to the reality of evil and forcing her to deal with it as more than simply a folkloric image or an outdated theological construct.

The only real limitation to Russell's work, and it is more a matter of emphasis than a true failing, is the insignificant space he gives to modern popular culture or, indeed, to the American context at all beyond literature. This is in part because of a palpable disdain for most popular expressions of interest in Satan. His description of the influence of heavy metal is typical. In *Mephistopheles*, he suggests that it has little or no serious value, having a "decomposing effect on weak and silly minds." At the same time he, astonishingly, raises the possibility that it has been the cause of "appallingly degenerate crimes, including the violation of children and the mutilation of animals (257)." The urban legends of the satanic panic clearly made their way into the scholar's study.

On the other hand, there are aspects of Russell's discussion of Satan in American literature that I consider definitive and seemed to make it unnecessary for me to explore much twentieth-century literary fiction. I would point especially to his discussion of the work of Flannery O'Connor in *Mephistopheles* (see 286–95).

The relationship between American religion and American popular culture is key to this study. A full exploration of the nature of popular culture can be found in Jack Nachbar and Kevin Lause's *Popular Culture: An Introductory Text* (Bowling Green, OH: Bowling Green State University Popular Press, 1977). Nachbar and Lause emphasize the idea, common to most historians of pop culture, that the popularity of "cultural elements" reflects some of the deeply held values of any given society. The intersection of religion and popular culture has been explored in a variety of sources. R. Laurence Moore's *Selling God: American Religion in the Marketplace of Culture* (New York: Oxford University Press, 1994) is the best place to begin.

CHAPTER 1

The role of the devil in the Atlantic world in the age of exploration and discovery grows apace. One of most important recent new books in Atlantic studies, Jorge Canizares-Esguerra's *Puritan Conquistadors: Iberianizing the Atlantic, 1550–1770* (Palo Alto, CA: Stanford University Press, 2006), explores the emergence of a common discourse about the role of Satan in the New World that influenced both English Puritan and Spanish Catholic conceptions of the Amerindian. The author believes that common discourse emerged "from a shared, centuries-old tradition of Christian holy wars" (119). What Canizares-Esguerra calls "the Satanic epic" of the New World prepared the ground for hundreds of years of demonizing the Other in the Americas. Two other important works explore the role of the Counter-Reformation in shaping conceptions of the demonic in the Atlantic world, essentially functioning as the beginnings of a historiography of the Inquisition and the European witch trials in the Atlantic. Nora Jaffery's *False Mystics* (Lincoln and London: University of Nebraska Press, 2004) examines the little-studied functions of the Spanish Inquisition in eighteenth-century Mexico. These efforts, conducted along with Spain's attempts to root out resistance to the Catholic Crown in the home country, led to accusing practitioners of native Mexican folk magic of being "crypto Jews." Martha Few's *Women Who Live Evil Lives* (Austin: University of Texas Press, 2002) looks at female sorcery in colonial Guatemala, and the attention it received from the Inquisition.

Much of the most important work on the Puritans and the supernatural (especially relating to the Salem witchcraft trials) appears in the endnotes to chapter one. Important to highlight, however, is that the study of Salem has begun to expand into study of the role of the supernatural in colonial life more generally. Richard Godbeer's *The Devil's Dominion* (Cambridge: Cambridge University Press, 1994) offers a new paradigm for understanding the trials in the context of the European folk beliefs about Satan and witchcraft in colonial New England. This exciting new trend was really begun by the work of a former professor of mine at Harvard Divinity School, David D. Hall, in *Worlds of Wonder, Days of Judgment* (Cambridge, MA: Harvard University Press, 1990). Hall examined Puritan ideas about the reader and the text, meteorology, and the relationship between luck and providence in order to map a Puritan popular culture in which older Puritan folk traditions, including the magical tradition, could flourish.

Outside of Godbeer and Hall's work on the Puritans, the larger story of colonial tradition concerned with the devil has received little scholarly attention. Jon Butler's *Awash in a Sea of Faith: Christianizing the American People* (Cambridge, MA: Harvard University Press, 1990) offers one of the few general histories of early American religion that gives much attention to the role of folk magic and the occult. Beliefs about Satan, and how they interacted with these folk beliefs, unfortunately, are not examined.

Folklorists and anthropologists have done the primary work on "the Jersey Devil." The interested reader should consult the works on Satan in American folklore mentioned above, as well as James F. McCloy's *Phantom of the Pines: More Tales of the Jersey Devil* (Moorestown, NJ: Middle Atlantic Press, 1998).

CHAPTER 2

The historiography of American revivalism has become increasingly complex and sophisticated, both from an anthropological and a historical standpoint. I have noted the most significant works in the texts and endnotes. I would like to highlight Christine Leigh Heyrman's *Southern Cross: The Beginnings of the Bible Belt* (New York: Knopf, 1997) as it is one of the few works on that period that give ample attention to the role of diabology in shaping the evangelical message.

A number of important works deal more generally with the role of evangelicalism in American history and culture. An interested reader should begin with the work of George Marsden, including his *Religion in American Culture* (San Diego: Harcourt Brace and Jovanovich, 2000). Also useful is his biography of Jonathan Edwards entitled *Jonathan Edwards: A Life* (New York: Oxford University Press, 1980).

The theological concept of redemption, so crucial to understanding emerging concepts of spiritual warfare, is most fully explored in Linda Munk's *The Devil's Mousetrap: Redemption and Colonial American Literature* (New York: Oxford University Press, 1997). Also useful in acquiring a broad, transatlantic understanding of the relationship between revivalism, conversion, and the new evangelical identity is Reginald W. Ward's *Early Evangelicalism: A Global Intellectual History, 1670–1789* (New York: Cambridge University Press, 2006).

The role of gendered constructions of Christianity in the late nineteenth and early twentieth centuries is fully explored in an excellent essay collection edited by Donald E. Hall, *Muscular Christianity Embodying the Victorian Age* (New York: Cambridge University Press, 2006). I also made use throughout this work of Edward J. Blum's discussion of how religion, race, and empire forged conceptions of masculinity at the turn of the twentieth century in *Reforging the White Republic: Race, Religion, and American Nationalism, 1865–1898* (Baton Rouge: Louisiana State University Press, 2005). More work deserves to be done on the myriad roles played by the devil in the career of Billy Sunday. Robert Francis Martin's *Hero of the Heartland: Billy*

Sunday and the Transformation of American Society, 1862–1935 (Bloomington: Indiana University Press, 2002) is the place to begin. However, neither Martin's fine work nor my brief treatment here does justice to the way in which language about the devil became a central component of one of the central figures of twentieth century American religion.

CHAPTER 3

Numerous works on the various movements for moral reform proved useful in putting together this chapter. The seminal work is Ronald G. Walters's *American Reformers, 1815–1860* (New York: Hill and Wang, 1978). The endnotes of this chapter testify to how heavily I depended on the work of James A. Morone in *Hellfire Nation: The Politics of Sin in American History* (New Haven, CT: Yale University Press, 2004). Morone not only looks at the beginnings of nineteenth-century moral reform but also creates a comprehensive interpretation of concepts of sin, morality, and the construction of the Other throughout American history.

A more comprehensive study of the devil and temperance could likely yield a number of interesting results. In addition to the famous "Deacon Giles" account discussed in the text, other popular temperance tracts included William Henry Burleigh's *The Devil and the Grog Seller: A Ditty for the Times* (Philadelphia: Merrihew and Thompson, 1848) and Evangeline Blanchard's *The Devil's Dream: A Temperance Story, Founded on Facts* (Andover, NY: C.B. Brown, 1889). While generally available only on microfilm, they offer a good starting point for a larger study of how temperance reformers understood, and made use of, the notion of demonic power. One of the best new interpretations of the temperance movement is Scott C. Martin's *Devil of the Domestic Sphere: Temperance, Gender, and Middle-Class Ideology, 1800–1860* (DeKalb: Northern Illinois University Press, 2008).

The work on the major American writers briefly discussed in this chapter is voluminous to say the least. I have cited in the endnotes for chapter 3 some of the work I found most helpful for this study. A good general introduction to the topic is Patricia Ten Broeke's "The Shadow of Satan": A Study of the Devil Archetype in Selected American Novels from Hawthorne to the Present Day" (PhD dissertation University of Texas, 1967). Also useful is Anne Shapiro's *Unlikely Heroines: Nineteenth-Century American Women Writers and the Woman Question* (New York: Greenwood Press, 1987).

Two of the authors discussed certainly deserve more than I was able to explore here on the question of Satan, evil, and American innocence. Nathanial Hawthorne's obsession with seeming innocence and inward evil (as well as the obverse) is explicated in Agnes McNeill Donohue's *Hawthorne: Calvin's Ironic Stepchild* (Kent, OH: Kent State University Press,

1985). The best new book on Hawthorne is Larry J. Reynolds, *Devils and Rebels: The Making of Nathanial Hawthorne's Damned Politics* (Ann Arbor: University of Michigan Press, 2008). Reynolds describes a profound resistance in Hawthorne to the American tradition of violence that made him a true public intellectual and moral prophet. This is a useful corrective to some of the simplistic interpretations of Hawthorne in the past. On both authors, see *Hawthorne, Melville, and the American Character: A Looking Glass Business* (New York: Cambridge University Press, 1984). Also highly recommended is Andrew Delbanco's introduction to *Moby Dick, or The Whale* in the 2003 Penguin Classics edition. I did not examine that most celebrated of American novels in part because its connection with satanic imagery and the idea of evil has been so thoroughly explicated elsewhere. See Helen P. Trimpi's "Melville's Use of the Devil and Demonology in *Moby Dick*," *Journal of the History of Ideas* (1969), 543–62.

I have cited already some of the best works dealing with Mark Twain's fascination with the figure of Satan. However, the reader interested in exploring further should also consult two works: Maxwell Geismar's *Mark Twain: An American Prophet* (Boston: Houghton Mifflin, 1970) and Everett Emerson's *Mark Twain: A Literary Life* (Philadelphia: University of Pennsylvania, 2000).

Abortion has become one of the most contested moral and cultural questions in contemporary America, so I thought it useful to briefly explore the early emergence of the controversy and its relationship to concepts about the devil. James C. Mohr's *Abortion in America: The Origins and Evolution of National Policy, 1800–1900* (New York: Oxford University Press, 1979) provides a useful primer for understanding the complex history of a complex moral question.

CHAPTER 4

A full discussion of the changes in American religion at the end of the nineteenth century can be found in the works cited in the endnotes. Marsden's *Religion in American Culture* prove helpful, especially 96–139 (5th edition). On the rise of natural sciences and higher criticism (and the degree to which it was challenged or welcomed) several works are useful. David N. Livingstone's *Darwin's Forgotten Defenders: Evangelical Theology and Evolutionary Thought* (Vancouver, BC: Regent College Publishing, 1984) provides an excellent introduction to a forgotten moment in American religious history, so crucial in many ways for shaping both the mainline Protestant tradition and, later, the rise of Fundamentalism. An article by David C. Lindberg and Ronald L. Numbers, "Beyond War and Peace: A Reappraisal of the Encounter Between Christianity and Science," *Church History* 55 (September 1986): 338–54, furthers the discussion on the growth of religious liberalism and its relationship to advances in scientific knowledge.

I depended heavily on Grant Wacker's *Heaven Below* for my discussion of Pentecostalism and the devil. Harvey Cox's *Fire from Heaven* (New York: Da Capo Press, 2001) provides the general reader with an introduction to the movement as a global phenomenon with a special emphasis on how the theology of the movement is lived in daily life, culture, and politics. Donald W. Drayton's *Theological Roots of Pentecostalism* (Grand Rapids, MI: Francis Asbury Press, 1987) provides the best introduction to the theological background and context for the movement. Robert Mapes Anderson places the movement in its social and cultural context in *Vision of the Disinherited: The Making of American Pentecostalism* (New York: Oxford University Press, 1979). David Martin's *Pentecostalism: The World Their Parish* (Malden, MA: Blackwell Books, 2002) places the Pentecostal movement in a global framework. All of these works give some attention to the Pentecostal emphasis on "deliverance from demons."

Douglas W. Frank's *Less Than Conquerors: How Evangelicals Entered the Twentieth Century* (Grand Rapids, MI: Eerdmans, 1986) gives the reader a sense of the disarray among conservative religious movements in America before World War II, underscoring their rapid rise since that period. On the growth of evangelicalism, see Robert Wuthrow's *The Restructuring of American Religion: Society and Faith since World War II* (Princeton, NJ: Princeton University Press, 1988).

One significant thinker on the question of evil and Satan not explored here is James Garrison's discussion *The Darkness of God: Theology after Hiroshima* (Grand Rapids, MI: Eerdmans, 1983), which raises uncomfortable questions about the nature of the universe and the nature of God, particularly the notion of true evil as the "shadow" of God. Although Garrison centered his discussion on the questions of recent history, it received little or no attention beyond theological circles, perhaps because of the profound existential discomfort his questions raised.

CHAPTER 5

Materials on the idea of the devil in twentieth-century America, outside of theological/religious literature, are very limited. At the same time, there is a profusion of materials that deal with the intersection of popular religion and popular culture. In many of these works, the devil can be found lurking in the shadows.

A large body of work exists on the blues and its relationship to African American folklore, religion, and identity. In edition to Francis Davis's classic work, the reader should also consult Gayle Wardlow's *Chasing That Devil Music: Searching for the Blues* (San Francisco: Miller Freeman Books, 1998). For more, specifically, on Robert Johnson and his "deal with the Devil," see Patricia R. Schroeder's *Robert Johnson: Mythmaking and Contemporary American Culture* (Urbana: University of Illinois Press, 2004). An interesting recent study that places the blues in historical context is Guido van Rijn's *The Truman and Eisenhower Blues: African-American Blues and Gospel Songs, 1945–1960* (New York: Continuum, 2004). All of these works make some use of black folklore related to Satan.

The chapter's discussion of the 1950s is not meant to replicate some of our simplistic conceptions of that era. At the same time, it's important to remember that the stereotypes of the 1950s we hold today are largely dependent on how television, advertising, and a wide variety of cultural ideologies from that era sought to shape its image. Several books on this point are useful, including James Burkhart Gilbert's *Men in the Middle: Searching for Masculinity in the 1950s* (Chicago: University of Chicago Press, 2005) and Alan J. Levine's *"Bad Old Days": The Myth of the 1950s* (New Brunswick, NJ: Transaction Publishers, 2008).

The popularity of Billy Graham helped to define the shape and growth of evangelicalism in the 1950s. Darryl G. Hart provides a good introduction to the topic in *Deconstructing Evangelicalism: Conservative Protestantism in the Age of Billy Graham* (Grand Rapids, MI: Baker Academic, 2004). Marshall Frady's *Billy Graham: A Parable of American Righteousness* (Boston: Little, Brown, 1979) provides an instructive discussion of Graham's relationship to some of the crucial social issues of the 1950s, 1960s, and beyond. The changes to this movement in the postwar era are placed in a larger historical perspective in Randall Herbert Balmer's *Blessed Assurance: A History of Evangelicalism in America* (Boston: Beacon Press, 1999). Unfortunately, most of these works only include a passing discussion of how the concept of the devil helped shaped evangelical identity.

Those interested in understanding the relationship between the "monster movie" that became popular in the 1930s and American culture should consult, first, David J. Skal's corpus. He is the highly readable, preeminent historian of horror in American film. Other useful and interesting works include Gregory W. Mank's *It's Alive: The Classic Cinema Saga of Frankenstein* (San Diego, CA: A.S. Barnes and Company, 1981).

The fiction of Ray Bradbury is fully examined in Robin Anne Reid's *Ray Bradbury: A Critical Companion* (Westport, CT: Greenwood Publishers, 2000). The larger topic of dissent against the alleged cultural consensus of the 1950s can be found in an essay collection edited by Josh Lukin entitled *Invisible Suburbs: Recovering Protest Fiction in the 1950s United States* (Jackson: University of Mississippi Press, 2008).

CHAPTER 6

The American conception of evil arose out of some specific political and cultural construction in the last quarter of the twentieth century. Assessments of the cultural and political malaise of the late 1960s and 1970s, and it relationship to the so-called Reagan Revolution are plentiful. In addition to works already cited, the reader should look at the recent work by Rick Perlstein, *Nixonland: The Rise of the President and the Fracturing of America* (New York: Scribner, 2008). Perlstein shows that many of the cultural divides, and perhaps the origins of the so-called culture wars themselves, lay in this era. Another useful work that looks at some of the same issues in a regional perspective is Dan T. Carter's *The Politics of Rage: George Wallace, the Origins of the New Conservatism, and the Transformation of American Politics* (Baton Rouge: Louisiana State University Press, 1995).

Film historians and critics have most frequently remarked on the increasing fascination with demonic themes in popular culture since the 1960s (at least outside of controversial literature that views the rise of interest in such matters as a sign of growing American decadence). Nickolas Schreck's work *The Satanic Screen* (London: Creation Books, 2001) provides basic information about these films, although his own understanding of how Satan and Satanism should be portrayed makes his analysis mostly tendentious. Charles P. Mitchell's *The Devil on Screen: Feature Films Worldwide, 1913–2000* (Jefferson, NC: McFarland and Company, 2002) provides a more complete catalog of these films.

The origin and growth of the Christian Right, and its influence over several presidential administrations has been examined in a variety of works. For specific information on the role played in the Reagan White House, see Clyde Wilcox and Carin Robinson's *Onward Christian Soldiers: The Religious Right in American Politics* (Boulder, CO: Westview Press). Ruth Murray Brown's *For a Christian America: A History of the Religious Right* (Amherst, NY: Prometheus Books, 2002) provides a look at the historical origins of the movement. Chris Hedges's *American Fascists: The Christian Right and the War on America* contains a detailed survey. His title, while seemingly sensationalist, should not obscure the fact that he exposes in detail the lineaments of an ideology that has at least a cousinship with twentieth-century right-wing nationalisms. Mark Lewis Taylor has sketched the religious right's relationship (and contribution) to the "War on Terror" in *Religion Politics and the Christian Right: Post-9/11 Powers in the American Empire* (Minneapolis, MN: Augsburg Fortress Press, 2005).

Work on the "satanic panic" of the 1980s has, thankfully, exploded the myths and urban legends that caused so much damage to lives and reputations. Many of the key works are cited in the endnotes but the interested reader should also examine Stanley Cohen's *Folk Devils and Moral Panics*

(New York: Routledge, 2003). This classic work was updated in order to include discussion of the "satanic panic." Jean La Fontaine examines the ways in which the panic became a transatlantic witch hunt in *Speak of the Devil: Tales of Satanic Abuse in Contemporary England* (Cambridge: Cambridge University Press, 1998). Sara Scott's study of the larger phenomenon of alleged "ritual abuse" in relation to sociological ways of knowing and political structures of the female subject provides a theoretical interpretation of the "satanic panic" and other "moral panics." See Scott's *The Politics and Experience of Ritual Abuse* (Philadelphia: Open University Press, 2001). Finally, Lawrence Wright provides a close study of a single case within the panic in *Remembering Satan: A Tragic Case of Recovered Memory* (New York: Vintage Press, 1995).

There have been a number of important studies that have examined how societies attempt to control social deviance through its definition of crime and the application of punishment. David Garland's *The Culture of Control: Crime and Social Order in Contemporary Society* (Chicago: University of Chicago Press, 2002) reveals how "mainstream America" uses the language of crime to mete out what amounts to social and cultural vengeance. The results of this symbolic effort can be found in Bruce Western's *Punishment and Inequality in America* (New York: Russell Sage Foundation Publishing, 2007). I hope my connection between these concepts and the "satanic panic" intervenes in this discussion.

The brief discussion here of comics is largely dependent on works cited in the endnotes. Another useful discussion of cultural and religious symbols as they appear in comics is *Superheroes and Gods: A Comparative Study from Babylonia to Batman* (Jefferson, NC: McFarland and Company, 2008). The final chapter explores the relationship of figures of horror to the concept of the comic book hero, suggesting a useful paradigm for examining evil in popular culture. A discussion of comics in relation to both religion and popular culture can be found in an essay collection edited by B. J. Oropeza, *The Gospel According to Superheroes: Religion and Popular Culture* (New York: Peter Lang, 2005).

Finally, the "demonic dangers" allegedly found in youth culture are placed in historical context in John Springhall's *Youth, Popular Culture, and Moral Panics: Penny Gaffs to Gangsta Rap, 1830–1997* (New York: Palgrave Macmillan, 1999).

CHAPTER 7

The place to begin understanding the American fascination with the apocalypse is Paul Boyer's *When Time Shall Be No More: Prophecy Belief in Modern American Culture* (Cambridge, MA: Harvard University Press,

1994). A large body of literature has developed on the relationship of the Left Behind novels (and their imitators) and the American concept of apocalypse. In addition to those cited in the chapter, the reader should also see Glenn W. Shuck's *Marks of the Beast: The Left Behind Novels and the Struggle for Evangelical Identity* (New York: New York University Press, 2005) and Jason Bivins's *Religion of Fear: The Politics of Horror in Conservative Evangelicalism* (Oxford: Oxford University Press, 2008).

A surprisingly large amount of scholarly literature exists on *Buffy the Vampire Slayer*. I have used the most relevant to this study in the text, though the interested reader should also see Matthew Pateman's *The Aesthetics of Buffy the Vampire Slayer* (Jefferson, NC: McFarland and Company, 2006) and Lorna Jowett, *Sex and the Slayer: A Gender Studies Primer for the Buffy Fan* (Middletown, CT: Wesleyan University Press, 2005).

No film discussed in this, or any, chapter has received as much public and scholarly discussion as Mel Gibson's *The Passion of the Christ*. Theologians, film critics, historians, and others have all joined in the public controversy. In addition to the works cited in the endnotes, readers who seek to learn more about this controversy should consult my article on *The Passion of the Christ* in *The Encyclopedia of American Movies and Culture* edited by Phillip DeMare (Santa Barbara, CA: ABC-Clio Press, 2009).

Although Margot Adler's work began the serious study of neo-paganism as a religious phenomenon, newer works have expanded the field. Sarah M. Pike's ethnographic study is useful for a further understanding of how neo-pagans situate themselves vis-à-vis charges of "Satanism." See her *Earthly Bodies, Magical Selves: Contemporary Pagans in Search of Community* (Berkeley: University of California Press, 2001), especially 87–132.

American foreign policy in the early twenty-first century was crafted around the concept of demonic evil. A number of works have examined how the Bush administration played on the concept of the American Satan on a global scale. The most relevant for a look at how religion and beliefs about evil influenced foreign policy are Jacob Weisberg's *The Bush Tragedy* (New York: Random House, 2008) and Glenn Greenwald's *A Tragic Legacy: How a Good vs. Evil Mentality Destroyed the Bush Presidency* (New York: Three Rivers Press, 2008). The most comprehensive account of the results of this mentality can be found in Jane Mayer's *The Dark Side: The Inside Story of How the War on Terror Turned into a War on American Ideals* (New York: Doubleday, 2008). See also Robert Rapley's *Witch Hunts: Salem to Guantanamo Bay* (Montreal: McGill-Queen's University Press, 2005). A very detailed and sophisticated discussion of how the idea of "evil individuals" has oversimplified foreign policy and represents a modern type of "magical thinking" can be found in David Keen's *Endless War? Hidden Functions of the War on Terror* (London: Pluto Press, 2006).

EPILOGUE

The theological, literary, and philosophical literature on the nature of evil spans many centuries. Here, I will, by necessity, only cite a few that the contemporary reader will find useful to look at in conjunction with the present study. Jeffrey Burton Russell's discussion of evil and the concept of Satan in the final chapter of his book *Mephistopheles* is especially useful. Russell uses the concept of evil as "negation" (an Augustinian category) to explore the role of evil in history. One of the most interesting and lucid recent philosophical accounts I have come across is Daryl Koehn's *The Nature of Evil* (New York: Palgrave Macmillan, 2007). Koehn makes the connection between literature and contemporary events, including September 11. A thoughtful discussion of the theological and philosophical issues raised by the question of evil can be found in N. T. Wright's *Evil and the Justice of God* (Downers Grove, IL: InterVarsity Press, 2006). Also worth examining is social psychologist Philip Zimbardo's *The Lucifer Effect: Understanding How Good People Turn Evil* (New York: Random House, 2008). Zimbardo, the researcher behind the infamous "Sanford Prison Experiment," also served as an expert witness at the trial of the guards in the Abu Ghraib system. My own thinking about evil and its relationship to the concept of the devil has been deeply informed by the writings of Swiss social critic Denis de Rougemont, whose work *The Devil's Share* (New York: Meridian Books, 1956) manages to avoid the literalism of the Fundamentalist and the oversimplifications, and naïveté, of secular rationalism.

Literature has been, above all, the place where the nature of evil has been most fully explored. The work of Flannery O'Connor, more than any American writer except for Hawthorne, deserves to be read by an anatomist of evil. Ian McEwan's *Black Dogs* (London: Vintage Books, 1998) is revelatory on a number of topics related to the nature of evil, especially its connection to history, memory, and folklore. Jayne Anne Phillips's *Shelter* (New York: Vintage Books, 1994) explores the construction of evil amid economic, cultural, and psychological isolation. *Shelter* also bears out, in narrative form, something I have suggested throughout this study: belief in the devil can open the door to truly devilish brutality and horror.

American historians have not, as of yet, been able to speak meaningfully about the reality of evil in national history. There are some important exceptions to this, but for the most part we have left such things to the theologians and the poets. This is a failing in the profession. For too long, allegedly rejected notions of "American exceptionalism" and "American innocence" have blinded both the amateur public and the professional historian to the darker chapters of our history. Where for example is the American counterpart to Daniel Jonah Goldhagen's *Hitler's Willing Executioners: Ordinary Germans and the Holocaust* concerned with the genocidal destruction of the Amerindian, with slavery, or with Jim Crow? Only when American historians reject the vestiges of national myth and equally acidic myths of "historical objectivity" can American historiography undergo a much-needed exorcism.

Index

About the Author

W. Scott Poole is assistant professor of history and director of the graduate program in history at the College of Charleston. In addition to various articles and book chapters, he is the author of *Never Surrender: Confederate Memory and Conservatism in the South Carolina Upcountry* and *South Carolina's Civil War: A Narrative History*. Poole is also the coeditor of *Vale of Tears: New Essays in Religion and Reconstruction* and coauthor of the forthcoming *South Carolina: A Short History*. He lectures widely, has appeared in the History Channel series, "The States," and contributes articles on topics ranging from NASCAR to comics to the influential Web journal PopMatters.com.